Green Mangoes
AND Lemon Grass

Southeast Asia's Best Recipes from Bangkok to Bali

by Wendy Hutton
foreword by Charmaine Solomon
photos by Masano Kawana
styling by Christina Ong and Magdalene Ong

PERIPLUS

contents

a tropical culinary adventure

At last, here is the book I have long awaited from a food writer I really trust. Wendy Hutton is one of the too few Western food writers on Asian food who knows her subject inside out. She takes the trouble to research painstakingly, and then conveys her knowledge and enthusiasm for Southeast Asian food with recipes that really work.

I have known Wendy for almost 30 years, and from the moment we met, recognized in each other a kindred spirit. She was half the editing team who worked on my *Complete Asian Cookbook*, making an onerous task one of great satisfaction.

Her *Singapore Food* is the only other cookbook (besides mine) that I keep in my kitchen and actually cook from. We consult each other on matters culinary and track down elusive ingredients with the enthusiasm of bloodhounds. Wendy has a much more adventurous attitude to food than I have, and often sends me jottings from the wild, as it were, where her descriptions of dishes she has tried during her travels in Asia fill me with awe.

While we might not all live in a tropical country with mangoes dropping from the trees and lemon grass growing happily in the garden, thanks to immigration, a wide range of Asian ingredients is now readily available in most Western countries. This book will open the door to those exciting hot, sweet, sour, salty, spicy, and sometimes bitter flavors which make the food of Southeast Asia such a palate-awakening experience. Even for those whose culinary aspirations are limited, this book is an inspiring read as Wendy Hutton shares her experiences and her recipes.

Charmaine Solomon

fabulous flavors from bangkok to bali

Southeast Asia is my adopted home. I came intending to stay two or three years. Thirty-five years later, I'm still here. How could I possibly tear myself away from such a fascinating region which also — or could this be the main reason? — offers some of the world's most sublime food.

When I think of the countries I have explored throughout Southeast Asia, I find it difficult to separate the people and places from the food. Cambodia is the slap-in-the-face odor of a jar of fermented fish on a houseboat on Tonle Sap lake. Thailand brings back my amazement at learning just how many wild plants are edible while helping forage for our evening meal with a hill tribe. Laos reminds me of facing skewers of tiny whole frogs in a morning market when I really wanted something less challenging for breakfast.

Burma sparks memories of a version (pretty dreadful too, to be honest) of British Christmas fare in a colonial-era guest house in the misty hills, with local kids singing carols outside. Bali is recollections of helping prepare endless intricate food offerings for a temple festival, while the sophisticated side of Singapore takes a back seat to memories of countless great meals whipped up in a wok at the local food stalls.

You might wonder how could there be any common thread running through the cuisines of places as far apart as Burma and Bali, a region with literally hundreds of different ethnic groups. And it's not just the people that are different. Southeast Asia is not all lush green paddy fields and waving coconut palms. Central Burma, for example, is downright arid, a dramatic contrast to the fertile corridor of the Mekong river, threading through Laos, Thailand, and Cambodia before sprawling in a maze of waterways in the Mekong delta of Vietnam. But despite variations caused by quirks of geography, most of Southeast Asia is hot and humid, so the basic foods are similar everywhere from Burma to Bali.

The way people put these ingredients together in the kitchen is partly the result of history. The region has seen the rise and fall of mighty Hindu and Buddhist kingdoms, leaving awe-inspiring remains such as stone stupas studding the plain of Pagan in Burma; astonishing temples, gateways and moats in Angkor, Cambodia; and exquisite Hindu remains in Java, Indonesia.

But history is about people as well as kingdoms and monuments, and it is the people who produce the cuisine. The mosaic of ethnic groups in some parts of Southeast Asia today is the result of different tribes from southern China moving gradually into Laos, Vietnam, and Thailand. More recent waves of immigration brought hundreds of thousands of Chinese to what was then Malaya, to Singapore, Indonesia, and Thailand. Indians spread across the border into Burma, while thousands of southern Indians were brought as laborers to Malaya and Singapore. These immigrants — and also the period of colonialism, which only Thailand escaped — introduced new ingredients and cooking styles, helping shape the food of Southeast Asia to varying degrees.

If you were to use just one phrase to sum up Southeast Asian cuisine, it would be "hot, sour, sweet, and salty," a concept is surprisingly similar to the Chinese principle of "balancing the five flavors" (adding bitter to the four flavors of Southeast Asia). Sometimes this blending of hot, sour, sweet, and salty comes altogether in just one dish, or it is spread over a series of dishes served with rice. For example, order a simple bowl of noodle soup in Thailand, and you'll find everything you need to balance the flavors set out on the table before you: hot chilies, sour lime wedges or rice vinegar, sweet cane sugar, and salty fish sauce (and, for a textural contrast, coarsely crushed toasted peanuts).

There's no denying the Chinese influence, especially in the towns and cities. You'll see the conical Chinese wok

in countless local kitchens, and find cooks following the Chinese technique of stir-frying. And just about everywhere, you'll find bean sprouts, bean curd, salted soybeans, noodles and — where fish sauce does not reign supreme — soy sauce, all introduced by the Chinese.

But despite these influences, Southeast Asian cuisine is unique. For me, the secret lies not just in the blending of hot, sour, sweet, and salty seasonings but in the incredibly fresh flavor and herbal aroma. Fresh seasonings, which are often crushed to a paste, include juicy purple shallots, garlic, ginger, chilies of different colors and intensities, blindingly yellow turmeric, and blush-pink galangal.

Herbs are used with almost wild abandon. The tang of citrus is personified in the intense flavors of lemon grass and kaffir lime leaf. Wild jungly odors come through in polygonum or Vietnamese mint, in saw-tooth coriander and rice paddy herb. Several varieties of basil hint of aniseed or other spicy savors, while the mint seems more pungent than any Western variety. There's also the distinctive fragrance of fresh coriander leaf, spring onions, and dill — and these are just the most commonly used herbs.

Although some dishes (especially in Thailand) are uncompromisingly hot, chilies are generally used sparingly in main dishes, appearing in a side-dish such as a sambal, as dried chili flakes or pickled, so you can adjust the heat to suit your taste.

Unlike Indian cuisine, Southeast Asian food doesn't normally contain large quantities of spices, with the exception of parts of Indonesia, Malaysia, and Burma. Elsewhere, cooks usually restrict themselves to a little freshly ground coriander, a pinch of turmeric, a stick of cinnamon and a whole star anise, or black pepper crushed with garlic and coriander root.

The appetite-sharpening sourness of many dishes has a wonderful fruitiness and fragrance so much richer than any vinegar; this comes from limes, tamarind juice, or wild acidic fruits, as well as tomatoes, star fruit, and pineapple. A perfect balance is often struck with palm sugar, fragrant as well as sweet, although regular cane sugar is also widely used.

There's no denying there's something fishy going on in Southeast Asian kitchens. Various forms of fermented fish are used throughout the region, yet amazingly, their alchemy is such that the resulting dishes don't actually taste of fish. Rather, they have a saltiness, an aroma, and a complex note that is difficult to isolate. First and foremost is fish sauce, an amber, fragrant, and salty liquid made from fermented fish, while in Cambodia, Laos, and southern Thailand, the pungency of fermented fish paste is particularly appreciated. Another fishy essential used virtually all the way from Burma to Bali is dried shrimp paste, added sparingly but with great effect. Dried prawns also add a wonderful depth and texture to many dishes.

So what do cooks combine with all these herbs and seasonings? The staple food throughout most of the region is rice, eaten with cooked and raw vegetables, as well as unripe fruits which are eaten in salads or cooked. There's fish from the rivers, lakes, and sea, and to a lesser extent, poultry and meat. This is generally pork (in non-Muslim countries), water buffalo, or beef, although in isolated rural districts, wild game and all kinds of less conventional creatures are tossed into the cooking pot or onto the grill.

Fresh and dried noodles are popular. These are mostly made from rice flour, although wheat noodles and transparent jelly-like noodles made from mung beans are also found. Rice flour is also used to make both fresh and dried wrappers for food, particularly in Vietnam.

Along the coasts and in the more fertile regions, coconuts provide creamy rich milk for many soups, stews, curries, and desserts. If we leave aside coconut milk (which, sadly, is fat-saturated), most Southeast Asian food is healthy. Lots of vegetables are eaten, many of them raw. Grilling, steaming, and simmering are the most commonly used cooking methods, and although some food is deep-fried, it is much more common to find ingredients stir-fried in just a trace of oil.

Despite so many shared elements, every country in Southeast Asia has its own special ingredients and dishes. The food of Burma has been influenced by its powerful neighbors, India and China, as well by geography. The coastal people prefer fish in all its forms, while the Burmese living in the dry central plains around Mandalay and on the Shan plateau replace fermented fish and prawn pastes with distinctive fermented bean wafers or fermented lentil sauces.

The cuisine of Thailand is probably the most varied in Southeast Asia, ranging from the generally hot, sour food of the north, through the simple yet striking dishes of the poorer northeast, down to rich coconut-milk dishes in the south, with sophisticated royal cuisine found in the capital. Thai food is the most emphatically flavored of all Southeast Asian cuisines, almost always a little hotter, sourer, sweeter, and saltier, yet always perfectly balanced.

Vietnam, Laos, and Cambodia were all part of what the French colonials referred to as Indochina, yet they are quite different. This is cleverly summed up by the local saying: "the Vietnamese plant rice, the Lao watch it grow and the Cambodians listen to it growing." One thing they share in common is excellent French bread, a most welcome colonial legacy.

Vietnamese food is scintillating, sophisticated, and often deceptively simple, with a subtle balance of flavors. The Vietnamese have a passion for wrap and roll, using wafer-thin dried rice papers, freshly steamed rice pancakes or lettuce leaves to enclose an amazing range of food. Rolls and barbecued meat are eaten with a platter of fresh herbs, bean sprouts, and salad leaves that accompanies just about every meal, even a simple bowl of noodle soup.

Most Laotians prefer glutinous or sticky rice to normal rice as their staple (as do the Thais living on the Lao border). Water buffalo is the most popular meat, but there is still a remarkable array of anything that slithers, jumps, and flies — frogs, eels, tiny birds, grasshoppers — in local markets. A large percentage of Lao plants are still gathered in the wild, including bamboo shoots, young leaves, rhizomes, flowers, and even a type of river algae.

Cambodia food is perhaps the most "pure" in the region, using fewer introduced ingredients than its neighbors. It is also the only country in the Southeast Asia where black pepper (the original source of heat before chilies were introduced) is still largely preferred. Fresh lemon grass, galangal, kaffir lime leaf are the most popular herbs, and freshwater fish (especially from the huge Tonle Sap lake) is much more common than meat.

Malaysia and Singapore share many culinary similarities, largely the result of waves of Chinese and Indian immigrants. The original inhabitants, the Malays, form around 50 percent of the population of Malaysia, while Singapore is predominantly Chinese. Like most Indonesians, the Muslim Malays do not eat pork; their food is often rich in coconut milk, generously spiced and frequently chili-hot.

The earliest Chinese immigrants to Singapore, and to Penang and Malacca (both now part of Malaysia) gave birth to an exciting cross-cultural cuisine blending Chinese and Malay ingredients and cooking styles. Known as Nonya cuisine (after the term for the women who created it), this sometimes contains Burmese, Thai, and Indonesian influences as well — a true Southeast Asian synthesis.

Indonesian cuisine differs considerably from one region to another. Best known, perhaps, are the mild, often sweet flavors of Java and the richly spiced, chili-hot and fragrant food of West Sumatra. Hindu Bali — the only area in the world's largest Muslim nation to enjoy pork — offers some of Indonesia's most exciting dishes.

Over the years, I have been amazed by the generosity of cooks throughout Southeast Asia. I don't think anyone has ever refused to let me peer over their shoulder, or been reluctant to explain an ingredient or a technique. I have been able to pass on some of this in books I've written about almost every individual Southeast Asian cuisine, but I feel it's now time to put some of my favorite recipes together in just one book.

This highly personal selection includes only a fraction of my favorites (my publisher refused to let me include them all). I've resisted the temptation to include purely Chinese or Indian food found in places like Singapore and Malaysia, concentrating on the indigenous dishes, or those which show a fusion of foreign and local cuisines. And I've avoided the most esoteric recipes as I know it's not always easy to find such things as fresh palm heart, turmeric flowers and fermented sticky rice in your local Asian store.

I've had a fabulous time "living the food," gathering, cooking, and enjoying these recipes over the years. I just hope you have half as much fun trying them out in your own kitchen.

You may find that the grouping of recipes within this book somewhat different from the conventional approach. It is worth remembering that in Southeast Asia, unless a one-dish meal such as noodles is being served, all dishes served with rice are generally placed on the table at the same time, for everyone to share.

This means that the grouping of dishes is not a hard and fast rule. Thus, within this book, snacks, starters, and soups are grouped into one chapter, as are salads, rice, and noodles. Because some recipes take much longer than others to prepare — and because time is often an important factor in busy modern lives — I've grouped various poultry, seafood, and meat dishes into two categories. A Flash in the Pan includes dishes that can be whipped up in under 30 minutes, while Time to Impress includes those recipes which take a lot longer, either in preparation time or actual cooking. Side dishes, which include various dips, relishes, pickles and cooked vegetable dishes, are grouped in the chapter A Little Something on the Side. The last category, Sweet Endings, says it all: delicious sweets that can either bring a meal to a close or be served, Southeast Asian-style, as a between-meal snack.

So free up your approach to food. Everything is flexible. Enjoyment is paramount. Welcome to the feast!

how to prepare the basics

The preparation of various Southeast Asian ingredients (such as shallots, lemon grass, etc) is described in Southeast Asian Ingredients (page 212). Some other important tasks which are a little more complex or take longer to describe are discussed here in greater detail.

Banana Leaf
If you are fortunate enough to have access to a whole banana plant, cut off an entire leaf. Cut down either side of the thick central rib to obtain two long leaf halves, then trim these to the required size using a pair of scissors. Most cooks will have to make do with packets of either fresh or frozen banana leaf. To prepare banana leaf for cooking, wash the leaves, then cut to the size specified in each recipe. To make banana leaf pliable for folding around food or for fashioning into little cups, it must be softened by passing it briefly through a gas flame (you can watch the moisture starting to rise and the color turn brighter), or by soaking the leaves in boiling water until they soften. When using banana leaf as a wrapper, keep the upper, more shiny side on the outside. (Aluminum foil can be used as a substitute, but it does not provide the moisture, nor the subtle flavor, that are characteristic of banana leaf.)

Crushed Dried Chili Flakes
You can make these by dry-frying whole dried chilies (the large type, not dried bird's-eye chilies) in a wok, turning them until they darken and become crisp. Take care not to burn them, however, as they cook very quickly. After frying, discard the stem end, break the chilies into smaller pieces, and process both the chilies and the seeds in a spice grinder until they are coarsely ground. Cool, then store in an airtight container; they'll keep indefinitely in the freezer.

Coconut Milk
If you can obtain freshly grated or frozen grated coconut, it's worth making your own coconut milk, especially for desserts or cakes. Put about 4 cups of room-temperature grated coconut (about 1 large coconut or 400–500 g) in a bowl and add $1/2$ cup (125 ml) of warm water. Squeeze with your hand for about a minute, then transfer the coconut and liquid to a cheese cloth set over a bowl. Grab the ends of the cloth together, tighten them and squeeze firmly to extract as much juice as possible to obtain thick coconut milk. To obtain coconut cream, let the thick coconut milk stand in the refrigerator for 10 to 15 minutes, then spoon off the rich cream that rises to the top.

To get thin coconut milk, put the squeezed coconut back in the bowl, add $2^1/_2$ cups (625 ml) of tepid water squeeze firmly with your hand for at least 1 minute (you could process it in a food processor at low speed for about 30 seconds if you prefer). Put the coconut back in the cheesecloth and squeeze firmly to extract all the liquid. For regular coconut milk, combine the thick and thin coconut milk without skimming off the coconut cream.

Freshly grated coconut and coconut milk are perishable, and will start to turn sour in a few hours. A pinch of salt slows the process (hence the faintly salty taste in many Southeast Asian cakes). However, even if refrigerated, coconut milk will be unusable after 24 hours unless first slowly heated to boiling point. Some cooks add $1/2$ to 1 teaspoon of cornflour to coconut milk or cream and stir it slowly until it comes almost to the boil. It can then be cooled and kept refrigerated for a day or so. (See also Coconut, page 212)

Crisp-fried Shallots & Garlic, and Flavored Oil
Peel shallots or garlic and slice thinly and evenly; this is important so that they will cook evenly. Heat enough vegetable oil to cover the shallots or garlic in a wok. When it is just warm, not hot, add the sliced shallots or garlic and cook over low heat, stirring frequently, until they are golden brown and crisp. It is essential to keep the temperature low otherwise the shallots or garlic will brown before they are cooked through; shallots may take around 6 to 8 minutes of slow cooking, garlic a little less. Lift out and dry on paper towel and when completely cold, store in an airtight jar; do not add salt as this will turn them limp. The flavored shallot or garlic oil is kept and used as a seasoning oil, drizzled over cooked food.

Dry-roasted Grated Coconut
This can be done using either fresh or desiccated coconut; the latter will turn golden much more quickly than freshly grated coconut. Put the coconut in a heavy dry wok and put over low heat. Cook, stirring frequently, until golden all over, about 8 to 10 minutes for fresh coconut, 3 to 4 minutes for desiccated. Remove immediately and cool completely before storing in an airtight container. Sometimes, roasted coconut is pounded while still hot until it turns into any oily paste.

Dry-roasted Peanuts

Roast the peanuts in a dry wok, preferably with the skins intact, in the same fashion as for coconut, for about 8 to 10 minutes. After cooking, leave the peanuts until cool enough to handle, then take outside and rub the skins vigorously to loosen the skin. Toss the peanuts a little, blowing to dislodge the skins (or let the wind do it for you).

Toasted Dried Shrimp Paste

Dried shrimp paste is almost always cooked, except in a few Thai dips. Sometimes, it is added raw to other pounded ingredients which are then fried or simmered, but more often, it is cooked on its own before being added to the dish. Even the most ardent shrimp paste lover will agree that it has an incredibly pungent smell during cooking, so to avoid having to do the job too often, and to have a stock of cooked dried shrimp paste on hand, I suggest toasting 1 to 2 tablespoons and keeping it in a sealed jar (you seldom need more than 1 teaspoon per recipe). Do not, however, use ready-toasted dried shrimp paste for dips and sambals; the full flavor of freshly cooked shrimp paste is vital for these.

One of the best ways to cook dried shrimp paste without the smell forcing everyone out of the house is to put the required amount on a piece of foil, folding over a flap and pressing down to make a thin layer. Tuck the edges of foil in loosely to make a packet, then set this on a wire grill directly over a medium gas flame, or under a broiler or grill. Cook for about 2 minutes, then turn and cook the other side for another couple of minutes. Open the packet to check that the shrimp paste has lost its wet, raw look and smells fragrant. If you don't have a grill or broiler, you can put the foil package into a wok or non-stick frying pan; it may need a little longer to cook.

Roasted Rice Powder

Put $1/4$ cup of raw long-grain rice in a heavy dry wok and put over low heat. Cook, stirring frequently, until the rice is golden-brown all over, about 8 to 10 minutes. While still hot, transfer to a mortar or spice grinder and grind or process to a sandy texture; do not grind finely as it is important for it to have a crunchy texture. I prefer to use a mortar to be able to monitor closely just how fine the rice is getting; around 30 seconds of turning the pestle firmly is generally enough. When the rice powder is completely cold, store in an airtight jar.

Preparing Ground Spices and Seasoning Pastes with a Spice Grinder

If you're ever tempted to use ground spices bought in a bottle or plastic pack, just try this test. Lightly toast in a dry pan some whole spice seeds (coriander, for example) for about a minute, or until they start to smell fragrant. Transfer them to a spice grinder and process to a fine powder. Lift the lid and sniff the result, then compare this with commercially available ground coriander that was processed goodness knows how long ago, and has gone from the factory to the store to your cupboard and been kept there until you're about to use it. I'm certain that after doing this test, you'll be convinced that it's best to grind your own spices. Heating spices before grinding crisps them slightly, making them easy to grind, and it also helps release the fragrance and flavor in the volatile oils.

Freshly roasted and ground spices can be cooled before being stored in an airtight container in the freezer, where they keep every bit of their fresh fragrance. Since I use a lot of coriander and cumin, to save time, I prepare a batch of several tablespoons of freshly roasted and ground spices and freeze them; they do not freeze into a solid block but retain their powdery texture, and when used, taste as if they have been freshly toasted and ground.

Seasoning pastes are used in countless Southeast Asian dishes. When using a spice grinder (and, indeed, if using a mortar and pestle), it is important to slice or chop the ingredients before processing. If using dry spices as part of the paste, these should be ground first, then the fresh moist ingredients such as chilies, shallots, garlic, galangal, and lemon grass added.

If you are not including shallots, which give off a lot of moisture, you may need to add some liquid to the spice grinder to keep the ingredients turning. Process the ingredients to break them up, switch off the grinder and scrape down the sides and lid with a rubber spatula, and process again. Keep repeating this, adding a little oil, water or coconut milk (each recipe suggests which is appropriate) if needed. Don't overload the jar of your spice grinder; divide the ingredients into two or even three batches if needed and process each until completely ground.

Cutting a Chicken

The chicken is usually cooked still on the bone, and most cooks begin with a whole fresh chicken, which is cut it in to manageable portions before going into the cooking pot. You'll need a sharp heavy cleaver and a wooden chopping board for the task. In Southeast Asia, when you buy a chicken in the market, you get the whole bird, head, feet and all. Remove these, or start with a trimmed Western-style chicken. Cut off both the legs at the joint where they join the body, then cut each leg, separating the thigh from the drumstick. in half. Put these four pieces to one side. Cut off the wings, taking a generous portion of the breast where they join the body. Cut off the wing tips and reserve for stock. Cut lengthways down the body, to one side of the back bone, then chop across each half to make a total of six pieces. You will now have 12 pieces of chicken; if the thighs seem large, you could cut these in half so you have a total of 14 pieces.

Steamed Rice

Throughout Southeast Asia, where a meal is synonymous with rice, a common greeting is "have you eaten rice yet?" Steamed white rice — usually fragrant long-grain rice but sometimes glutinous or sticky rice — is most commonly cooked by the absorption method. In a few areas (such as Java), it is first boiled briefly in lots of water, then transferred to a conical woven basket, set over boiling water and steamed. Thousands of women in the cities and towns use a rice cooker; rural cooks and those who don't have a rice cooker follow this basic method for cooking rice. Choose a saucepan with a heavy base and allow $1/2$ cup uncooked rice per person. This should be enough for four.

2 cups (400 g) long-grain rice, preferably Thai jasmine
water to cover (see below)

Put the rice in the saucepan and cover it with cold water. Rub the rice with your hand for a few seconds, then pour out the cloudy water. Repeat this process two or three times until the water runs clear. This step is important as it removes any loose starch caused by the grains rubbing together during packing and transit, and helps make sure that your rice won't stick together in an unpalatable mess when cooked.

Add sufficient fresh water to the pan so that it comes up to the first joint of your forefinger when you set it on the surface of the rice. Cover the pan and bring the rice to the boil over high heat. Put the lid slightly to one side, lower the heat a little and continue boiling until all the liquid has been absorbed and you see small "craters" appearing on the surface of the rice; this will probably take around 5 minutes.

Lower the heat to the absolute minimum, cover the pan firmly and cook the rice for 10 minutes. Remove the lid, wipe off any moisture underneath, and fluff up the rice with a fork or chopstick. Cover the pan again, remove from the heat and stand 10 minutes, or up to 1 hour, before serving.

Basic Chicken or Pork Stock

This simple, lightly seasoned stock is the basis of countless soups and other dishes in Southeast Asia. Vietnamese cooks like to add a pinch of sugar; some cooks omit the peppercorns; others use either onion or spring onion, while some use both, and Lao cooks often add a whole fresh coriander plant (root, stems, and leaves). This is the recipe I normally use, taking care to keep the salt content low in case I want to season it with salty fish sauce later. I find it's worth making a double quantity and deep-freezing it in 2 cups (500 ml) portions for future use.

1 teaspoon vegetable oil
1 clove garlic, crushed and minced
2 chicken carcasses, chopped in half, any skin and fatty
  deposits discarded, or 1 kg meaty pork bones
10 cups (2.5 liters) water
1 medium onion, minced
2 spring onions, minced
4 thin slices ginger
10 black peppercorns
$1/2$ teaspoon salt

Put the oil in a very large saucepan and heat. Add the garlic and stir-fry over low heat until it turns golden brown. Lift out the garlic and discard, leaving the garlic-flavored oil in the pan. Add the chicken or pork and water. Bring to the boil, then simmer uncovered for 10 minutes, skimming off any scum that rises to the surface.

Add all other ingredients, cover the pan and simmer very gently for 1 hour. Remove the lid and continue simmering very gently until the stock is reduced by half, about another hour. It is important not to let the stock boil, or the result will be cloudy rather than clear. Strain the stock into a large bowl, cool, then refrigerate for several hours. Scrape off any fat that solidifies on the surface, then transfer the stock into a covered container. Refrigerate or deep-freeze.

Note: This basic stock can be transformed into a simple soup to serve with any rice-based meal. Season it with a little fish sauce, soy sauce or salt, a sprinkle of white or black pepper, then add a little of what you fancy: a few leafy greens; bean sprouts; diced bean curd; sliced fresh or soaked dried black mushrooms; a few fresh prawns or slivers of chicken or pork. Simmer until the ingredients are cooked, and serve piping hot.

snacks, starters, and soups

It's often said that Asians are always eating, munching throughout the day and on into the night, stopping to buy savory nibbles or sweetmeats from itinerant vendors or roadside stalls. And why not? There are just so many irresistible goodies out there.

Some of the snack and starter recipes included here are perfect for serving with drinks, such as slices of Spicy Dried Beef, or Crispy Rice Cakes that you can dunk into one of the dips you'll find in the chapter, A Little Something on the Side.

If you're looking for an impressive start to a meal, you can't do better than succulent satay made from beef (Sate Istimewa). Unless, of course, you decide to serve scrumptious Thai Prawn Satay. Then again, you would consider one of the wonderful palate-tickling recipes such as Leaf-wrapped Savory Nibbles or Tuna Carpaccio.

For party snacks, you could try various types of roll-ups, including ever-popular Vietnamese Deep-fried Spring Rolls, or the refreshingly different Tangy Marinated Fish Roll-ups. And for a really substantial snack which makes a great lunch, you won't find anything more satisfying than Vietnamese Happy Pancakes. Unless, of course, it's an Indochinese Sandwich, where French *baguette* meets Southeast Asian meats, salads, and spreads.

Many of these snacks and starters could also be served as part of a main meal with rice, especially the various types of satay as well as Cambodian Fragrant Grilled Chicken Wings, Thai Sweet Corn Fritters, and Deep-fried Prawn or Fish Cakes.

In Southeast Asia, soup is a liquid dish of broth or coconut milk containing vegetables, fruit, seafood, poultry, or meat, served together with rice, and rarely eaten as a separate course. When you get used to eating soup the Asian way, spooning some of the solids on to your rice, and either sipping the broth from the soup bowl or pouring a little directly over the rice, the logic of soup becomes apparent. Steamed rice on its own is dry. Add the liquid from your soup and it is just so much easier to eat. As many of the locals say, soup "helps the rice down."

You can cook just about anything in a soup. Your main protein for the meal might come in Vietnamese Bouncy Beef Ball Soup, Cambodian Chicken Soup with Lime, Chili & Basil, or Thai Chicken & Coconut Milk Soup. Put some of your vegetables into Creamy Pumpkin Soup, or make Indonesian Sour Mixed Vegetable Soup, or healthy Spinach Soup with Sweet Corn. And don't stop at vegetables. You can enjoy fruit in the Piquant Fish Soup with Pineapple & Bean Sprouts.

(Noodle soups are generally eaten alone, rather than served with rice, and are therefore included in a separate chapter.)

deep-fried spring rolls *cha gio*

One of the things that makes these delightful Vietnamese spring rolls different to the Chinese variety is the wrapper of delicate rice paper. The filling is a lightly seasoned combination of pork, prawns, and transparent bean thread noodles, plus some crabmeat if you like. The *coup de grâce* is the way they are eaten, tucked in a cool lettuce leaf with fragrant herbs and crunchy bean sprouts, then dipped in salty, sour, sweet, and hot Vietnamese Fish Sauce Dip.

30 wedge-shaped rice papers, or 20–25 small round rice papers (5–6 in or 14–16 cm in diameter)
2–3 cups (500–750 ml) oil for deep frying

Accompaniment
lettuce leaves
1 cup mint sprigs
1 cup polygonum sprigs (long-stemmed Vietnamese mint or *rau ram*)
1 cup fresh coriander sprigs
1 cup (80 g) bean sprouts
1 cup (250 ml) Vietnamese Fish Sauce Dip (page 175)

Filling
2 shallots, minced
1 clove garlic, minced
4 oz (125 g) lean pork, diced
$^1/_2$ lb (250 g) small or medium raw prawns, peeled (or 4 oz or 125 g peeled raw prawns)
4 oz (125 g) cooked crabmeat, or additional 4 oz (125 g) pork
1 spring onion, minced
4 teaspoons fish sauce
$^1/_4$ teaspoon freshly ground black pepper
handful (1 oz or 30 g) transparent noodles, soaked in hot water to soften, drained, cut in $^3/_4$ in (2 cm) lengths

Prepare the Filling by processing the shallots, garlic, and pork in a food processor until the pork is finely ground. Add the prawns, crabmeat (if using), spring onion, fish sauce, and pepper and process until smooth. Transfer to a bowl and stir in the noodles.

Put a large bowl of warm water and a clean kitchen towel on a bench or table. Dip a rice paper in the water for 4 to 5 seconds, remove it, and spread on the towel; if you are using wedge-shaped rice papers, put the pointed end facing away from you. Smooth the rice paper with your fingers until soft and pliable. Repeat until you have six to eight softened rice papers on the towel.

Put about 2 teaspoons of the Filling across the wider part of a wedge rice paper, or across each round rice paper, placing it about 1$^1/_4$ in (3 cm) from the bottom edge. Wet your fingers slightly and shape each portion of filling into a cigarette shape about 2 in (5 cm) long. Rinse and dry your hands and then fold up the end closest to you. Tuck in both sides, squeezing gently to make sure there isn't any air trapped, then roll up firmly. Put on a plate, making sure rolls do not touch each other. Repeat until all the rolls are prepared.

To prepare Accompaniment, wash, drain, and dry lettuce, both lots of mint and coriander. Divide between two large serving plates. Wash and drain bean sprouts and add to herbs. Put fish sauce dip into small sauce bowls.

Heat a wok for 30 seconds, then add oil for deep frying. When the oil is moderately hot (but not smoking), add several of the spring rolls, one at a time, taking care not to overcrowd the wok. Fry over medium heat until golden brown and cooked, about 5 minutes, stirring occasionally to prevent them sticking together and to ensure they are golden brown all over. Drain and serve hot with the dip and salad platter and prepared accompaniments.

To eat, each person puts a spring roll on a lettuce leaf, adding some of the herbs and bean sprouts. The leaf is tucked up and dipped in the sauce before eating.

Note: If you want to prepare the spring rolls in advance, cook them until light golden, about 3 minutes. Drain them on paper towel and keep at room temperature. Just before serving, re-heat the oil until very hot, then fry the spring rolls for about 1 minute until golden brown and crisp.

Serves: **4-6**   Preparation time: **45 min**   Cooking time: **25 min**

barbecued pork balls *nem nuong*

When the wonderful fragrance of grilling meat fills the streets of Vietnam each evening, chances are that these pork balls will be among the items sizzling away. Balls of lightly seasoned minced pork threaded onto skewers are cooked over charcoal, giving off little bursts of fragrance as drops of oil hit the hot coals. The pork balls are served with fresh herbs, lettuce, and bean sprouts, and normally accompanied by Vietnamese Salted Soybean & Peanut Sauce; you could, however, serve Vietnamese Fish Sauce Dip if you prefer.

$3\frac{1}{2}$ oz (100 g) hard pork fat, in one piece
$1\frac{1}{4}$ lb (600 g) lean pork shoulder or leg, thinly sliced
4 shallots, finely minced
4 cloves garlic, crushed and minced
2 tablespoons fish sauce
2 teaspoons sugar
1 teaspoon freshly ground black pepper
$\frac{1}{2}$ teaspoon salt
2 tablespoons roasted rice powder (page 18)
3 tablespoons vegetable oil
Salted Soybean, Pork & Peanut Sauce (page 178) or Vietnamese Fish Sauce Dip (page 175)

Accompaniments
2 butter lettuce, washed, leaves separated
$1\frac{1}{4}$ cups (100 g) bean sprouts
sliced cucumber
1–2 small star fruit, thinly sliced across, optional
1 cup loosely packed mint sprigs
1 cup loosely packed Asian basil or coriander leaf

Put the pork fat into a small saucepan with water to cover. Bring to the boil, simmer 10 minutes, then drain. When cool enough to handle, chop the fat into tiny pieces the size of a rice grain. Put the fat in a large bowl and add the pork, shallots, garlic, fish sauce, sugar, and pepper, mixing well. Cover and refrigerate at least 1 hour, or overnight if preferred.

Process the marinated mixture until it forms a paste. Add the toasted rice powder, pulse for 3 to 4 seconds to blend, then transfer the pork mixture to a bowl. Put the oil into a small bowl and smear some on the palms of your hands. Rub oil onto a plate.

Shape the pork paste into balls about $\frac{3}{4}$ in (2 cm) in diameter, squeezing firmly, then put the pork balls on the oiled plate. When all meat balls have been prepared, thread onto bamboo skewers, leaving at least $\frac{1}{2}$ in (1 cm) between each meat ball.

Put all the accompaniments (washed and dried where relevant) on a serving plate. Heat a table top griller or barbecue until very hot. Cook the skewers of pork, turning to brown all over, until done, about 10 minutes. Serve with the Accompaniments and individual bowls of dip. To eat the pork balls, slide them off the skewers, and put 1 or 2 at a time in a lettuce leaf with some of the herbs, bean sprouts, and cucumber. Spoon over a little of the sauce then roll up, dunking the roll into more of the sauce or the dip before eating.

Serves: **4** Preparation time: **30 min + 1 hour marinating** Cooking time: **15 mins**

extraordinary beef satay   *sate istimewa*

When I lived in Indonesia, I discovered that the best satay were invariably served in private homes. Friends from Southern Sulawesi kindly shared their family recipe; the name, *istimewa*, aptly translates as "extraordinary." Cubes of beef are marinated in sweet soy sauce, garlic, ginger, lime juice, spices, and grated kaffir lime rind, with a dash of vodka or brandy (my friends are Christian, so the Muslim ban on alcohol doesn't apply). There's so much flavor in the satay that there's no need to serve it with a peanut dip.

$^1/_3$ cup (85 ml) sweet soy sauce
3 tablespoons lime juice
3 tablespoons vodka or brandy
$1^1/_2$ tablespoons peanut or vegetable oil
1 teaspoon freshly ground coriander powder
1 teaspoon freshly ground cumin powder
2 cloves garlic, crushed and minced
2 teaspoons finely grated ginger
1 teaspoon finely grated kaffir lime or
   lemon rind
$^1/_2$ teaspoon salt
$1^1/_2$ lb (750 g) rump steak, in $^1/_2$ in (1.5 cm)
   slices, cut in 1 in (2.5 cm) squares
bamboo skewers, soaked in cold water
   30 minutes

Put the soy sauce, lime juice, vodka or brandy, 2 teaspoons of the oil, coriander, cumin, garlic, ginger, lime rind, and salt into a bowl. Add the beef, stirring to coat thoroughly. Cover and refrigerate for minimum 2 hours or up to 8 hours, stirring a couple of times while marinating.

Grease the grill of a barbecue or gas or electric griller with oil. Heat until very hot. Remove the beef from the marinade and thread onto bamboo skewers, first soaked in water for 30 minutes. Grill over high heat, turning frequently, until the beef is cooked to your taste, about 5 minutes.

Serves: **4-6**   Preparation time: **12 min + 2 hours marinating**   Cooking time: **6-10 min**

spiced dried beef *saiko niet*

I first came across Lao-style dried beef in a simple thatch restaurant in Vientiane, where it was served with mugs of wonderfully cold beer. It's not surprising that different versions dried beef are found in most of Southeast Asia, for in rural areas where refrigeration is non-existent, thin slices of marinated beef are sun-dried as a method of preservation. The dried beef is grilled to make a savory snack and can also be shredded and added to salads or served with rice. Don't worry if you can't sun-dry the beef — there are alternative methods.

1 lb (500 g) striploin or topside, in one piece
2 tablespoons minced ginger or 2 tablespoons very thinly sliced lemon grass
1–2 large red chilies, sliced
2 cloves garlic, minced
2 tablespoons sugar
1 tablespoon fish sauce
1 tablespoon light soy sauce
1 teaspoon salt
1 teaspoon freshly ground coriander powder
1 tablespoon vegetable oil

Chill the beef in the freezer for 30 minutes, then slice it thinly across the grain. Process the ginger or lemon grass, chilies, garlic, and sugar to a smooth paste, adding a little of the fish sauce if needed to keep the mixture turning. Transfer to a bowl and stir in the fish sauce, soy sauce, salt, coriander, and oil, mixing well. Add the beef strips and massage with your hand for about 30 seconds to mix thoroughly. Cover the bowl with plastic wrap and refrigerate 4 hours.

Spread the meat in a single layer on bamboo tray or on a metal rack and dry in the sun, turning the meat after a few hours. Leave in the sun until the meat is completely dry; this will take around 8 hours of full sunshine. Alternatively, you can put the rack of meat slices in a large baking dish and cook in the lowest possible oven until meat has completely dried out, about 4 hours. To serve, the dried beef can be cooked briefly over hot charcoal, about 2 minutes on both sides, or under a very hot grill. If you prefer, you could cook it on racks in a hot oven (425°F or 200°C) until crisp, about 10 minutes.

Serves: **4**   Preparation time: **15 min**   Drying time: **4-8 hours**   Cooking time: **4-10 minutes**

steamed pork sausage *cha lua*

You might think that the colonial French introduced the art of making *paté* and sausages to Vietnam, but sausages wrapped in banana leaf or stuffed into animal casings have been around Southeast Asia for generations. This silky steamed sausage is usually purchased in Vietnam, but it's easy to make at home with a food processor. Don't be put off by the amount of fat included; as any good *charcutier* (French or Vietnamese) will tell you, you must have plenty fat to make a good moist sausage.

1 lb (500 g) lean leg or loin pork, thinly sliced
4 shallots, minced
1 clove garlic, minced
1 teaspoon crushed rock sugar or white
  sugar
4 teaspoons tapioca flour
1 teaspoon bicarbonate of soda (baking soda)
$^1/_2$ teaspoon freshly ground black pepper
$^1/_3$ cup (85 ml) fish sauce
$3^1/_2$ oz (100 g) hard pork back (loin) fat,
  boiled in water 10 minutes, diced to about
  the size of a rice grain
2 pieces of banana leaf, 12 in (30 cm) square,
  softened in boiling water or a gas flame

Put the pork in a bowl. Process the shallots and garlic to a paste, then add this together with the sugar, tapioca flour, baking soda, pepper, and fish sauce to the pork. Massage with your hands for about a minute so that the marinade is absorbed. Cover the bowl, refrigerate and leave to marinate for 4 to 6 hours, or overnight if preferred.

Transfer the bowl of pork to the freezer for 15 minutes, then put the pork and every bit of its marinade into a food processor and blend until very fine and smooth. Add the pork fat and pulse just two or three times, until it is well mixed.

Put the pork mixture in the middle of one piece of banana leaf and with wet hands, shape it to make a fat roll about 8 in (20 cm) long. Lift the two ends of the banana leaf up (leaving the sides open for the moment) and fold over about $1^1/_4$ in (3 cm) on the top. Roll this down until the sausage is completely enclosed, then tuck in the sides. Put the roll on the second piece of banana leaf and repeat the rolling process, starting with the sealed side of the roll face down. Tie the double-wrapped roll loosely with string around the sides and ends (not too tightly as the sausage will swell during cooking).

Put the roll on a perforated disk or in a steamer set over a wok of boiling water, making sure the water does not touch the roll. Steam over boiling water for 2 hours, adding boiling water to the wok frequently to make sure it does not dry out. Leave the cool completely, then refrigerate until required.

The pork sausage is sliced thinly and served as a snack with pickles or tangy relish, or put inside French bread to make a typical Indochinese Sandwich (see below).

Serves: **6-8**   Preparation time: **1 hour + marinating 4 hours**   Cooking time: **2 hours**

indochinese sandwich

This fantastic snack is found everywhere that the French left their wonderful bread. It's a flexible recipe, with variations within each country as well as between neighboring countries. You need small loaves of crusty bread (crisped over a charcoal brazier in Laos and Cambodia), a spread, a filling of one or two types of meat or *paté*, crunchy vegetables, and herbs to finish it all off. Below are some of the options so you can compose your own variation on an Indochinese theme.

(1) small French loaves or *baguettes*, halved
  lengthways
(2) a spread of either mashed boiled eggs
  (a Cambodian favorite), chicken liver paté,
  soft pork paté, Onion/Chili Spread (see
  right), butter or mayonnaise
(3) slices of pork sausage such as Steamed
  Pork Sausage (above), Chinese red-
  roasted pork (*char siew*), chicken sausage
  or pieces of cooked chicken
(4) freshly grated green papaya (or chayote/
  choko) or sliced cucumber, plus shredded
  Long White Radish and Carrot Relish
  (page 178)
(5) fresh herbs such as coriander, mint, or
  spring onion

Onion/Chili Spread
1 tablespoon vegetable oil
2 large red or brown onions, finely minced
2-4 teaspoons Roasted Thai Chili Paste
  (page 179)
$^1/_4$ cup (60 ml) water

Heat the oil in a small saucepan and stir-fry the onion over low-medium heat until transparent, about 2 minutes. Add the chili paste, cover, and cook 5 minutes. Add the water, stir and continue cooking until the onion is very soft, about another 10 minutes, stirring occasionally. Transfer to a bowl and leave to cool.

Serves: **4-6**   Preparation time: **15 min**
Cooking time: **$1^1/_4$-$1^1/_2$ hours**

crispy rice cakes *khao tong*

One of the reasons I've never got around to buying a rice cooker is that I love to cook steamed rice until it forms a dry crust on the bottom of the pan. I sun-dry this the next day, then store it for frying into crisp, crunchy rice cakes which are perfect with all kinds of dips. Here's another way of making these rice cakes which may be easier if you happen to use a rice cooker, or if you don't have a steady supply of sunlight.

2 cups (400 g) uncooked long-grain rice
2 teaspoons oil

Serves: **8-10**   Preparation time: **10 min**
Drying time: **2 hours**   Cooking time: **45 min**

Cook the rice in the usual way (page 19). You can now either use two frying pans, each about 8¹/₂ in (22 cm) and preferably non-stick, or double your length of cooking time by doing the next stage of cooking in two batches. Assuming you are using two frying pans, put 1 teaspoon of the vegetable oil in each. Heat the oil, then swirl it around to grease the pan over the sides and base, then tip out any excess oil and reserve.

Add half the rice to each greased frying pan. Grease a spatula with oil and press it down very firmly on the surface of the rice so that the grains stick together to make a compact cake. Put the frying pans over the lowest heat possible and cook for 10 minutes, pressing down on the surface of the rice several times. Slide the rice cake onto a large plate and invert it over the pan, so the rice cake goes back in with the cooked side facing up. Press down again on the top of the rice with your spatula and cook for another 10 minutes.

Slide each rice cake onto a baking tray lined with baking paper and cook in the oven set to the lowest possible heat until thoroughly dry, about 1¹/₂ hours to 2 hours. Cool the rice cake completely, then break up into chunks of about 2 in (5 cm). Store in an airtight container for several months.

To cook the rice cakes, heat vegetable oil for deep-frying in a wok until very hot. Add 2 or 3 rice cakes at a time and cook until puffed up and golden brown on both sides; this should take less than a minute. Drain on paper towel and serve with any kind of dip, or simply sprinkle with a little salt and a few crushed dried chili flakes.

tangy marinated fish roll-ups *goi ca*

With its intriguing balance of flavors and textures, this is one of the most refreshing appetizers I've come across. But be warned: it really gets the appetite going, so be sure you have plenty of other food to follow. Strips of fish are "cooked" in vinegar, then combined with onions, herbs, crunchy peanuts, and deep-fried shallots. Look for the freshest whole fish you can find (don't buy fillets unless you're absolutely sure of their freshness). If you want to try the Vietnamese version, wrap everything up in a rice paper, or go the Laotian way and use lettuce leaves.

10–13 oz (300–400 g) fresh white fish fillets (grouper, whiting, or other fine-fleshed fish)
1 cup (250 ml) rice vinegar
1 red or brown onion, halved and very thinly sliced
4 teaspoons caster sugar
2 teaspoons salt
1 heaped tablespoon finely minced mint
1 heaped tablespoon finely minced polygonum (long-stemmed Vietnamese mint)
1 fresh red chili, seeded and minced
3 tablespoons crushed dry-roasted peanuts
1 tablespoon crisp-fried shallots
12–16 small rice papers, 5½–6½ in (14–16 cm) in diameter, or 12–16 soft lettuce leaves
2 under-ripe star fruit (carambola) or 2 green tomatoes, thinly sliced

Wash the fillets, dry thoroughly with paper towel, then cut into thin slices about ½ x 2 in (1 x 5 cm). Put the fish in a bowl and pour over the vinegar. Stir and leave to marinate at room temperature for 1 hour.

After fish has been marinating 30 minutes, put the onion into a separate bowl. Sprinkle with sugar and 1 teaspoon of the salt, massaging the onion with your fingers. Marinate for 30 minutes.

When the fish has marinated 1 hour, transfer to a sieve and rinse briefly under running water. Drain well and pat the fish dry with paper towel, then put into a bowl. Squeeze the onion to remove as much liquid as possible, but do not rinse. Combine the onion, fish, remaining 1 teaspoon of salt, herbs, chili, peanuts, and shallots, mixing well with your hand.

If using rice papers, dip them one at a time into a bowl of warm water for 3 to 4 seconds. Remove and place on a kitchen towel, smoothing them with your fingers. Add some of the fish mixture to each rice paper (or lettuce leaf), roll up to form a cigar shape, and put on a serving plate. Garnish with star fruit or green tomato.

Serves: **4-6**   Marinating: **1 hour**   Preparation time: **10 min**

lacy malay pancakes   *roti jala*

In the old days, Malay cooks used to make these lacy pancakes by putting their hand in the batter and then swirling it over the frying pan, letting the batter dribble down their fingers. Then sophistication struck and the *roti jala* cup was born, a cup-like funnel with four spouts. You could use a regular kitchen funnel, or a Japanese soy sauce dispenser to get the appropriate lacy look to these pancakes, which are fabulous for mopping up curry gravy.

1 1/2 cups (185 g) plain flour
1/2 teaspoon salt
2 eggs, lightly beaten
2 1/2 cups (560 ml) coconut milk or fresh milk
vegetable oil for greasing pan
roti jala cup or kitchen funnel

Sift the flour into a bowl and stir in the salt and eggs. Add the coconut or fresh milk gradually, stirring to make a smooth batter.

Lightly grease a frying pan, preferably non-stick, with a little oil. Hold a *roti jala* cup, a Japanese soy sauce dispenser with a narrow hole, or a regular kitchen funnel with the end partly closed with one finger to let through a thin stream of batter, over the frying pan. Use the other hand to pour in about 1/4 cup of the batter, swirling the cup or funnel rapidly in circles over the pan to make a lacy pattern as the batter goes in. Allow the pancake to set on top, then turn over and cook for another 30 seconds. Use a spatula to fold the pancake in half, then half again, and transfer to a plate. Continue, greasing the pan after each pancake, until all the batter has been used up. If the batter thickens towards the end, add a little more milk. Serve with any curry.

Serves: **4**   Preparation time: **7 min**   Cooking time: **40 mins**

prawn satay *satay kung*

Satay — skewers of seasoned meat, poultry, or seafood grilled to perfection over charcoal — is most commonly associated with Malaysia and Indonesia, but the Thais also prepare some amazingly good satay in the south. In this version, the natural sweetness of prawns is accentuated by the marinade of coconut cream, galangal, lemon grass, and spices. You could eat these with a peanut dipping sauce, but I think a squeeze of lime or lemon juice is all that's needed (and it's fat-free as well).

4 teaspoons coriander seeds, lightly toasted
1 teaspoon cumin seeds, lightly toasted
2 teaspoons very finely minced fresh
  galangal
2 stems lemon grass, tender inner part of
  bottom 3 in (8 cm) only, thinly sliced
4 teaspoons sugar
1 teaspoon salt
$^1/_2$ teaspoon white pepper
$^1/_4$ teaspoon turmeric powder
$^1/_2$ cup (125 ml) coconut cream
$^1/_4$ cup (60 ml) water
2 lb (1 kg) large or medium raw prawns,
  peeled and deveined, leaving head and
  tail intact
bamboo skewers, soaked in cold water
  30 minutes
1 tablespoon vegetable oil
1 large lime or lemon, quartered

Put the coriander and cumin seeds in spice grinder and process until fine. Add galangal, lemon grass, sugar, salt, pepper, turmeric, and 1 tablespoon of the coconut cream and process to a smooth paste.

Transfer the spice paste to a bowl and stir in the remaining coconut cream and water, mixing to make a smooth marinade. Add prawns and stir to coat with the marinade. Cover with plastic wrap and marinate at room temperature minimum 30 minutes, or refrigerate for up to 4 hours.

Grease the grill of a barbecue or broiler with oil. Heat until very hot. Thread a prawn horizontally onto each skewer, then cook over high heat for 2 minutes. Turn and cook another 2 minutes; check to see if prawns are cooked. Serve accompanied by lime wedges.

Serves: **4-6**   Makes: **about 20 sticks**   Preparation time: **12 min**   Cooking time: **5 min**

deep-fried thai prawn or fish cakes *tod man kung/pla*

If you've ever visited any of the coastal areas of Thailand, you're sure to have encountered this popular street snack, fried on the spot for you at food stalls. Tod Man Kung (or Tod Man Pla, if you're using fish) has a characteristic springy texture, and is wonderfully flavored with kaffir lime, curry paste, and fish sauce. Serve the prawn or fish cakes with Thai sweet chili sauce, which you buy off the shelf at most supermarkets.

2 lb (1 kg) fresh prawns, peeled and de-veined,
  or 1¹/₄ lb (600 g) boneless white fish fillet,
  skinned and cubed
3–4 tablespoons Thai Red Curry Paste
  (page 164)
2 tablespoons cornflour
¹/₂ teaspoon bicarbonate of soda (baking soda)
2 tablespoons fish sauce
1 egg white
2–3 string beans, very finely sliced, optional
4 kaffir lime leaves, cut in hair-like shreds,
  or 2 spring onions, finely minced
2 medium ripe tomatoes
¹/₂ large or 1 small cucumber
vegetable oil for deep frying
Thai sweet chili sauce to serve

Put the prawns or fish into a food processor, add the curry paste, cornflour, bicarbonate of soda, fish sauce, and egg white, and process until smooth. Transfer to a bowl and stir in the long beans and kaffir lime leaves.

Wet your hands and shape about ¹/₄ cup of the prawn or fish mixture into a ball. Flatten it slightly to make a circle about ³/₄ in (2 cm) thick. Put on a plate and continue until all the mixture is used up.

Slice the tomatoes. Rake the cucumber lengthways with a fork to score the skin, then slice thinly. Arrange tomato and cucumber in alternating slices around the edge of a serving dish.

Heat oil in a wok. When it is hot, add a few prawn or fish cakes at a time and deep fry until cooked, turning so they turn golden brown all over, 3 to 4 minutes. Drain on paper towel and transfer to the serving dish.

Serves: **6-8**   Makes: **about 8 large pieces or 24 bite-sized pieces**
Preparation time: **25 min**   Cooking time: **15 min**

sweet corn fritters *tod man khao phod*

I thought sweet corn fritters were as American as apple pie until I came across an excellent Thai version in the southern city of Nakkorn Si Thammarat. Fresh sweet corn kernels are mixed in a batter with Thai curry paste, soy sauce, and fish sauce — and what a superb difference those seasonings make. If you can't get fresh sweet corn, you could use defrosted sweet corn kernels, but avoid the canned version as the texture is disappointingly limp. These tasty fritters are ideal as a snack or appetizer, or you could just as easily serve them as part of a main meal.

4 tablespoons plain flour
4 tablespoons rice flour
1 1/2–2 tablespoon red curry paste or curry powder
1 tablespoon fish sauce
1 tablespoon light soy sauce
1/4 teaspoon salt
2 large eggs
3 cups (400 g) raw sweet corn kernels (cut from 3–4 corn cobs) or defrosted sweet corn kernels
vegetable oil for shallow-frying

Put both lots of flour, curry paste, fish sauce, soy sauce, and salt in a bowl and stir in the eggs, mixing well. Add the sweet corn kernels and stir; if the batter seems to dry, add 1 to 2 tablespoons water.

Heat enough oil to cover the bottom of a frying pan by about 1/4 in (0.5 cm). Drop in about 2 heaped tablespoons of the corn mixture, pressing lightly with a spatula to flatten it into a round cake (or make tiny fritters from about 2 teaspoons of batter if serving as finger food). Fry the fritters over medium heat, a few at a time, until golden brown on both sides and cooked through, 4 to 5 minutes. Drain on paper towel and serve warm or at room temperature. These sweet corn fritters go very well with Vinegared Cucumber Salad (page 182).

Serves: **4** Preparation time: **7 min** Cooking time: **5 min**

happy pancakes with pork & prawns *bahn khoai*

This is one of several types of savory pancake sold by street vendors and market stalls in Vietnam. In line with the Vietnamese passion for fresh flavors, the pancakes are eaten with lettuce and herbs, with Salted Soybean & Peanut Dip drizzled over (but they're just as good with the ubiquitous Vietnamese Fish Sauce Dip). The pancakes are usually prepared from scratch for each person in Vietnam, but I find it's quicker to cook all the pork and prawn filling in advance when you're serving pancakes for several people.

$1/_2$ lb (250 g) lean pork, shredded
1 lb (500 g) small to medium fresh prawns, peeled and deveined
2 teaspoons fish sauce
2 teaspoons minced garlic
1 teaspoon Chinese rice wine (preferably Shao Hsing), optional
$1/_2$ teaspoon freshly ground black pepper
2 spring onions, green and white portions separated, minced
2 cups (320 g) rice flour
1 teaspoon salt
1 teaspoon caster sugar
$3/_4$ teaspoon turmeric powder
$2^1/_4$ cups (560 ml) water
3 large eggs
3 cups (250 g) bean sprouts, washed and drained
1 red or brown onion, halved and sliced very thinly across
$1/_2$ cup (125 ml) vegetable oil

Accompaniments
2 whole butter lettuce, leaves washed and dried
1 cup firmly packed mint leaves
1 cup firmly packed coriander leaves
2 small star fruit or 1 small cucumber, thinly sliced across
Salted Soybean, Pork & Peanut Sauce (page 178) or Vietnamese Fish Sauce Dip (page 175)

Put the pork and prawns in a bowl and add the fish sauce, garlic, rice wine, pepper, and the white portion of spring onions. Mix well with your fingers and set aside.

Combine the rice flour, salt, sugar, and turmeric in a bowl and gradually stir in the water to make a very thin batter. Put the eggs in a bowl and beat lightly with a fork. Set near the stove.

Prepare the Accompaniments. Arrange the lettuce leaves, mint, coriander, and star fruit on a serving platter. Divide the dip between four to eight small bowls.

Heat 2 tablespoons of oil in a wok. When hot, add the pork and prawn mixture and stir-fry for 3 minutes. Transfer to a plate and divide into eight portions. Put the green portion of spring onions, bean sprouts, and onion in a bowl and gently toss with your fingers, then add to the portions of pork and prawn.

Heat 1 tablespoon oil in a large frying pan, preferably cast-iron or non-stick, swirling it around to completely grease the base and sides. Tip out the excess oil and save it for greasing the pan next time. Re-heat the pan and when very hot, stir the batter, then measure $1/_3$ cup and pour it quickly into the frying pan, tilting the pan so that it spreads over the bottom; don't worry if there are a few small gaps. Scatter over one portion of the pork, prawn, and bean sprout mixture. Cover the pan and cook over medium heat for 2 minutes.

Uncover the pan and drizzle over about 2 tablespoons of the beaten egg, filling in any gaps that might have been left in the pancake. Cover and cook over medium heat for 1 minute. Remove the lid and cook uncovered for about 1 minute, to make sure the bottom is crispy, then fold the pancake in half and transfer to a serving plate (see Note). Repeat, adding oil to the pan and stirring the batter each time until you have made eight pancakes. Serve with the Accompaniments and dip. The pancakes are normally broken into pieces and tucked in a lettuce leaf with the herbs, a slice or two of star fruit or cucumber and a dollop of sauce, then rolled up and eaten.

Note: Ideally, each pancake should be served immediately and eaten while still hot and crisp. A frying pan set on tabletop burner would be ideal, saving you from running back to the kitchen repeatedly; alternatively, you could use two frying pans and cook two pancakes at the same time to speed things up.

Serves: **4-8**   Makes: **about 8 pieces using a $8^1/_2$-in (22-cm) frying pan**
Preparation time: **20 min**   Cooking time: **40 min**

thai tuna carpaccio

Wafer-thin slices of beef marinated in lime juice and seasonings can be found in northern Thailand but in this modern variation, fresh tuna replaces the beef and is marinated not only with lime juice but olive oil, like the well-known Italian beef carpaccio. All you need for this recipe is spanking fresh tuna, lime juice, olive oil, freshly ground black pepper, and fresh coriander leaf. It's amazingly easy to prepare, and bound to be a success as a part of either a Southeast Asian or Western meal.

$1/2$ cup (125 ml) extra virgin olive oil
$1/4$ cup (60 ml) lime or lemon juice
2–3 teaspoons fish sauce
$1/4$ teaspoon freshly ground black pepper
13 oz (400 g) *sashimi*-quality fresh tuna, thinly sliced
3 tablespoons minced fresh coriander leaf

Combine the olive oil, lemon juice, fish sauce, and black pepper in a small bowl, whisking to blend. Pour half of the dressing onto a flat plate large enough to hold tuna slices in one layer. Arrange the tuna on top of the dressing, then spoon the remaining dressing over the top. Cover the plate with plastic wrap and refrigerate 20 to 30 minutes.

Transfer the tuna slices to a serving plate, sprinkling with fresh coriander leaf.

Serves: **4**   Preparation time: **8 min**

mussels with lemon grass, lime leaves & basil *hoy mangpoo ob mor din*

This is quite the most delicious way of preparing mussels you'll ever try. The fragrance of kaffir lime leaves, lemon grass, and Asian basil totally transforms the mussels, which are briefly simmered in the herb-seasoned stock and eaten with sweet Thai chili sauce. The mussels can be served with rice and also make a perfect first course for a Western meal, served with crusty French bread and a good Sauvignon Blanc.

3 cups (750 ml) water
6 kaffir lime leaves, torn
3 stems lemon grass, bottom 6½ in (16 cm) only, bruised and cut in 4 pieces
1 teaspoon salt
2 lb (1 kg) mussels, preferably green-lipped variety, scrubbed to remove grit, washed and drained
1–2 large red chilies, sliced
½ cup firmly packed Asian basil sprigs
sweet Thai chili sauce

Put the water into a wok or large saucepan and add the kaffir lime leaves, lemon grass, and salt. Bring to the boil, lower heat, and simmer uncovered for 5 minutes. Add the mussels and continue simmering, stirring frequently, removing each mussel immediately the shell opens and transferring it to a serving bowl. Discard any mussels which do not open.

Pour the stock through a cloth-lined sieve. Put 2 cups of the strained stock back into the wok and bring to the boil. Add the chilies and basil and simmer uncovered for 1 minute.

Pour the stock over the mussels and serve with sweet Thai chili sauce as a dipping sauce.

Serves: **4**   Preparation time: **15 min**   Cooking time: **8 mins**

fresh summer rolls *goi cuon*

The Vietnamese are famous for their superb rolls, the savory fillings wrapped in wafer-thin rice papers or tucked up in freshly steamed rice crêpes. There's no denying that you need time to prepare this recipe. I once spent over an hour making Summer Rolls for a party of about 50 in France, and swore I'd never do it again. But when they were devoured in preference to other elegant French appetizers, I was ready to make them all over again for the next party. You could serve the rolls as a starter at dinner, or as finger food for parties.

$^1/_2$ cup (125 ml) water
$^1/_4$ cup (60 ml) rice vinegar
4 teaspoons Chinese rice wine (preferably Shao Hsing)
1 teaspoon fish sauce
8 medium-sized raw prawns (about $^1/_2$ lb or 250 g), or 16–20 if using small rice papers
10 oz (300 g) pork loin or fillet, in one piece
8 large Vietnamese rice papers (about 8 in or 20 cm diameter), or 16–20 small rice papers (6$^1/_2$ in or 16 cm diameter)
8 lettuce leaves
1 cup (80 g) bean sprouts
1$^1/_2$ oz (50 g) rice vermicelli, soaked, soaked in hot water to soften, cut in 2 in (5 cm) lengths
$^1/_2$ cup loosely packed mint leaves
$^1/_2$ cup loosely packed coriander leaves
$^1/_2$ cup loosely packed Thai basil leaves (optional)
small bunch garlic chives or spring onions, cut in 4–5 in (10–12 cm) lengths (optional)

Bring the water, vinegar, wine, and fish sauce to the boil in a small pan. Add the prawns and simmer until just cooked, 2 to 3 minutes. Remove the prawns, leaving the liquid in the pan. When prawns are cool, peel, devein, and cut in half lengthways.

Put the pork in the reserved liquid in the pan, adding just enough water to barely cover the meat. Bring to the boil, cover, and simmer gently until tender, about 10 minutes for fillet and 25 minutes for loin. Drain, discarding the liquid. When the pork is cool, shred finely.

Shortly before serving, set a bowl of warm water and a kitchen towel on a bench. Dip a rice paper in the water for 3 to 4 seconds, remove and place on the towel. Smooth the rice paper with your fingers. Repeat with another three rice papers.

Put a lettuce leaf across the center of each of the soaked rice papers and add 2 prawn halves. Spread over some of the pork, bean sprouts, vermicelli, mint, basil, and coriander. Lay two lengths of garlic chives across the top.

Roll up the rice paper, tucking in the edges to make a cigar shape and completely enclose filling. Alternatively, you could leave one side open, so that the garlic chives stick out and look more decorative. Repeat with the remaining rice papers. Serve whole if using small rice papers, or cut diagonally in three bite-sized portions if using large rice papers.

Makes: **8 large or 16-20 small rolls**   Preparation time: **35 min**   Cooking time: **15-30 min**

fragrant grilled chicken wings   *slab mouan kroeung*

The first night I investigated a cluster of food stalls in Siem Reap in Cambodia, the kerosene lighting was so dim that I wasn't quite sure what I was ordering. Luckily, I chanced upon these succulent chicken wings, marinated in a delightful blend of lemon grass, galangal, chilies, fish sauce, and other seasonings. These make ideal finger food (don't forget the paper napkins as they're quite sticky), and the marinade could even be used for a whole chicken, oven-roasted in the usual Western style.

2 lb (1 kg) chicken wings, pricked all over
  with a fork
1–2 tablespoons vegetable oil for brushing

Marinade
2 stems lemon grass, tender inner part of
  bottom 3 in (8 cm) only, thinly sliced
2 shallots, minced
2 large red chilies, sliced
3–4 cloves garlic, minced
1 tablespoon ground galangal
1 tablespoon vegetable oil
$1/4$ teaspoon turmeric powder
1 tablespoon sugar
1 teaspoon salt
3 tablespoons fish sauce

Prepare the Marinade. Process the lemon grass, shallots, chilies, garlic, and galangal until finely ground, adding a little of the oil if needed to keep the mixture turning. Transfer to a bowl and stir in the rest of the Marinade ingredients. Add the chicken wings to the Marinade, mixing well with your hand to ensure the wings are evenly coated. Cover and marinate at least 2 hours or refrigerate overnight.

Brush a barbecue or gas grill or broiler with oil and heat. Grill the chicken wings over moderate heat, turning several times until they turn golden brown and crisp all over, about 15 to 20 minutes. Brush a couple of times with oil during the cooking. Drain on paper towel and serve warm. If preferred, cook the chicken wings on a rack set inside a baking dish in a hot oven (about 500°F or 220°C) for 15 minutes, then turn the wings and continue cooking until they are done, another 10 to 15 minutes.

Note: It's a good idea to prepare a double batch of these chicken wings, and deep-freeze half of them after marinating. Let the wings thaw to room temperature before grilling.

Serves: **4-6**   Preparation time: **10 min**   Cooking time: **30 min**

leaf-wrapped savory nibbles   *miang kham*

This delightful appetizer (the whole of which is definitely greater than the sum of its parts) is normally made using wild pepper leaves (*cha plu* in Thai, *bo la lot* in Vietnam). Don't worry if you have to substitute these with lettuce — the unexpectedly piquant flavors and contrasting textures of the filling still taste great. There's a fair amount of preparation, but this can be done in advance and at the last minute, all you need do is arrange the ingredients decoratively and serve.

6 shallots, finely minced
4 in (10 cm) young ginger, minced
$1/2$ cup (75 g) dry-roasted peanuts, skinned
$1/2$ cup (50 g) dried prawns, soaked in water
  to soften, minced
3 tablespoons Crisp-fried Garlic (page 17)
I large lemon, skin washed and dried, skin
  and flesh finely diced, seeds discarded
8–10 red or green bird's eye chilies,
  chopped, or 1–2 large red or green chilies,
  minced
$1/2$ cup (50 g) freshly grated or desiccated
  coconut, toasted in a dry wok until golden
  brown
wild pepper leaves or butter lettuce leaves

Sauce
3 tablespoons dry-roasted peanuts
I tablespoons dried prawns, soaked in warm
  water to soften
3 tablespoons freshly grated or desiccated
  coconut
3 shallots, minced
I stem lemon grass, tender inner part of
  bottom 3 in (8 cm) only, thinly sliced
I teaspoon finely minced ginger
I teaspoon finely minced galangal
2 teaspoons dried shrimp paste, toasted
$1 1/4$ cups (300 ml) water
$1/3$ cup (60 g) finely minced palm sugar
$1/2$–I teaspoon salt

Prepare the Sauce first. Process the peanuts to a fine powder in a spice grinder, then transfer to a saucepan. Do the same for the prawns, and then again for the coconut. Add the shallots, lemon grass, ginger, galangal, and shrimp paste and process to a smooth paste, adding a little of the water if needed to keep mixture turning.

Transfer the paste to the saucepan and add water, palm sugar, and salt. Bring to the boil, stirring. Reduce heat and simmer uncovered, stirring frequently, until the Sauce thickens and is reduced to about $3/4$ cup, around 15 minutes. Leave to cool, then transfer to four small serving bowls.

Arrange separate piles of shallots, ginger, peanuts, dried prawns, garlic, lemon, chilies, and coconut on a large serving dish. (If you like, you can prepare these ingredients in advance and keep them in covered containers for about an hour, although it is best to cut the lemon just before serving.)

Arrange the wild pepper or lettuce leaves on a plate and serve with the filling ingredients. Everyone adds a little of the ingredients, then spoons over some of the Sauce, before tucking up the leaf and eating (usually with sighs of pleasure).

Serves: **6-8**   Preparation time: **45 min**   Cooking time: **10 min**

straw mushroom soup with lemon grass & chili *tom yum hed*

Straw mushrooms, which have a firm yet slippery texture, are grown on a large scale in Thailand and have a wonderful woodsy perfume. They're excellent in this hot sour soup, which uses freshly made vegetable stock, although you could substitute this with chicken stock (preferably home-made) if you prefer. If you can't get fresh straw mushrooms, try the canned variety or use fresh button mushrooms.

1–2 tablespoons Roasted Thai Chili Paste (page 179)
1 stem lemon grass, bottom 7 in (18 cm) only, bruised and cut in 4–5 pieces
3 kaffir lime leaves, torn
3 tablespoons lime or lemon juice
4 teaspoons fish sauce
1 teaspoon sugar
3^1/$_2$ oz (100 g) fresh straw mushrooms, halved if large
1 medium ripe tomato, quartered
2–3 bird's-eye chilies, lightly bruised
sprigs of coriander leaf to garnish

Vegetable Stock
5 cups (1.25 liters) water
1 medium onion, minced
1 large carrot, minced
1 stalk celery, sliced
1 whole coriander plant including roots, minced
1 teaspoon black peppercorns

Make the Vegetable Stock by combining the water, onion, carrot, celery, coriander, and peppercorns in a large saucepan. Bring to the boil, cover, lower heat, and simmer until the liquid has reduced to 3^1/$_2$ cups, about 30 minutes.

Strain the vegetable stock in a medium saucepan, or if using chicken stock, put in 3^1/$_2$ cups (875 ml). Stir in the chili paste, lemon grass, and lime leaves. Bring to the boil, lower heat, and simmer uncovered 3 minutes, stirring occasionally. Add the lime juice, fish sauce, sugar, mushrooms, tomato, and chilies. Bring to the boil, reduce heat and simmer uncovered until mushrooms are cooked, 3 to 4 minutes. If using canned mushrooms, simmer 3 minutes.

Transfer to a serving bowl and garnish with fresh coriander sprigs. Serve hot with steamed rice and other dishes.

Serves: **4**   Preparation time: **10 min**   Cooking time: **40 min**

creamy pumpkin soup *gaeng lian fak thong*

This easy and delicious soup is a Thai recipe, but I've enjoyed similar soups in both Laos and Cambodia. I'm not sure of the reason, but this soup is recommended "for nursing mothers and children." However, I've found that everyone loves it. Do try to find Asian basil, which has a marvelous aniseed flavor lacking in sweet European basil.

2 tablespoons dried prawns, soaked in hot
  water to soften
1/2 teaspoon dried shrimp paste, toasted
3 shallots, minced
1–2 large red or green chilies, sliced (some
  seeds removed if desired)
3 cups (750 ml) thin coconut milk
10 oz (300 g) butternut, kabocha, or other
  brightly colored pumpkin, peeled and diced
1/4 cup (60 ml) coconut cream
1 tablespoon fish sauce
1/2 cup Asian basil leaves

Process the prawns to a powder in a spice grinder, then add the shrimp paste, shallots, and chilies. Process to a smooth paste, adding a little of the thin coconut milk if needed to keep the mixture turning. Transfer to a saucepan and stir in the coconut milk. Bring to the boil over medium heat and stir constantly. Add the pumpkin pieces and simmer with the pan uncovered until are soft. Add the coconut cream and fish sauce, stirring gently for about 1 minute. Add the basil leaves and serve immediately.

Serves: **4**   Preparation time: **10 min**   Cooking time: **15 min**

spinach soup with sweet corn *sayur bayam*

When I lived in Central Java in the mid-1970s, our cook, 'Bu Hardi, often prepared this delicious soup. I think it's nicest with English spinach, but I sometimes use amaranth (also called Chinese spinach); you could even substitute silver beet (Swiss chard) or Chinese flowering cabbage. Indonesians always use large chunks of sweet corn on the cob, but it's easier to eat if you add fresh or frozen corn kernels. Do try to find salam leaf for that distinctive Javanese flavor.

3 cups (750 g) chicken stock
3 shallots, thinly sliced
1/2 in (1 cm) sliced galangal, lightly bruised
2 cloves garlic, crushed and minced
1/4 teaspoon turmeric powder
1 fresh or dried salam leaf
1 teaspoon finely minced palm sugar
1 cup (125 g) fresh or defrosted sweet
  corn kernels
10 oz (300 g) English spinach, washed and
  coarsely chopped
salt to taste

Put the stock, shallots, galangal, garlic, turmeric, *daun salam*, and sugar in a saucepan and bring to the boil. Cover and simmer 5 minutes, then add the sweet corn, and simmer the pan partially covered until the corn is tender, 7 to 8 minutes. Add the spinach and simmer until it is tender. Add salt to taste and serve hot with rice and other dishes.

Serves: **4**   Preparation time: **10 min**   Cooking time: **15 min**

sour mixed vegetable soup with peanuts *sayur asam*

When I first tried this popular West Javanese soup, I was intrigued by the spray of red-skinned oval nuts and leaves floating in it. As I've subsequently learned, *melinjo* nuts, and leaves are hard to find outside of Indonesia, but even without these, this mixture of vegetables and peanuts in sour broth tastes really great. Do try, however, to find fresh or dried salam leaves, which really make a difference to the flavor.

$^1/_4$ cup (40 g) raw peanuts
$^1/_2$ teaspoon dried shrimp paste, toasted
6 shallots, thinly sliced
1 clove garlic, thinly sliced
1 large red chili, seeded and sliced
4 thick slices galangal, bruised
2 fresh or dried salam leaves
4 cups (1 liter) light chicken or beef stock
7 oz (200 g) minced cabbage
1 small zucchini or chayote (choko), peeled and diced
$3^1/_2$ oz (100 g) green beans, cut in short lengths
2–3 tablespoons tamarind pulp, soaked in $^1/_2$ cup warm water, squeezed and strained to obtain juice
minced palm or soft brown sugar to taste
salt to taste

Put the peanuts in a small saucepan with water to cover. Bring to the boil, reduce heat, and simmer 10 minutes. Drain and set aside.

Put the shrimp paste into a saucepan with the shallots, garlic, chili, galangal, salam leaves, and stock. Bring to the boil, cover, reduce heat, and simmer 5 minutes. Add the peanuts and vegetables and return to the boil. Lower the heat, cover, and simmer until vegetables are cooked, 10 to 15 minutes. Add the tamarind juice and simmer for about 1 minute. Add sugar and salt to taste; if you prefer a really sour soup, sugar will not be necessary. Remove galangal and salam leaves, then transfer to a serving bowl and serve with steamed rice; this is particularly good with grilled fish or poultry.

Serves: **4**   Preparation time: **10 min**   Cooking time: **20 min**

chicken & coconut milk soup *gaeng tom kha gai*

In Thailand, this wonderfully creamy soup is often served in an unglazed terracotta pot with a curved bottom, placed on a charcoal brazier to keep it warm throughout the meal. The galangal, lemon grass, and kaffir lime leaves give a heavenly fragrance, and as there are only a few bruised chilies, the flavor is fairly mild. Serve with rice and Simple Thai Fish Sauce & Chili Dip, which lets you intensify the heat as much as you like.

5 cups (1.25 ml) thin coconut milk
2 in (5 cm) galangal, bruised and thickly sliced
4 stems lemon grass, bottom 7 in (18 cm)
  only, bruised and cut in 4–5 pieces
1 ¹/₂ lb (750 g) chicken pieces, cut through the
  bone into bite-sized pieces, or 1 lb (500 g)
  boneless breast or thigh fillet
¹/₂ cup (125 ml) thick coconut milk
¹/₄ cup (60 ml) lime juice
¹/₄ cup (60 ml) fish sauce
4–5 kaffir lime leaves, torn
4–6 red or green bird's-eye chilies, bruised
sprigs of coriander leaf
Simple Thai Fish Sauce & Chili Dip (page 175)

Put the thin coconut milk, galangal, and lemon grass into a saucepan and bring slowly to the boil, stirring frequently. Simmer gently with the pan uncovered for 5 minutes, then add the chicken and simmer gently, uncovered, until the chicken is tender.

Add the thick coconut milk, lime juice, fish sauce, lime leaves and chilies and bring almost to the boil, stirring. Transfer to a large bowl and garnish with coriander. Serve with the Simple Thai Fish Sauce & Chili Dip in separate bowls and allow everyone to add according to taste.

Serves: **4**   Preparation time: **10 min**   Cooking time: **20 min**

chicken soup with lime, chilies & basil   *s'ngao muan*

If you're looking for a tangy soup as a foil to rich food (such as seafood or meat cooked in coconut milk, or fried fish or meat), this clear chicken soup is just the thing. It has lots of lime juice and Asian basil, with a few hot chilies for extra zing. You can make it in advance, and re-heat just before serving. (Incidentally, I find it intriguing that the name for this type of sour Cambodian soup, *S'ngao*, is almost the same as the Filipino equivalent, which is called *Sinigang*.)

I lb (500 g) chicken pieces (breast and thigh),
  skinned but left whole with the bones
  still intact
6 cups (1.5 liters) water
2 stems lemon grass, bottom 7 in (18 cm),
  bruised and cut in 3–4 pieces
2 cloves garlic, smashed and minced
2–4 red or green bird's-eye chilies, bruised
2 teaspoons sugar
2 tablespoons fish sauce
salt to taste
3–4 tablespoons lime juice
$^1/_2$ cup loosely packed Asian basil leaves,
  coarsely chopped

Put the chicken, water, lemon grass, garlic, chilies, and sugar in a saucepan and bring to the boil. Partially cover the pan and simmer for 5 minutes, removing any scum that rises to the surface. Cover the pan completely and simmer gently until the chicken is cooked, 25 to 30 minutes.

When the chicken is cooked, leave it in the stock until cool enough to handle (if you're in a hurry, you can remove it from the stock to cool). Remove the lemon grass pieces from the stock and discard. Shred the chicken meat, then return it to the stock. If you're preparing the soup well in advance, cool, then refrigerate the soup until required.

Shortly before serving, heat the soup, add the fish sauce, salt, and lime juice to taste, then add the basil. Stir and immediately transfer to a serving bowl.

Serves: **4-6**   Preparation time: **15 min**   Cooking time: **30 min**

spicy beef soup   *tom yam neua*

A Thai girlfriend taught me how to make this soup back in the early days when I was just beginning to learn about Thai food and thought that soups began and ended with the ubiquitous Tom Yam Kung, the hot sour soup made with prawns. I think this beef soup — which has similar seasonings — is just as good, and in areas where prawns are expensive or hard to find, an excellent alternative. Saw-tooth coriander looks like a wide blade of grass with serrated edges; if you can't find it, regular coriander leaf is fine.

4 cups (1 liter) water
2 stems lemon grass, bottom 7 in (18 cm) only, bruised and cut in 4–5 pieces
1¼ in (3 cm) galangal, thinly sliced
4–5 kaffir lime leaves, torn
4–6 bird's-eye chilies, lightly bruised
2–3 tablespoons Roasted Thai Chili Paste (page 179)
1½ tablespoons fish sauce
1 medium ripe but firm tomato, cut in 8 wedges
2 tablespoons lime or lemon juice
7 oz (200 g) fillet or striploin beef, chilled in the freezer 30 minutes, very thinly sliced across the grain
salt to taste
several saw-tooth coriander leaves, torn, or fresh coriander leaves to garnish

Put the water, lemon grass, galangal, lime leaves, and chilies into a saucepan. Bring to the boil, lower the heat, and simmer uncovered for 5 minutes. Stir in the chili paste, fish sauce, tomato, and lime juice. Simmer 1 minute, then add the beef, and cook just until the beef is done.

Taste and add salt, if desired, and a little more lime juice if it is not sour enough. Sprinkle with coriander leaves and serve hot with rice and other dishes.

Serves: **4-6**   Preparation time: **10 min**   Cooking time: **8 min**

bouncy beef ball soup   *sup bo vien*

The region's most famous beef ball soup is found in the southern Thai town of Haadyai (though I'm not too reassured by the fact that Haadyai is also famous for bull fights). I prefer the fragrant beef ball soup of Vietnam, where the beef is marinated then ground to a smooth paste with a touch of bicarbonate of soda to help give a characteristic springy texture. This soup is usually served as part of a main meal with rice, but you could transform it into a noodle soup (see Note). Beef balls are also added to beef stock with a mixture of other cuts (tripe, intestines, brisket, slivers of tender beef) to make what is sometimes irreverently called "spare parts soup."

10 oz (300 g) lean topside beef, thinly sliced
2 teaspoons sesame oil
2 tablespoons minced fresh coriander leaf
liberal sprinkling of freshly ground
   black pepper

Marinade
1 tablespoon fish sauce
1 tablespoon iced water
2 teaspoons lime juice
1 teaspoon tapioca flour or cornflour
$1/2$ teaspoon bicarbonate of soda
   (baking soda)
$1/4$ teaspoon freshly ground black pepper
$1/4$ teaspoon sugar

Stock
6 cups (1.5 liters) beef stock, preferably
   home-made
1 tablespoon fish sauce
1 medium red or brown onion, minced
1 clove garlic, smashed and minced
1 stem lemon grass, sliced
1 whole star anise
$1/2$ teaspoon black peppercorns
salt to taste

Put the sliced beef in a bowl and add the Marinade ingredients, massing well with your hand until the liquid is completely absorbed. Cover the meat and refrigerate for at least 4 hours, or overnight if preferred.

To make the Stock, put all the ingredients except salt in a pan and bring to the boil. Cover the pan, lower the heat, and simmer for 20 minutes. Strain, discarding the solids, then return the stock to the pan. Taste and add salt if desired.

Transfer the marinated beef to a food processor and process to a very smooth paste. Put the sesame oil in a small dish and use it to moisten your hands. You can use both hands to shape the mixture into very small balls about $3/4$ in (2 cm) in diameter. Alternatively, you can try doing it the Vietnamese way, taking a handful of the beef mixture in one oiled hand and making a circle with between your thumb and forefinger. Squeeze out some of the meat, scraping off the small ball that emerges with a teaspoon held in your other (non-oiled) hand. Repeat until you have used up the beef mixture and set the balls aside on a plate. (You should have around 30 beef balls.)

Reheat the stock, add the beef balls, and bring to the boil. When the beef balls have risen to the surface of the stock, lower the heat and simmer with the pan partially covered for 3 minutes. Transfer to individual soup bowls, sprinkle with coriander leaf and black pepper, and serve immediately as an accompaniment to rice.

Note: If you'd like to convert this into a noodle soup, increase the amount of stock to 7 cups (1.75 liters) and add 7 oz (200 g) cooked rice vermicelli or wheat noodles before serving. You could add a handful of bean sprouts too, if you have them handy.

Serves: **4-6**   Preparation time: **30 min + 4 hours (or overnight) marinating**
Cooking time: **25 min**

piquant fish soup with pineapple & bean sprouts *samlor machou khmer*

As the Cambodian name for this dish (*samlor*) indicates, this is a soupy stew eaten with rice. What the name doesn't tell you is how absolutely delicious it is. The delicate seasoning of galangal, lemon grass, other herbs, and fish sauce is joined by the full-on flavor of crisp-fried garlic. The unusual addition of a beaten egg gives a lovely smooth texture to the soup, which has fresh pineapple and tomato for a touch of acidity. All in all, this has to be one of my favorite fish recipes.

4 cups (1 liter) chicken stock
1 heaped tablespoon tamarind pulp
1 tablespoon finely minced galangal
2 stems lemon grass, bottom 5–6 in
 (12–14 cm) only, bruised and cut in 4 pieces
1 thick slice of fresh pineapple (about ¼ lb or
 250 g), peeled, cored, and cut in very small
 wedges
1 large ripe tomato, cut in 12 wedges
3 tablespoons fish sauce
1 tablespoon sugar, or more to taste
13 oz (400 g) boneless fish fillets (catfish if
 possible), cut in bite-sized pieces
2–3 tablespoons Crisp-fried Garlic (page 17)
1¼ cups (100 g) bean sprouts, tails removed
½ cup Asian basil leaves, coarsely chopped
¼ cup coarsely chopped rice paddy herb or
 coriander leaf
1 egg, lightly beaten, optional
freshly ground black pepper to taste
1 tablespoon sliced bird's-eye chilies

Put the chicken stock, tamarind pulp, galangal, and lemon grass into a saucepan and bring to the boil. Lower the heat, cover and simmer for 10 minutes. Pour through a sieve, discarding the solids, and return the stock to the pan.

Add the pineapple, tomato, fish sauce, and 1 tablespoon of sugar. Bring to the boil, cover and simmer for 5 minutes. Add the fish and continue simmering uncovered until the fish is cooked, about 5 to 8 minutes depending on the thickness and type of fish. Add crisp-fried garlic to taste, bean sprouts, Asian basil, and rice paddy herb (if using coriander, do not add yet). Stir for a few seconds, until the sprouts start to wilt slightly. Taste and add a little more sugar if desired; this will depend on the sweetness of the pineapple.

Pour in the egg in a slow steady stream, stirring slowly until it sets. Add the coriander, if using, then transfer the soup to a large bowl and serve hot with rice, accompanied by the chilies in a separate bowl for adding to taste. If you like, the soup can be transferred to individual bowls, and spooned over the rice as required while eating.

Note: Chicken stock made with stock cubes or powder could be used, although home-made stock is preferable.

Serves: **4**   Preparation time: **15 min**   Cooking time: **25 min**

hot, sour & fragrant prawn soup   *tom yam kung*

This is one of the all-time favorite Thai dishes in restaurants around the world (and yes, even in Thailand too). With the fragrance of kaffir lime, galangal, and lemon grass, the saltiness of fish sauce, the sour bite of lime juice, and the heat of chilies, this dish epitomizes the best of Southeast Asian food. All that and luscious prawns too.

1 tablespoon vegetable oil
1 lb (500 g) medium-large raw prawns, peeled and deveined, heads and shells reserved
5 cups (1.25 liters) light chicken stock, preferably home-made
3 stems lemon grass, bottom 7 in (18 cm) only, bruised and cut in 4–5 pieces
2 in (5 cm) galangal, thinly sliced
2 shallots, minced
2 tablespoons Roasted Thai Chili Paste (page 179)
4–6 kaffir lime leaves, torn
4–8 bird's-eye chilies, lightly bruised
1 medium tomato, cut in 8–10 wedges
2 tablespoons fish sauce
2–3 tablespoons lime juice

Heat the oil in a saucepan, then add the prawn heads and shells, and stir-fry until they turn pink. Add the stock, lemon grass, galangal, and shallots. Bring to the boil, cover, lower the heat and simmer for 15 minutes. Pour through a sieve, pressing down firmly with a spoon to extract as much liquid as possible.

Put the chili paste in the saucepan and slowly stir in the strained stock. Add the kaffir lime leaves, chilies, and tomato and bring slowly to the boil, stirring all the time. Put in the prawns and simmer for just 2 to 3 minutes, taking care not over-cook. Stir in fish sauce and lime juice to taste. Serve hot with rice and other dishes.

Serves: **4-6**   Preparation time: **15 min**   Cooking time: **20 min**

salads, rice, and noodles

Salads are among some of the most exciting and creative food of Southeast Asia. To start with, the variety of vegetables found in most local markets is astonishing, and cultivated vegetables aren't the only option. Rural cooks have an impressive knowledge of wild edible plants, and go on a daily forage to pluck young leaves from trees and shrubs, pick herbs growing beside a stream or a paddy field, or gather wild ferns and immature fruits.

In most regions, cultivated and wild vegetables are often preferred raw in salads, or served with a spicy dip, rather than eaten cooked. Salads are by no means confined to vegetables: sour fruits, poultry, meat, fish, rice, noodles, cashew nuts — just about anything that will excite your palate while doing great things for your health ends up in a salad. Dressings are often piquant with lime juice, fish sauce, garlic, and chilies, or sometimes come in the form of a creamy peanut sauce.

Most salads are served at the same time as rice and other main meal dishes, their fresh flavor, crisp texture, and bright green color adding a pleasing balance to the meal. For a genuine Southeast Asian meal, try to include a salad as part of every main, even if it's just a platter of raw vegetables (lettuce, cabbage, young long beans, for example) and an array of fresh herbs.

Rice — the symbol of fertility and the embodiment of the life force — is so much more than the grain which nourishes millions throughout Southeast Asia. The Rice Goddess, who hovers over paddy fields and dry hillside rice plantations, is honored in countless festivals related to the rice cycle. Rice is cooked with the respect it deserves: steamed to a soft, fragrant and fluffy mound; stir-fried; enriched with coconut milk; turned into a salad; or made into a type of soup.

Southeast Asians adore noodles, especially those made from rice flour, but you'll also find wheat noodles and transparent noodles made from mung beans. Noodles come in different shapes and sizes and are truly versatile; they can be served stir-fried (as in the classic Thai Rice-stick Noodles), bathed with a rich meaty sauce (try Malay Mee Rebus) or swimming in huge bowls of noodle soup. These substantial noodle soups, ranging from Vietnamese Beef & Noodle Soup to Penang Nonya Hot Sour Noodle Soup or the incredible Singapore Laksa are enough to get you going for the day, to buck you up at lunch time, or to have as a late-night snack, just to make sure you're not going to be awake hungry during the night.

crisp & tangy cabbage salad   *gawbi lethoke*

The Burmese have perfected the art of making salads, first choosing the vegetables, then adding extra ingredients for saltiness, texture, fragrance, and acidity. In this simple yet really tasty recipe, shredded cabbage is mixed with onion, dried prawns, and lime juice, together with crisp-fried shallots or, even better, Burmese Crispy Dried Prawn Sprinkle.

$^3/_4$ lb (375 g) round cabbage or Chinese
   celery (Napa) cabbage, finely shredded
1 medium red or brown onion, halved
   lengthways, thinly sliced across
1 teaspoon salt
3 tablespoon dried prawns, dry roasted over
   low heat 4–5 minutes, blended to a fine
   powder, or 3 tablespoons Burmese Crispy
   Dried Prawn Sprinkle (page 176)
2–3 tablespoons lime juice
1 tablespoon vegetable oil, preferably shallot-
   or garlic-flavored oil (page 17)
1 large fresh green chili, thinly sliced, or
   1 teaspoon crushed dried chili flakes
1–2 tablespoons Crisp-fried Shallots (omit if
   using Burmese Crispy Dried Prawn
   Sprinkle)

Put the cabbage in a bowl, cover with cold water, and refrigerate 1 hour. Combine the onion with salt, mixing well. Stand for 30 minutes, then rinse briefly and squeeze out the moisture. Set onion aside.

Drain the soaked cabbage thoroughly, then put in a bowl. Add the onion, dried prawn powder (if using), 2 tablespoons lime juice, oil, and chili. Mix thoroughly by hand, squeezing the cabbage slightly to bruise it. Taste and add more salt and lime juice if desired. Put the cabbage in a serving bowl and scatter with the crisp-fried shallots or Burmese Crispy Dried Prawn Sprinkle. Serve immediately with rice and other dishes.

Serves: **4-6**   Preparation time: **20 min + 1 hour soaking**   Cooking time: **5 min**

green mango & cashew salad *yam mamuang*

This salad is so superb that even though green mangoes are usually a fairly esoteric item outside of Southeast Asia, they're well worth tracking down just to make this recipe. The sourness of the mango is offset by a touch of sugar, a heady aroma provided by kaffir lime leaves and other herbs, with a splash of fish sauce for salty fragrance and chilies to give a bit of a bite. The cashew nuts add crunchy sweetness to the salad, which is great with just about anything, especially grilled or fried food. This recipe is a specialty of southern Thailand and northern Malaysia, where cashew trees are cultivated.

4–5 unripe green mangoes (about 1 1/4 lb or
  600 g), peeled
2–3 teaspoons caster sugar, or more to taste
2 kaffir lime leaves, in hair-like shreds
2 tablespoons minced fresh coriander leaf
1 spring onion, thinly sliced
2–3 red or green bird's-eye chilies, thinly sliced
3 shallots, thinly sliced
2 tablespoons fish sauce
1/3 cup (45 g) raw cashews, dry roasted until
  golden and crisp

Hold a peeled mango over a shredder and grate to make matchstick shreds. Alternatively, hold the mango in the palm of one hand and with a sharp knife in your other hand, make vertical cuts down to the stone, keeping the cuts close together. Hold the knife horizontally and slice across to make shreds. Repeat on the other side of the mango.

Put the mango shreds in a bowl and sprinkle with sugar. Massage with your fingers for about 30 seconds, then add all other ingredients except the cashews, tossing to mix well. Taste and if the mangoes seem too sour, add more sugar. Add the cashews, toss and serve immediately. (This salad can also be used as a topping for grilled fish, see page 148.)

Serves: **4-6** Preparation time: **10 min**

green papaya salad *som tum*

Versions of this hot, sour, salty green papaya salad are made for you on the spot at food stalls in Thailand, Vietnam, Cambodia and Laos. I was once asked in Central Thailand if I wanted it local style, with a pickled crab (shell and all) added. My policy is to always to try something at least once, so I did, but I still wish they'd shelled the crab first. The traditional way to make this salad is using a mortar and pestle to bruise the ingredients — for once, a food processor just won't do.

3–4 cloves garlic
4–6 red or green bird's-eye chilies
2 tablespoons dried prawns, soaked to soften
2 teaspoons sugar
1 small tomato, diced
2 long beans ($^3/_4$ oz or 50 g) or green beans, cut in $^3/_4$ in (2 cm) lengths
1 unripe green papaya (about 10 oz or 300 g), peeled and shredded
2 tablespoons fish sauce
2 tablespoons lime juice
2–3 tablespoons coarsely crushed dry-roasted peanuts
4–6 cabbage leaves, washed and torn into several pieces, optional

Divide the garlic, chilies, and dried prawns into two batches. Put half into a mortar, add 1 teaspoon of sugar into a mortar and pound until well broken up. Add half of the long beans and pound a little to bruise, then add half of the chopped tomato and pound a few times just until they are broken up. Add half the papaya to a mortar, a little at a time, pounding until lightly bruised. Transfer the mixture to a bowl and repeat with the remaining garlic, chilies, dried prawns, sugar, tomato, beans, and papaya.

Add the fish sauce, lime juice, and peanuts to the bowl of papaya mixture, tossing to mix well. Taste and add a little more lime juice, fish sauce, or sugar if you like, and serve immediately. The salad is often eaten with cabbage leaves (served separately on a plate, with ice cubes to keep them cool and crisp), each person using a piece of the cabbage to scoop up the papaya.

Serves: **4-6**   Preparation time: **25 min**

thai mixed vegetable salad with chicken & prawns *yam yai*

This substantial mixture, known as "Big Salad," is also found in Laos, although some of the traditional ingredients there (such as boiled pig's heart) don't appeal as much as this Thai version. Most of the preparation can be done in advance, and all you need to do is just toss it the ingredients together with the sauce at the last minute. This salad is great for buffets (you may want to double the amounts), and as an accompaniment to barbecued poultry or fish.

4 in (10 cm) long white daikon radish, shredded (60–75 g)

1 teaspoon salt

1¼ cups (100 g) bean sprouts, straggly tails removed

1 small cucumber, skin left on, seeds removed, flesh julienned

1 oz (30 g) transparent (bean thread) noodles, soaked in hot water to soften, cut in 2 in (5 cm) lengths

3 pieces dried wood ear fungus, soaked in hot water to soften, hard portions discarded, cut in bite-sized pieces

7 oz (200 g) boneless cooked chicken breast, shredded

7 oz (200 g) cooked lean pork, thinly sliced

7 oz (200 g) cooked small prawns, peeled and deveined

2 hard-boiled eggs, peeled and sliced

½ cup loosely packed mint leaves, washed and drained

Sauce

¼ cup (60 ml) fish sauce

1½ tablespoons lime or lemon juice

2 teaspoons sugar

1 teaspoon finely minced or crushed garlic

1–2 teaspoons crushed dried chili flakes

Put the long white radish in a small bowl, sprinkle with salt and mix well with your fingers. Stand 15 minutes, rinse, drain and squeeze.

Scatter the bean sprouts in a wide serving bowl and spread radish on top. Add cucumber, noodles, wood ear fungus, chicken, pork, and prawns, scattering evenly. Arrange eggs slices on top and scatter with mint. (If preparing in advance, cover with plastic wrap and refrigerate.)

To make the Sauce, combine the fish sauce, lime juice, sugar, garlic, and chili in a small bowl, stirring to dissolve sugar. Just before serving, pour over the prepared salad and toss.

Note: You could also add 3 to 4 sliced water chestnuts or ½ cup grated yam bean (*jicama*) to the salad. For a more decorative appearance, try using eight to twelve hard-boiled quail eggs, left whole, instead of hen eggs.

Serves: **4-6**   Preparation time: **30 min**   Cooking time: **20 min**

vegetable & bean curd salad with peanut sauce *gado gado*

For some reason I've never tracked down, Indonesians usually prefer their salads with lightly cooked rather than raw vegetables. *Gado gado* (sometimes served as a snack at *warung* or food stalls) is a mixture of vegetables, boiled egg, and fried bean curd drenched in spicy peanut sauce, the whole lot topped with crunchy prawn crisps (*krupuk*). This hearty salad is good for a light lunch; you could serve it with steamed rice for a more substantial meal, and perhaps even add some grilled fish or poultry.

2 cups (500 ml) water
$^1/_2$ lb (250 g) small waxy potatoes, washed, skins left on
7 oz (200 g) long beans or green beans, cut in 1$^1/_4$ in (3 cm) lengths
7 oz (200 g) cabbage, coarsely shredded
3$^1/_2$ oz (100 g) water spinach, English spinach, or silver beet
7 oz (200 g) bean sprouts, straggly tails pinched off
7 oz (200 g) cucumber
$^1/_2$ teaspoon salt
2 hard-boiled eggs, quartered
1 cake hard bean curd (4 oz or 125 g), deep fried until golden brown, sliced
crisp-fried prawn crackers (*krupuk udang*) to garnish

Peanut Sauce
8 dried chilies, cut in 1 in ($^1/_2$ cm) lengths, soaked in hot water to soften
8 shallots, minced
1 clove garlic, minced
1 tablespoon finely minced galangal
1 stem lemon grass, tender inner part of bottom 3 in (8 cm) only, thinly sliced
3 tablespoons vegetable oil
1 heaped tablespoon tamarind, soaked in $^1/_4$ cup water, squeezed and strained to obtain juice
$^1/_2$ cup (75 g) raw peanuts, dry-roasted, ground until moderately fine, or $^1/_2$ cup chunky peanut butter
1 cup (250 ml) coconut milk
1 tablespoon sugar
1 teaspoon salt, optional

To make the Peanut Sauce, process the chilies, shallots, garlic, galangal, and lemon grass until finely ground. Heat the oil in a small pan and add the ground mixture, stir-frying over low-medium heat for 4 to 5 minutes. Add the tamarind juice, peanuts, coconut milk, sugar, and salt. Bring to the boil, stirring, then lower the heat, and simmer until the sauce thickens. Transfer the sauce to a bowl and leave to cool.

Bring the water to boil in a small saucepan. Add the potatoes and simmer until tender, about 15 minutes. When cool enough to handle, peel and slice $^1/_2$ in (1 cm) thick. Bring the water back to the boil, add the beans, and simmer 3 minutes. Remove the beans with a slotted spoon and drain in a colander.

Cook the cabbage in the same water until just tender, about 3 minutes. Remove the cabbage with a slotted spoon and drain. Repeat for the spinach, cooking for 2 minutes only. Blanch bean sprouts in boiling water for 5 seconds, drain, and plunge into a bowl of iced water to refresh. Drain thoroughly.

Let the cooked vegetables cool to room temperature. Scrape the cucumber skin with the tines of a fork and massage in the salt for 30 seconds. Rinse under running water, wipe dry, and cut the cucumber in thin slices or diagonal chunks.

Arrange the potatoes, beans, cabbage, spinach, bean sprouts, cucumber, boiled eggs, and fried bean curd in separate piles on a large serving platter. Just before serving, pour the peanut sauce over the vegetables and garnish with the prawn crackers.

Serves: **6-8**   Preparation time: **30 min**   Cooking time: **35 min**

thai beef salad with herbs & spicy dressing *yam neua*

If you happen to have any left-over grilled steak or roast beef, this recipe is really quick to prepare, and it takes only a little longer if you need to grill the steak just before you want to serve the salad. The room-temperature beef is sliced and mixed with a fragrant bouquet of lemon grass, coriander, mint, and lime leaves, then tossed with a spicy dressing of fish sauce, lime juice, garlic, and chilies. Arrange the meat on a bed of lettuce and serve it as part of a meal with rice.

1 lb (500 g) roast, grilled or barbecued beef, preferably medium-rare, cut in thin slices 2 in (5 cm) in length
1 stem lemon grass, tender inner part of bottom 3 in (8 cm) only, very thinly sliced
4 shallots, thinly sliced
1 tablespoon minced coriander leaf
2 tablespoons mint leaves, coarsely torn
4 kaffir lime leaves, very finely shredded
6–8 lettuce leaves, washed and dried
1 firm ripe tomato, sliced
cucumber slices
4 sprigs of mint

Sauce
2 cloves garlic, minced
2 large red chilies, sliced
1 tablespoon sugar
$^1/_4$ cup (60 ml) lime juice
2 tablespoons fish sauce

Put the beef slices in a bowl and add lemon grass, shallots, coriander, mint, and kaffir lime, tossing to mix well.

Prepare the Sauce by blending garlic, chilies, and sugar in a spice grinder, adding a little of the lime juice if needed to keep mixture turning. Transfer to a bowl and stir in lime juice and fish sauce. Pour the sauce over the beef and herbs, mix well. Cover with plastic wrap and leave to marinade 10 minutes.

Line a serving plate with lettuce leaves, put the beef (at room temperature, not chilled) on top, and surround with tomato and cucumber slices. Garnish with mint sprigs and serve.

Serves: **4**   Preparation time: **20 min**   Cooking time: **5 min**

sweet, sour, and spicy fruit & vegetable salad   *rujak*

When hunger pangs suddenly strike during the day in Bali or Java, you can stop at roadside stall and indulge in this marvelous healthy snack of under-ripe fruit and vegetables mixed with a pungent sauce (a blend of shrimp paste, chilies, sweet palm sugar, and sour tamarind). Toss it with your choice of under-ripe fruit, cucumber, and yam bean (*jicama*) with the sauce and enjoy the quintessential flavors of Southeast Asia.

Prepare about 4–6 cups of the following
  ingredients, peeled, cut in bite-sized pieces
  about $^3/_4$ in (1$^1/_2$ cm) thick:
  under-ripe pineapple
  under-ripe mango, or sour green apple
  pomelo or grapefruit, membranes removed
    from each segment
  under-ripe papaya
  cucumber
  yam bean (*jicama*)

Sauce
1 teaspoon dried shrimp paste, toasted
$^1/_2$ cup (90 g) minced palm sugar
1–2 large red chilies, minced, or 2–3 bird's-
  eye chilies, bruised
$^1/_2$ teaspoon salt
2–3 tablespoons tamarind pulp
1 cup (250 ml) water

Make the Sauce by combining all ingredients in a small pan. Bring to the boil, stirring to dissolve the sugar. Lower the heat and simmer uncovered until the sauce has thickened, about 12 to 15 minutes. Pour through a sieve, pressing to extract as much liquid as possible, and leave to cool completely. (The prepared sauce can be refrigerated for several days.)

Just before serving, put the prepared fruits and vegetables in a bowl. Pour over the sauce, toss to mix well, and serve immediately. *Rujak* is normally eaten as a snack, but you could serve it with rice and a simple grilled chicken or fish for a main meal.

Serves: **4-6**   Preparation time: **20 min**   Cooking time: **15 min**

vietnamese cabbage & chicken salad *ga xe phay*

I don't know anyone who doesn't love the fresh flavors and herbal aroma of this excellent salad (a dish that my friends insist I always bring along on picnics and boat trips). It's worth trying to track down polygonum (long-stemmed Vietnamese mint or *rau ram*) for the unique flavor it adds. The Vietnamese normally use long white Chinese or Napa cabbage, but I find regular round white cabbage is also very good. Some cooks add up to 50 percent more chicken, but I prefer the balance in this recipe.

13 oz (400 g) chicken thighs, or 7 oz (200 g) boneless thigh fillets, skin and fat removed
2 teaspoons salt
1 very large or 2 small to medium red or brown onions, halved lengthways, very thinly sliced across
13 oz (400 g) long white Chinese celery or Napa cabbage, or round white cabbage, cored and finely shredded
$1/4$ cup firmly packed coriander leaves, coarsely chopped
$1/4$ cup firmly packed mint leaves, coarsely chopped
$1/4$ cup firmly packed polygonum (long-stemmed mint), coarsely chopped, or another $1/4$ cup regular mint
liberal amount of freshly ground black pepper

Sauce
4 tablespoons lime juice
3 tablespoons fish sauce
3 tablespoons caster sugar
1 tablespoon rice vinegar
1 large red chili, minced

Put the chicken thighs in a saucepan with 1 teaspoon of the salt and add just enough water to cover. Bring to the boil, cover, and simmer until the chicken is cooked. Cool in the stock if you have time, then remove the meat from the bones and shred the flesh into fine, lengthwise strips with your fingers. Keep the stock for some other purpose.

While the chicken is cooking, sprinkle the remaining teaspoon of salt over the onion, rub with your fingers, and set aside for 30 minutes. To prepare the Sauce, combine all ingredients in a small bowl, stirring to dissolve the sugar. Set aside for the flavors to blend.

Just before serving, put the cabbage and herbs in large bowl. Rinse the salted onion under running water, then squeeze dry and add to the cabbage. Add the chicken and Sauce, tossing to combine well. Grind over a liberal amount of black pepper, toss again, and serve with other dishes.

Note: If you're preparing the salad in advance, put the mixed cabbage, chicken, and herbs in a sealed container, with the sauce in a separate container. Combine immediately before serving.

Serves: **4-6**   Preparation time: **20 min**   Cooking time: **10 min**

barbecued pork, cashew & herb salad   *yam chu yuk kan*

Seasoned and slightly sweetened pork, beaten into wafer-thin slices and grilled over charcoal, can be found in most Chinatowns around the world. In this creative Thai recipe, the pork (known in Chinese as *chu yuk kan*) is combined with cashews and lashings of herbs to make a remarkable salad. The flavors are perfectly offset by plain rice; you can also serve a couple of other dishes for a complete meal.

$5^1/_2$ oz (150 g) barbecued pork slices, cut in narrow strips
1 cup (150 g) raw cashews, toasted in a wok over low heat until golden brown and crisp
2–3 shallots, thinly sliced
1 stem lemon grass, tender inner part of bottom 3 in (8 cm) only, very thinly sliced
1–2 stalks of Chinese celery, stems cut in $^3/_4$ in (2 cm) lengths to make $^1/_3$ cup (do not use the leaves)
$^1/_3$ cup loosely packed coriander leaves, coarsely chopped
$^1/_3$ cup loosely packed mint leaves, coarsely chopped
1 spring onion, thinly sliced
1 tablespoon lime juice
1 tablespoon fish sauce
$^1/_2$–1 teaspoon crushed dried chili flakes

Put all ingredients in a bowl and toss to mix thoroughly. Serve immediately. The sweetness, crunch, and herbal aroma of this salad would be ideal partnered with Chicken & Coconut Milk Soup (page 51), steamed rice, and a simple cooked green vegetable dish.

Serves: **4**   Preparation time: **15 min**

southern thai rice salad *khao yam pak thai*

Want something refreshingly light, healthy, and herbal for lunch or a warm evening? This lovely Thai salad has a refreshing mixture of tastes and textures. Start off with cooked rice, then add toasted coconut, bean sprouts, cucumber, and long beans for a lovely crunch. Shredded omelette, dried prawns, and sweet-sour pomelo join the party, with plenty of sour, fragrant notes in the lime juice and herbs. The salad looks really pretty if you arrange each portion of rice and accompaniments separately on individual serving plates.

1 teaspoon vegetable oil
4 cups (520 g) room-temperature cooked
  rice (made using 2 cups raw long-grain
  fragrant rice)
1 cup (100 g) freshly grated or desiccated
  coconut, toasted in wok until golden brown,
  cooled
1 cup (125 g) shredded pomelo or grapefruit
  segments (juice drained off if using grapefruit)
1 1/4 cups (100 g) bean sprouts, straggly tails
  removed
2 eggs, lightly beaten and cooked to make
  2 thin omelettes, shredded
1/3 cup (35 g) dried prawns, soaked in hot
  water to soften, drained and minced
1 cup (100 g) thinly sliced young long beans
  or green beans
1 cup (100 g) finely diced cucumber
4 stems lemon grass, tender inner part of
  bottom 3 in (8 cm) only, very thinly sliced
1 tablespoon minced red or green bird's
  eye chili
1/2 cup loosely packed coriander leaves
1 large lime, quartered
2 kaffir lime leaves, cut in hair-like shreds

Sauce
2 tablespoons preserved fish or 3 tablespoons
  chopped canned anchovies
2 tablespoon ground palm sugar
2 tablespoons ground galangal
4 shallots, finely minced
1 stem lemon grass, bottom 4 in (10 cm) only,
  thinly sliced
2 kaffir lime leaves, torn
2 teaspoons dark soy sauce
1 cup (250 ml) water

To prepare the Sauce, put all the ingredients in a small saucepan, and bring to the boil, stirring. Lower the heat and simmer very gently, with the pan uncovered, until the liquid is reduced by half, 10 to 15 minutes. Pour through a sieve into a small bowl, pressing with the back of a spoon to extract as much juice as possible. Leave the liquid to cool, discarding the solids.

You can either arrange the rice in the center of one large serving plate, putting all the other ingredients around it, or you can prepare individual servings. To do the latter, lightly grease a small bowl with oil. Add 1 cup rice, pressing down to make grains adhere, then invert the bowl over a plate. Repeat, putting each portion of rice on a separate plate. Put small piles of pomelo, bean sprouts, omelette, dried prawns, snake beans, cucumber, lemon grass, bird's-eye chili, and coriander leaves around each rice mound. Add 1 lime quarter to each plate, and top the rice with kaffir lime shreds.

Divide the Sauce between four small sauce dishes and serve with the salad for everyone to drizzle over according to taste. The garnish ingredients are normally mixed through the rice just before eating.

Serves: **4**   Preparation time: **30 min**   Cooking time: **15 min**

smoked fish & green mango salad *yoam makah trey ang*

This is one of the first local dishes I ate in Cambodia, sitting under a shady tree in an open-air restaurant along the banks of the Mekong just north of Phnom Penh. It shows just how flavorful a dish can be with only a few seasonings — shallots, chilies, fresh mint, fish sauce, and lime juice — but when you're starting with sour green mango and combining it with deep-fried smoked fish, it's hard to go wrong.

I long-leaf Asian or butter lettuce leaves separated, washed and dried
vegetable oil for deep-frying
7 oz (200 g) boneless smoked fish, cut in bite-sized pieces (smoked mackerel or trout can be used)
3–4 unripe green mangoes (about 1 lb or 500 g), peeled
1 tablespoon sugar
1 tablespoon fish sauce, or more to taste
3 shallots, thinly sliced
2–3 red or green bird's-eye chilies, thinly sliced
lime juice to taste
2 tablespoons minced mint or coriander leaf

Place the lettuce leaves on a serving plate and set aside.

Heat oil in a wok and when very hot, add the smoked fish and deep-fry until it becomes crisp and brown. Drain on paper towel and leave to cool.

Hold each peeled mango over a shredder and grate to make matchstick shreds. Alternatively, hold the mango in the palm of one hand and with a sharp knife in the other hand, make vertical cuts down to the stone, keeping the cuts close together. Hold the knife horizontally and slice across to make shreds. Repeat on the other side of the mango. Put mango shreds in a bowl.

Sprinkle with sugar, rub with your fingers to soften the mango slightly, then add fish sauce, shallots, chilies, and the cooled fish. Toss and taste, adding more fish sauce (you may not need this if the smoked fish is very salty), and a little lime juice only if the mangoes are not sufficiently sour. Toss in the mint and serve in a bowl, together with the lettuce leaves. Each person puts some of the salad into a lettuce leaf and rolls it up to eat with the hand.

Serves: **4**   Preparation time: **7 min**   Cooking time: **5 min**

spicy nonya rice vermicelli salad *kerabu beehoon*

One of my friends in Singapore, whose grandmother was a Nonya, gave me her basic recipe for this salad, which is a fabulous mixture of rice vermicelli, toasted coconut, bean sprouts, shallots, herbs, lime juice, fish sauce, and the favorite local condiment, Sambal Belacan. Julia also adds dried prawns and salted fish, and sometimes throws in chopped bird's-eye chilies for those who like it hot. As she says, "It's up to you, lah!"

7 oz (200 g) rice vermicelli
1 cup (100 g) freshly grated coconut, or
  1 cup (80 g) desiccated coconut
1/3 cup (35 g) dried prawns, lightly toasted
  until fragrant, processed to a powder
1/2 cup (40 g) thinly sliced salted fish, fried
  until crisp and golden, coarsely crumbled
2 cups (160 g) bean sprouts, straggly tails
  discarded
8 shallots, thinly sliced
2 stems lemon grass, tender inner part of
  bottom 3 in (8 cm) only, thinly sliced
4–5 kaffir lime leaves, cut in hair-like shreds
2 spring onions, finely minced
1/4 cup minced coriander leaf
1 ginger bud, thinly sliced, optional
1/4 cup (60 ml) lime juice
2–3 tablespoons Malay Chili & Dried Shrimp
  Paste Dip (page 175)
2 tablespoons fish sauce
1 1/2 tablespoons sugar
1 teaspoon sesame oil
salt to taste
black pepper to taste

Do not pre-soak the rice vermicelli but put it dry into a saucepan of boiling water and simmer until it is just cooked but still firm, about 3 to 4 minutes, separating the noodles as they start to soften. Drain, rinse under cold running water, then drain thoroughly and set aside.

Put the coconut in a dry wok and cook over very low heat, stirring constantly, until it turns golden brown. Transfer to a plate and leave to cool.

To finalize the salad, cut the rice vermicelli into 3 in (8 cm) lengths, then put in a large bowl and add the coconut, dried prawns, salted fish, bean sprouts, shallots, lemon grass, lime leaves, spring onions, coriander, and ginger bud (if using). Toss gently.

Combine the lime juice, Sambal Belacan, fish sauce, sugar, and sesame oil in a small bowl, stirring to mix well, then pour over the rice vermicelli, tossing gently to mix. Taste and add salt and pepper if you like, and a little more lime juice or sugar depending on the degree of acidity you enjoy. Toss again and serve immediately.

Serves: **4-6**   Preparation time: **20 min**   Cooking time: **8 min**

stir-fried vegetarian noodles *mee cha*

Although most Southeast Asian noodle dishes have a little meat, poultry, or seafood in them, here's an easy vegetarian version from Cambodia with bean curd, broccoli, mushrooms, carrot, and bean sprouts. There's just enough seasoning to give a delightful flavor to the combination, and you can adjust the amount of chili to suit your taste. This would be good for a quick and healthy lunch, especially if followed by fresh fruit.

12 oz (375 g) dried egg noodles
$1/2$ cup (125 ml) oil
2 cakes (200–250 g) hard bean curd
1 tablespoon crushed and minced garlic
1–2 large red chilies, finely minced
4 dried black Chinese mushrooms, soaked to
  soften, stems discarded, caps shredded
5 oz (150 g) broccoli, broken into very small
  florets
1 medium carrot (about $3^1/2$ oz or 100 g), cut
  in match-stick pieces
4 tablespoons light soy sauce
4 tablespoons dark soy sauce
$1^1/2$ teaspoons sugar
$1^1/4$ cups (100 g) bean sprouts
$1/2$ teaspoon salt
sprigs of coriander leaf to garnish,
  or 1 spring onion, thinly sliced

Bring a large pan of water to the boil and add the dried noodles. Boil rapidly, stirring from time to time to separate the noodles, until they are just soft. Transfer noodles to a colander and rinse well under cold running water. Drain and set aside.

Heat the oil in a wok for 30 seconds and when very hot, add the bean curd and fry until golden brown all over, about 2 minutes on each side. Remove and drain on paper towel. When cool enough to handle, cut each bean curd in half across, then slice thinly.

Remove all but 3 tablespoons of the oil from the wok. Heat, then add the garlic, and stir-fry for 5 seconds. Add the chili and mushrooms and stir-fry 30 seconds, then put in the broccoli and carrot and stir-fry for 1 minute. Add the drained noodles and stir-fry, mixing well, for 1 minute.

Sprinkle both lots of soy sauce and sugar over the noodles, then add the bean sprouts, reserved bean curd, and salt. Stir-fry for 1 minute, mixing thoroughly to incorporate the noodles and vegetables. Serve immediately garnished with fresh coriander leaf.

Serves: **4**   Preparation time: **10 min**   Cooking time: **3 min**

nonya-style noodles with pork and prawns   *mee goreng nonya*

Want to take out a little life insurance next time you celebrate your birthday? Then try this recipe, a mixture of typical Chinese ingredients with Malay garnishes. The Chinese custom of serving noodles (which symbolize a long life) at birthday dinners is continued by the Nonyas of both Malaysia and Singapore. But you don't have to wait for your birthday try this tasty noodle dish. Whatever you do, don't cut the noodles before eating them — this is considered very bad luck as it implies cutting your life short.

7 oz (200 g) belly pork, in one piece
2–3 cups (500–750 ml) water
2 tablespoons vegetable oil
3 shallots, finely sliced
1 clove garlic, crushed and finely minced
2 tablespoons salted soybeans
$\frac{1}{2}$ lb (250 g) small raw prawns, peeled and deveined
$\frac{1}{2}$ teaspoon salt
$\frac{1}{2}$ teaspoon sugar
$3\frac{1}{2}$ oz (100 g) Chinese flowering cabbage, cut in 2 in (5 cm) lengths
$1\frac{1}{4}$ cups (100 g) bean sprouts, straggly tails removed
13 oz (400 g) fresh wheat noodles, rinsed and drained (see Note)
Malay Chili & Prawn Paste Dip (Sambal Belacan) (page 179)

Garnish
1 egg, cooked to make a thin omelette, julienned
5 in (12 cm) piece cucumber, seeded, flesh cut in matchstick shreds
1 large red chili, sliced
1 tablespoon Crisp-fried Shallots (page 17)
sprigs of fresh coriander leaf
4 lime wedges

Put the pork and enough water to cover it in a small saucepan. Bring to the boil, cover the pan, lower heat, and simmer until the meat is tender. Cool and cut the pork into thin slices, reserving the stock. Measure the stock and add water if needed to make up 1 cup (250 ml). Set aside.

Heat the oil in a wok and add the shallots and garlic. Stir-fry until transparent, then add the salted soybeans and stir-fry 1 minute. Add the prawns and stir-fry just until they change color, then sprinkle with salt and sugar. Add the cabbage and stir-fry until it starts to soften, about 1 minute. Add the bean sprouts and stir-fry for a few seconds, then add the noodles and pork.

Stir-fry to mix well, then add the reserved stock and cook over high heat, stirring frequently, until the stock has been absorbed and the noodles are cooked, about 3 minutes. Transfer the noodles to a large serving dish and decorate with the Garnish ingredients. Sprinkle with lime juice to taste and serve with Sambal Belacan.

Note: If you prefer, you could use 12 oz (375 g) dried wheat or egg noodles, preferably thin and round; cook them in boiling water just until tender; rinse and drain thoroughly.

Serves: **4-6**   Preparation time: **25 min**   Cooking time: **12 min**

singapore-style hokkien noodles *fujian mien*

The majority of Singapore's Chinese population is Hokkien in origin, their ancestors coming from Fujian province in southern China. You won't be surprised to learn, then, that the nation's favorite noodle dish is this Hokkien mixture of fresh yellow noodles and rice vermicelli in a rich pork and seafood stock. It's always served with something you won't find in China: a side-dish of the very local Malay Chili and Dried Shrimp Paste Dip or Sambal Belacan.

1 lb (500 g) fresh thick yellow noodles
5$\frac{1}{2}$ oz (150 g) dried rice vermicelli, soaked in hot water to soften, cut in 3 in (8 cm) lengths
$\frac{1}{2}$ lb (250 g) belly pork, covered with water and boiled until cooked, stock reserved, meat thinly sliced
3 tablespoons oil
10 oz (300 g) small raw prawns, peeled and deveined, heads and shells reserved
$\frac{1}{2}$ lb (250 g) bean sprouts, washed and drained, straggly tails discarded
8–10 cloves garlic, crushed and minced
2 eggs, lightly beaten
1 teaspoon salt
$\frac{1}{4}$ teaspoon white pepper
$\frac{1}{4}$ cup minced Chinese chives or spring onions, cut in $\frac{3}{4}$ in (2 cm) lengths
Malay Chili and Dried Shrimp Paste Dip (Sambal Belacan) (page 175)
4 small round green limes (*limau kesturi*), top portion sliced off, or 1 regular lime, quartered

Put the fresh yellow noodles in a bowl and pour over boiling water. Stand 1 minute, then drain in a colander and put on a plate with the soaked and drained rice vermicelli.

Measure the reserved pork stock and add water if necessary to make up 1 cup (250 ml). Set aside.

Heat 1 tablespoon of oil in a saucepan and stir-fry the prawn heads and shells until they turn pink. Add the reserved pork stock to the prawn shells, bring to the boil, cover and simmer 5 minutes. Strain, pressing down on the prawns shells to extract as much juice as possible. Put the stock back in the pan, add the prawns and simmer until just cooked, about 3 minutes. Strain and reserve the stock and prawns separately. (The recipe can be prepared in advance to this stage, and all ingredients refrigerated for several hours.)

Heat the remaining 2 tablespoons oil in a wok and stir-fry the garlic until it turns golden brown and flavors the oil. Discard the garlic and raise the heat. When the oil is very hot, pour in the beaten eggs and stir for 1 minute. Add the noodles, bean sprouts, and $\frac{1}{2}$ cup of the reserved stock. Stir-fry over high heat for 1 minute, then add the pork, prawns, salt, and pepper. Stir-fry 2 to 3 minutes until everything is heated through and well mixed, adding a little more stock if the noodles threaten to stick.

Add the Chinese chives, stir for a few seconds, then transfer to a large serving dish. Serve with Sambal Belacan and limes, or, if preferred, small bowls of dark soy sauce with sliced large red chili.

Note: Some cooks like to add fresh squid to the noodles; substitute 5$\frac{1}{2}$ oz (150 g) of the prawns with squid; slice the squid and simmer together with the prawns.

Serves: **4**   Preparation time: **25 min**   Cooking time: **15 min**

fried rice-flour noodles with pork, prawns & squid *char kway teow*

There used to be a Chinese cook in a coffee shop opposite Singapore's Newton Circus where the version of fried rice-flour noodles was so fantastic that you could queue for as long as 30 minutes if you went during the lunch-hour rush. The cook and the coffee shop have long gone, but the basic way of cooking the noodles still remains. The addition of crisp-fried pork fat is a real no-no in these health-conscious days, but it gives a unique and authentic flavor to the noodles. (You could, however, omit this if you prefer.)

3$^1/_2$ oz (100 g) hard pork fat (cut from the back), cut in $^1/_2$ in (1 cm) dice (see Note)
2 tablespoons water
4 cloves garlic, crushed and minced
2 large red chilies, crushed to a paste, or 2 teaspoons crushed chili
7 oz (200 g) lean pork, shredded
13 oz (400 g) raw prawns, peeled and deveined
7 oz (200 g) squid, cleaned, peeled and sliced
1 tablespoon light soy sauce
1 tablespoon dark soy sauce
2 teaspoons oyster sauce
$^1/_2$ teaspoon salt
liberal sprinkling of white pepper
$^1/_2$ lb (250 g) bean sprouts, straggly tails removed
2 lb (1 kg) fresh wide rice-flour noodles, scalded in boiling water, rinsed and drained
1 large red chili, sliced
sprigs of coriander leaf

Put the pork fat and water in a wok and cook over medium heat, stirring from time to time, until the water has dried up and the oil run out. Keep cooking until the pieces of fat have turned crisp and golden brown, then remove and drain on paper towel. Leave 3 tablespoons of the pork oil in the wok and discard the remainder.

Heat the pork oil and stir-fry the garlic and chili over low-medium heat for about 30 seconds. Increase the heat, add the pork and stir-fry 2 minutes. Add the prawns and squid and stir-fry 2 minutes. Season with both lots of soy sauce, oyster sauce, salt, and pepper.

Add the bean sprouts and stir-fry 2 minutes, then put in the noodles and stir-fry until well mixed and heated through. Stir in the crisp pork fat and transfer to a serving dish. Garnish with chili and coriander.

Note: If you prefer, the pork crisps can be omitted, and 3 tablespoons vegetable oil used instead of the pork oil for frying.

Serves: **4**   Preparation time: **20 min**   Cooking time: **18 min**

rice noodles with beef & broccoli   *guey teow pad sei ew*

Fresh wide rice-flour noodles are the basis of this Thai dish, particularly popular in Bangkok (you could use dried noodles if the fresh ones aren't available). The silky noodles are mixed with beef and broccoli, both of which have strong flavors that seem to have been made for each other. Although this is similar to many Chinese stir-fried noodle dishes, the addition of fish sauce, chili, and crushed peanuts gives this recipe a true Thai accent.

10 oz (300 g) boneless sirloin or rump steak, thinly sliced across the grain, cut in bite-sized pieces
3 tablespoons vegetable oil
3 cloves garlic, crushed and minced
10 oz (300 g) broccoli, cut into small florets
$1/4$ cup (60 ml) water
2 tablespoons fish sauce
1 tablespoon dark soy sauce
$1^3/4$ lb (800 g) fresh wide rice flour noodles, blanched briefly in boiling water and drained (see Note)
3 tablespoons coarsely crushed dry-roasted peanuts
2 tablespoons dried chili flakes

Marinade
1 tablespoon cornflour
1 egg, lightly beaten
1 clove garlic, crushed and minced
1 tablespoon Chinese rice wine (preferably Shao Hsing)
1 tablespoon fish sauce
1 tablespoon oyster sauce
1 tablespoon sugar
1 teaspoon sesame oil
$1/2$ teaspoon white pepper

Put the beef in a bowl and prepare the Marinade. Sprinkle the beef with cornflour and toss to coat, then add all other Marinade ingredients, mixing well. Marinate for 10 minutes.

Heat the oil in a wok and stir-fry the garlic for 5 seconds. Add the beef and its marinade and stir-fry over very high heat until the meat starts to change color, about 1 minute. Add the broccoli and stir-fry for 1 minute, then put in the water and continue stir-frying until broccoli is just cooked, about 2 minutes. (The broccoli must be cut into very small pieces so it will cook quickly.)

Splash in the fish sauce and soy sauce, then add the noodles, stir-frying for about 1 minute to mix well and heat through. Transfer to a serving dish and sprinkle with peanuts. Serve hot with dried crushed chili served separately for adding to taste.

Note: If fresh noodles are not available, use 13 oz (400 g) dried wide rice-flour noodles or regular rice stick noodles, soaked in hot water to soften, then simmered until cooked.

Serves: **4**   Preparation time: **25 min + 10 min marinating**   Cooking time: **8 min**

thai stir-fried rice-stick noodles *pad thai*

This Thai classic combines rice-stick noodles with pork or chicken, prawns, and eggs, plus a little bean curd if you like. The fried noodles have a faint sweet-sour tang, thanks to the lime juice and sugar, as well as a lovely contrast in textures, with soft noodles snuggling up to crunchy bean sprouts and peanuts. You can vary the protein, using either pork or chicken, or adding bean curd. Served with Thai Fish Sauce & Chili Dip, these noodles make a great lunch.

$1/4$ cup (60 ml) vegetable oil
6 cloves garlic, crushed and minced
3–4 shallots, minced
1 teaspoon crushed dried chili flakes
7 oz (200 g) lean pork or chicken, shredded
$1/2$ lb (250 g) small or medium prawns,
  peeled and deveined
4 tablespoons fish sauce
2 eggs
13 oz (400 g) dried rice stick noodles, soaked
  in warm water to soften, drained
1 tablespoon lime juice
1 tablespoon sugar
$1 1/4$ cups (100 g) bean sprouts, straggly tails
  removed

Garnish
4 tablespoons coarsely crushed unsalted
  roasted peanuts
1 tablespoon dried prawns, toasted over low
  heat 4–5 minutes, processed to a powder
1 spring onion, finely sliced
2 tablespoons coarsely chopped coriander
  leaf
1 lime, quartered
$1 1/4$ cups (100 g) bean sprouts, straggly tails
  removed

Accompaniments
crushed dried chili flakes
Simple Thai Fish Sauce & Chili Dip (page 175)

Heat the oil in a wok, add the garlic, shallots, and chili and stir-fry for a few seconds. Add the pork or chicken and stir-fry over high heat for 2 minutes. Add the prawns and stir-fry just until they are just cooked, 2 to 3 minutes. Splash over the fish sauce, stir, then add the eggs, stirring briefly to break up the yolks. Leave for a few seconds until the egg starts to set, then mix it with the pork and bean prawns.

Push the cooked ingredients up the sides of the wok and put in the drained noodles in the centre. Leave them for a few seconds, then toss to mix well. Add the lime juice and sugar and give a quick stir. Put in the bean sprouts and stir-fry for just 30 seconds, mixing well.

Transfer immediately to a large serving dish or four individual dishes. Sprinkle with crushed peanuts, prawn powder, spring onions, and coriander sprigs. Arrange the bean sprouts and lime wedges around the edge of the noodles and serve together with chili flakes and Simple Thai Fish Sauce & Chili Dip.

Note: You could reduce the amount or pork or chicken to 4 oz (125 g) and add 1 cake hard bean curd (about 4 oz or 125 g); cut the bean curd in $1/2$ in (1 cm) dice and add as soon as the prawns have started to turn pink.

Serves: **4**   Preparation time: **20 min**   Cooking time: **7 min**

indonesian spicy chicken noodle soup *soto ayam*

Soto Ayam is one of the most popular noodles soups in Indonesia, sold by mobile vendors and in basic restaurants throughout the archipelago. The addition of hard-boiled egg, bean sprouts, and potatoes to the chicken, rice vermicelli and spiced chicken stock makes this a satisfying dish. Versions made at home often include potato croquettes or *pergedel* instead of sliced boiled potato.

1 1/4 lb (600 g) chicken pieces with the bone still in (preferably thigh)
4 cups (1 liter) water
1 teaspoon salt
3 tablespoons oil
1/2–1 teaspoon chicken stock powder, optional
1 cup (250 ml) coconut milk
2 kaffir lime leaves, edges torn
2 small waxy potatoes, boiled, peeled, and thickly sliced
2 hard boiled eggs, peeled and halved lengthways
1 1/2 cups (120 g) bean sprouts
7 oz (200 g) fine dried rice vermicelli, soaked in hot water to soften
3 tablespoons Crisp-fried Shallots (page 17)
2 tablespoons finely minced Chinese celery leaf or coriander
1 large lime, quartered

Seasoning Paste
1 teaspoon black peppercorns
1 teaspoon coriander seeds, lightly toasted
4 candlenuts, minced
6 shallots, minced
2 cloves garlic, minced
1 thin slice ginger, minced
1/2 in (1 cm) fresh turmeric, minced, or 1/4 teaspoon turmeric powder

Put the chicken, water, and salt in a saucepan. Bring to the boil, cover, lower heat, and simmer gently until the chicken is soft. When the chicken is cool enough to handle, discard the skin and remove the flesh from the bones, shredding it finely by hand. Set aside. Reserve the chicken stock.

Prepare Seasoning Paste by processing pepper and coriander to a powder in a spice grinder. Add remaining ingredients and process to a smooth paste, adding a little of the oil if needed to keep the mixture turning.

Heat the oil in a saucepan with a heavy base, then add the Seasoning Paste and stir-fry over low-medium heat until fragrant, about 4 minutes. Add the reserved chicken stock and bring to the boil. Lower the heat, cover the pan, and simmer 5 minutes. Add the coconut milk and kaffir lime leaves, then bring gently to the boil, stirring. Taste and add a little chicken stock powder if desired. Simmer with the pan uncovered for 5 minutes.

To serve, divide the noodles, potato, egg, bean sprouts, and chicken between four large noodle bowls. Add hot stock to each, then garnish with crisp-fried shallots and celery leaf. Serve with a lime wedge and, if preferred, a chili sambal.

Serves: **4**   Preparation time: **30 min**   Cooking time: **35 min**

creamy chicken noodle soup *kauk swee*

When I first tried these excellent noodles — basically, a very liquid chicken curry served in a bowl with noodles — in northern Thailand, I didn't realize that the recipe actually originated in Burma. I must admit I prefer the seasonings of this aromatic Thai version, which makes an excellent lunch or light meal, or could be served with a side salad and followed by dessert for a dinner.

$^1/_4$ cup vegetable oil
2 cups (500 ml) chicken stock
1 stem lemon grass, bottom 5 in (12 cm)
  bruised with a pestle or back of a cleaver,
  cut in 1 in (2 cm) lengths
13 oz (400 g) boneless chicken breast or
  thighs fillets, cut in $^1/_4$ in (5 mm) strips
  about 2 in (4 cm) in length
2 cups (500 ml) coconut milk
salt to taste
7 oz (200 g) dried round or flat egg noodles
1 large fresh red chili, seeded and sliced
1 spring onion, finely sliced
2 tablespoons Crisp-fried Shallots (page 17)
1 large lime, quartered lengthways

Curry Paste
2 teaspoons coriander seeds, lightly toasted
1 teaspoon cumin seeds, lightly toasted
1 teaspoon finely minced coriander root
2 tablespoons minced fresh galangal
2 cloves garlic, minced
2 teaspoons dried shrimp paste
$2^1/_2$ tablespoons curry powder
$^1/_2$ teaspoon chili powder
3 tablespoons water

Make the Curry Paste by processing the coriander and cumin to a powder in spice grinder. Add the coriander root, galangal, garlic, and shrimp paste and process until fine, adding a little of the water if needed to keep mixture turning. Transfer to a small bowl and mix in curry powder, chili powder, and water.

Heat the oil in a medium saucepan and stir-fry the curry paste over low-medium heat until fragrant and cooked, 4 to 5 minutes. Add the chicken stock and lemon grass and bring to the boil. Simmer uncovered for 5 minutes, then add the chicken and cook until tender, 10 to 15 minutes. Add the coconut milk and heat, stirring frequently, until it almost comes to the boil. Add salt to taste and keep warm.

Bring a saucepan of water to the boil, then add the noodles and boil until cooked, 3 to 4 minutes depending on the thickness of the noodles. Rinse, drain, and divide between four large bowls. Ladle the chicken curry mixture over the top of each portion of noodles. Garnish each with sliced chili, spring onions, and shallots. Serve lime wedges on separate plate for adding the juice to taste.

Serves: **4**   Preparation time: **25 min**   Cooking time: **30 min**

nonya rice vermicelli in spicy gravy   *mee siam*

The hot, sour, spicy flavor of many Nonya dishes makes them remarkably similar to some Thai food, a good example being this fragrant noodle soup. Although this Nonya version of Thai noodles (hence the name "Siam") takes a while to prepare, the spice paste, gravy, and garnishes can be done well ahead of serving. Then it's just a matter of a short time in the kitchen when you're ready to eat.

2 cups (160 g) bean sprouts, straggly tails removed
1/2 cup minced Chinese chives, cut in 3/4 in (2 cm) lengths
10 oz (300 g) cooked prawns, peeled, heads removed, halved lengthways
10 oz (300 g) dried rice vermicelli, soaked in hot water to soften, drained, cut in 2 1/2 in (6 cm) lengths
1 square (4 oz or 125 g) hard bean curd, deep fried until golden, halved crossways and thinly sliced
2 hard-boiled eggs, peeled and quartered
2 limes, quartered, or 4 small round green limes (*limau kesturi*), top portion sliced off

Spice Paste
8–10 dried chilies, soaked to soften, some seeds discarded if preferred, to reduce the heat
8 shallots, minced
6 candlenuts, minced
1/4 cup (60 ml) oil
1/4 cup salted soybeans, lightly crushed with the back of a spoon
3–4 teaspoons sugar

Gravy
4 cups (1 liter) water
3 tablespoons dried prawns, soaked to soften, blended to a powder
2 heaped tablespoons tamarind pulp, soaked in 1/2 cup warm water, squeezed and strained to obtain juice
sugar to taste

Prepare the Spice Paste by grinding the chilies, shallots, and candlenuts in a spice grinder, adding a little oil in needed to keep the mixture turning. Heat the oil in a wok for 30 seconds, then add the Spice Paste and stir-fry over low-medium heat, stirring frequently, for 4 minutes. Add the salted soybeans and stir-fry for 30 seconds, then sprinkle in sugar and cook another 30 seconds. Remove half the Spice Paste from the wok.

To prepare the Gravy, put half the Spice Paste in a large saucepan, reserving the remainder for frying the noodles. Add the water and dried prawn powder to the saucepan, bring to the boil, then add the tamarind juice. Taste and add a little sugar if desired. Simmer for 3 minutes. Remove from the heat but keep the gravy in the saucepan.

Heat the Spice Paste remaining in the wok, then add the bean sprouts and stir-fry over high heat for 30 seconds. Add half the garlic chives and half the prawns and stir-fry for 30 seconds. Add the rice vermicelli, a little at a time, stirring vigorously to mix it thoroughly with the other ingredients. Stir-fry for 2 minutes, then transfer to a large serving dish.

Arrange the remaining garlic chives and prawns decoratively on top of the noodles, and garnish with the bean curd, eggs, and lime. Re-heat the gravy and transfer to a deep bowl or jug. Serve hot. (Alternatively, you can divide the noodles, garlic chives, prawns, bean curd, and eggs between four large noodle bowls, topping each up with Gravy and adding two pieces of lime.)

Serves: **4**   Preparation time: **30 min**   Cooking time: **20 min**

spicy singapore noodle soup *laksa singapura*

Extravagant. Time consuming. Absolutely delicious. Of all the versions of the famous Laksa noodle soup prepared in Malaysia and Singapore, this is my favorite. The fragrant coconut milk gravy is laced with chilies and dried prawns, with the accompaniments giving even more flavor and texture. Serve this for a special lunch or dinner, followed by a delectable dessert and believe me, you won't regret it.

12–16 small fish balls, or 1–2 fish cakes, thinly sliced

1 1/2 lb (750 g) fresh round rice-flour (laksa) noodles, blanched in boiling water 30 seconds, drained (see Note)

160 g (2 cups) bean sprouts, straggly tails removed

13 oz (400 g) cooked prawns, peeled and deveined, tails intact

12 canned or fresh quail eggs, hard-boiled and peeled if fresh, or 2 hard-boiled eggs, quartered (see Note)

4 large pieces deep-fried dried bean curd, blanched in boiling water 1 minute, sliced (see Note)

sprigs of polygonum (long-stemmed mint) to garnish

Laksa Gravy

10–12 dried chilies, cut in 3/4 in (2 cm) lengths, soaked in hot water to soften

2–3 large red chilies, sliced

16 shallots, minced

2 in (5 cm) galangal, minced

6 cloves garlic, minced

1 in (2.5 cm) ginger, minced

3 stems lemon grass, tender inner part of bottom 4 in (10 cm) only, sliced

3/4 in (2 cm) fresh turmeric, or 1 teaspoon turmeric powder

1 1/2 teaspoons dried shrimp paste, toasted

1/3 cup (85 ml) vegetable oil

2 teaspoons coriander, lightly toasted and ground to a powder

1/2 cup (50 g) dried prawns, soaked to soften, ground to a powder

3 cups (750 ml) water

4 tablespoons finely minced polygonum leaves (long-stemmed mint)

1 1/2 teaspoons salt, or more to taste

1 1/2 teaspoons sugar, or more to taste

3 cups (750 ml) coconut milk

Accompaniments

4 tablespoons pounded fresh chili or Malay Chili & Dried Shrimp Paste Dip (page 175)

4 small round green limes (*limau kesturi*), stalk end sliced off, or 1 regular lime, quartered

To make the Laksa Gravy, process both lots of chilies, shallots, galangal, garlic, ginger, lemon grass, turmeric, and shrimp paste to a smooth paste, adding a little oil if needed to keep the mixture turning.

Heat the oil in a large saucepan, add the chili paste and stir-fry over low-moderate heat until fragrant and the oil starts to separate, about 10 minutes. Add the coriander powder and stir-fry 1 minute. Add the dried prawns and stir-fry 1 minute. Stir in the water, polygonum leaves, salt, and sugar. Bring to the boil, lower heat, and simmer uncovered for 5 minutes. Add fish balls and simmer another 5 minutes. Add the coconut and bring almost to the boil, then remove from heat. Taste and adjust salt and sugar if needed.

To serve, divide the noodles and bean sprouts between four large bowls. Fill each with hot gravy, then top with prawns, fish balls, quail eggs (or 2 egg quarters), and bean curd slices. Garnish with sprigs of polygonum and serve immediately with small dishes containing Chili and Dried Shrimp Paste Sambal (Sambal Belacan) and a lime.

Note: If boiling fresh quail eggs, add 1 tablespoon of salt to the water and boil for just 3 minutes; the salt makes it easier to peel off the shell. If fresh laksa noodles are not available, use 10 oz (300 g) dried laksa noodles, prepared according to directions on pack, or 13 oz (400 g) dried rice vermicelli, soaked to soften, then simmered about 1 minute until cooked. Deep-fried dried bean curd is sometimes called "tofu puff" or "tofu cube;" if you can't find this, use 1 square hard bean curd, deep-fried and thinly sliced.

Serves: **4**   Preparation time: **40 min**   Cooking time: **30 min**

cambodian pork & rice-stick noodle soup *k'tieu*

If you're prepared to brave the exhaust fumes from the endless flow of motorcycles weaving along Phnom Penh's busy streets, you can grab a bowl of this noodle soup at just about any food stall. K'tieu is to the Cambodians what Beef & Noodle Soup is to the Vietnamese, the national dish, slurped with pleasure at any time of day. Both pork fillet and minced pork are simmered in rich chicken or pork stock, which is poured over noodles and bean sprouts. Uniquely Cambodian touches come in the form of shredded salted cabbage and dried prawn powder, with chilies, fresh herbs, and crisp-fried garlic and shallots all adding their magic.

10 oz (300 g) pork fillet or loin, in one piece
6 cups (1.5 liters) chicken or pork stock
1–2 teaspoons sugar
$\frac{1}{2}$ teaspoon freshly ground black pepper
7 oz (200 g) ground lean pork
2 oz (60 g) finely shredded salted cabbage
$\frac{1}{2}$ lb (250 g) rice-stick noodles, soaked in hot water to soften, drained
2 cups (160 g) bean sprouts, straggly tails removed
12 cooked medium prawns, peeled and deveined
2 tablespoons Crisp-fried Shallots (page 17)
1–2 tablespoons Crisp-fried Garlic (page 17)
1 spring onion, finely minced
3 tablespoons minced coriander leaf or mint
3 tablespoons dried prawns, soaked in hot water to soften, processed to a powder
2–3 green or red bird's-eye chilies, minced

Pork the pork fillet or loin into a saucepan with the stock. Bring to the boil, cover, lower heat and simmer until tender, about 15 minutes for fillet, 30 to 40 minutes for loin. Remove the pork, slice thinly, and set aside, leaving the stock in the pan.

Add the ground pork to the stock and simmer until cooked, 4 to 5 minutes. Return the sliced pork to stock and add sugar, pepper, and salted cabbage. Bring to the boil, cover and remove from the heat.

Bring a large saucepan of water to the boil. Add the noodles and cook until done, 1 to 2 minutes. Drain, rinse under running water, drain again, then divide between four large bowls. Put $\frac{1}{2}$ cup of bean sprouts into each bowl. Add the stock and garnish each serving with shallots, garlic, spring onion, coriander, prawn powder, and chili. Serve immediately.

Serves: **4**   Preparation time: **10 min**   Cooking time: **30 min**

penang nonya hot sour noodle soup   *asam laksa penang*

Sour, fishy, fragrant, sweet, salty, and hot, this Penang favorite is very different to the coconut-milk Laksa found in the rest of Malaysia and Singapore. Some of the Penang Nonyas are descended from Chinese who migrated to this lovely island off the northwest Malay peninsula from southern Thailand in the 19th and early 20th centuries — and as this dish demonstrates, their food certainly shows it.

1 1/4 lb (600 g) small whole mackerel, cleaned
6 cups (1.5 liters) water
2 tablespoons tamarind pulp, soaked in
  1/2 cup warm water, squeezed and strained
  to obtain juice
1 teaspoon sugar, or more to taste
1 teaspoon salt, or more to taste
1 ginger bud, halved lengthways, thinly sliced
  across, optional
4 large stalks polygonum (long-stemmed
  mint)
1 1/4 lb (600 g) fresh thick rice flour noodles
  (see Note), or 10 oz (300 g) dried rice
  vermicelli

Seasoning Paste
4 shallots, minced
2 stems lemon grass, bottom 3 in (8 cm) only,
  finely sliced
3/4 in (2 cm) fresh turmeric, minced, or
  1/2 teaspoon turmeric powder
6–8 dried chilies, cut in 3/4 in (2 cm) pieces,
  soaked in hot water to soften
3 large red chilies, sliced
1 teaspoon dried shrimp paste, toasted

Garnish
1/2 small cucumber, halved lengthways, pulp
  discarded, flesh cut in matchstick strips
5 1/2 oz (150 g) pineapple, peeled and cored,
  cut in very small wedges
1 medium red or brown onion, halved
  lengthways, very thinly sliced across
1 large red chili, seeds discarded, sliced,
  optional
4 large sprigs mint, leaves coarsely torn
2 tablespoons thick black prawn paste
1 tablespoon warm water

Put the fish in a large saucepan and add the water. Bring to the boil, lower heat, and simmer uncovered until the fish is soft, about 5 minutes. Remove the fish and when cool enough, flake the flesh and keep aside, making sure you get rid of any tiny bones (local cooks use their fingers to be sure). Strain the stock back into pan and add tamarind juice, sugar, salt, ginger bud (if using), and polygonum.

Prepare the Seasoning Paste by processing all ingredients in a spice grinder, adding a little water if necessary to keep mixture turning. Add to the fish stock, bring to the boil, lower heat and simmer uncovered, 15 minutes. Taste and add more sugar or salt if desired. Return the flaked fish to the stock.

Heat a large saucepan of boiling water. Blanch the noodles for 30 seconds, drain and divide between four large noodle bowls. Add fish soup to each bowl, and garnish with cucumber, pineapple, onion, chili, and mint. Combine the prawn paste with water and serve in separate bowl for adding according to taste.

Note: If fresh laksa noodles are not available, use 10 oz (300 g) dried laksa noodles or dried rice vermicelli, prepared according to directions on pack.

Serves: **4**   Preparation time: **45 min**   Cooking time: **30 min**

vietnamese beef & noodle soup   *pho bo*

Variations of this classic noodle soup are found throughout Vietnam. It sounds simple: beef stock, slices of beef, noodles, bean sprouts, and herbs. But what a fabulously rich beef stock, bathing silky rice-flour noodles and crunchy sprouts, with morsels of rare beef, all perfumed with herbs and lime. This is a seriously satisfying soup. Eat it on its own for breakfast, lunch, or supper (or all three).

10 oz (300 g) beef brisket or gravy beef, in one piece
2 lb (1 kg) beef shin bones
10 cups (2.5 liters) water
2 in (5 cm) ginger, unpeeled
1 medium onion, unpeeled
2 whole star anise
3 in (8 cm) cinnamon
1 teaspoon salt
13 oz (400 g) fresh wide rice noodles, or 7 oz (200 g) dried rice stick noodles, soaked in hot water to soften, drained
$1/_2$ lb (250 g) sirloin or fillet steak, chilled in the freezer 30 minutes, cut in paper-thin slices
1 medium red or brown-skinned onion, cut in paper-thin slices
2 spring onions, thinly sliced

Accompaniments
$1^1/_4$ cups (100 g) bean sprouts
large handful of mint sprigs
large handful of Asian basil
1–2 large red chilies, sliced
1 lime, quartered
small bowls of fish sauce

Put the brisket beef and beef bones in a very large pan and add water to cover the meat. Bring to the boil, then simmer uncovered for 10 minutes. Pour off the water and then add the 10 cups fresh water.

While the beef is blanching, spear the ginger and the onion on a skewer and hold in a gas flame or place under a very hot grill. Cook, turning, until the ginger and onion are blackened. Do not remove the skin but add the whole piece of ginger and the onion, skin and all, to the pan. Add the star anise, cinnamon, and salt and simmer over very low heat, with the pan uncovered, for 3 hours. By this time, the meat will be almost falling apart. Remove the piece of brisket and set aside to cool. Discard the beef bones and pour the stock through a sieve into a clean pan. If desired, the stock can be made one to two days in advance and refrigerated.

Cut the brisket beef into thin slices. Re-heat the strained stock and keep warm. If using fresh noodles, plunge them in a large pan of boiling water for 10 seconds, then drain in a colander to drain.

To serve, put some of the noodles into the bottom of four large soup bowls. Top with sliced brisket beef and the raw sirloin slices. Fill each bowl with hot stock and scatter with a little thinly sliced raw onion and spring onions. Place the Accompaniments in the center of the table for each person to add to the noodle soup as desired.

Serves: **4**   Preparation time: **30 min**   Cooking time: **3-4 hours**

mimosa rice *com hua mimosa*

The Vietnamese name this beautifully presented rice dish after the yellow mimosa flower, which the garnish of egg yolk is supposed to resemble. The rice is cooked in coconut milk for a rich creamy taste, then mixed with seasoned diced chicken, pork, dried Chinese sausage, peas, and carrots. This recipe makes enough for a light meal with a simple salad, or you could serve it with a soup, salad, or another dish for a more substantial dinner.

2¼ cups (560 ml) coconut milk
¼ cup (60 ml) water
½ teaspoon salt
2 cups (400 g) long-grain rice, washed and drained
4 oz (125 g) chicken breast fillet, diced
4 oz (125 g) pork fillet or loin, diced
2 teaspoons fish sauce
¼ teaspoon sugar
sprinkling of freshly ground black pepper
2 dried Chinese sausages (*lap cheong*)
1 tablespoon peanut or vegetable oil
1 clove garlic, crushed and finely minced
2 spring onions, minced
½ cup (75 g) green peas, boiled 30 seconds, drained
1 small carrot, diced, simmered in boiling water 2 minutes, and drained
2 hard-boiled eggs, separated, yolks sieved and whites finely minced
sprigs of coriander leaf to garnish

Put the coconut milk and salt in a saucepan with a heavy base. Bring to the boil over low-medium heat, stirring constantly. Pour in the rice, stir, then partially cover the pan. Cook over low heat until coconut milk is completely absorbed, about 5 minutes.

Cover the pan firmly and remove from heat. Stand 5 minutes. Wipe the inside of the lid with a towel and cover again. Put over the lowest possible heat and cook for 20 to 30 minutes until tender. Remove from the heat, fluff up the rice with a fork, cover, and let it stand while preparing the rest of the ingredients.

Put the chicken and pork in a bowl and sprinkle with the fish sauce, sugar, and pepper. Toss, then set aside. Put the Chinese sausages in boiling water in a saucepan and simmer gently until softened, about 3 to 4 minutes. Remove and cut into ½ in (1 cm) slices.

Heat the oil in a wok, then stir-fry the garlic and spring onions for 10 seconds. Add the chicken and pork and stir-fry over a medium heat for 5 minutes. Add the peas, carrots, and Chinese sausage and stir-fry until cooked, 3 to 4 minutes.

Add the rice, stirring to mix well. Transfer to a well-oiled ring mold, pressing down lightly. Turn out onto a serving dish. Place the egg white in the center, then sprinkle the top of the egg white with half of the yolk. Scatter the remaining yolk over the rice and garnish with coriander leaf.

Serves: **4-6**   Preparation time: **40 min**   Cooking time: **1 hour**

thai fried rice with pork & prawns   *khao phad*

Thai fried rice dishes are usually quite mild, but are always pepped up by the accompanying Simple Thai Fish Sauce & Chili Dip or lots of dried crushed chili. There is no hard and fast recipe — cooks use whatever is on hand, taking their pick from pork, chicken, prawns, crabmeat, or bean curd. This recipe is a basic guideline, and makes enough to serve four for lunch or a light supper. It could also be served instead of steamed rice as part of a main meal for six to eight persons.

4 tablespoons vegetable oil
1 red or brown onion, halved lengthways,
  thinly sliced across
6–8 cloves garlic, crushed and finely minced
$^1/_2$ lb (250 g) lean pork or chicken, julienned
10–13 oz (300–400 g) raw prawns, peeled
  and deveined, halved lengthways if large
2 eggs, lightly beaten
3 tablespoons fish sauce
6 cups (800 g) cold cooked rice (made from
  3 cups uncooked Thai rice)
1 tablespoon lime juice
3$^1/_2$ oz (100 g) cooked crabmeat, flaked,
  optional
3 tablespoons coarsely chopped coriander
1 spring onion, julienned
freshly ground black pepper to taste
1 large ripe tomato, halved, then sliced across
12 slices cucumber
Simple Thai Fish Sauce & Chili Dip (page 175)

Heat the oil in a wok and add the onion and garlic. Stir-fry over moderate heat until softened, 1 to 2 minutes, then add the pork or chicken. Stir-fry until it changes color, then add the prawns, and stir-fry over high heat until cooked, about 3 minutes. Slowly pour in the eggs around the upper edges of the wok, stirring as they set.

Splash in the fish sauce, then add the rice and stir-fry for 2 to 3 minutes. Season with lime juice, then add the crabmeat (if using) and cook, stirring, until it is heated through. Sprinkle on the coriander, spring onion, and black pepper, stir, then immediately transfer the rice to a large serving dish. Arrange the tomato and cucumber slices around the plate and serve hot with the Simple Thai Fish Sauce & Chili Dip for adding to taste.

Serves: **4**   Preparation time: **10 min**   Cooking time: **7 min**

indonesian fried rice *nasi goreng*

Fried rice is a common breakfast throughout Indonesia. It is often very simple — cooked rice tossed with a seasoning paste of chili and a dash of sweet soy sauce — or can be more substantial, like this recipe, which adds beef instead of the pork often used in non-Muslim parts of Southeast Asia. You could also add some prawns, and top each serving with a fried egg (which the Indonesians call a "bull's-eye egg"). This is a quickly made lunch or supper dish.

$1/3$ cup (85 ml) vegetable oil
7 oz (200 g) sirloin or rump steak, thinly
   sliced across the grain, shredded
7 oz (200 g) small raw prawns, peeled and
   deveined, or add another 7 oz beef
6 cups (800 g) cold cooked rice (made from
   3 cups uncooked Thai long-grain rice),
   stirred with a fork to separate grains
2 tablespoons sweet soy sauce
1 teaspoon salt
4 eggs
2 tablespoons Crisp-fried Shallots (page 17)
1 spring onion, julienned
1 large ripe tomato, sliced

Seasoning Paste
6 shallots, minced
2 cloves garlic, minced
2–3 large red chilies, sliced
$1/2$ teaspoon shrimp paste, toasted

Prepare the Seasoning Paste by pounding or processing all the ingredients together to a coarse paste.

   Heat $1/4$ cup of the oil in a wok and add the Seasoning Paste. Stir-fry over medium heat until softened and fragrant, about 4 minutes. Increase the heat, add the beef and prawns (if using) and stir-fry until cooked, about 3 minutes. Add the rice and stir-fry over high heat 1 minute. Sprinkle with soy sauce and salt and stir-fry for another minute.

   Transfer the rice to a large bowl and keep warm. Use the remaining oil to fry the eggs, one at a time, in the wok, or cook them all at the one time in a frying pan. Transfer the rice to four plates. Top each serving with an egg and garnish with crisp-fried shallots and spring onion. Add a few tomato slices and serve with a chili sambal.

Note: As with all fried rice dishes, it is preferable to use rice that was cooked the previous day, so that it has completely dried out.

Serves: **4** Preparation time: **10 min** Cooking time: **10 min**

coconut rice   *nasi lemak*

Nasi Lemak is the Malay name for rice cooked in coconut milk, and also for the popular breakfast combination of coconut rice, cucumber, egg, crunchy deep-fried anchovies, and peanuts, plus a chili sambal. You could serve the coconut rice as part of a main meal (for a balance of flavors, make sure that the other dishes do not contain coconut milk), or go the whole way and serve the rice with the traditional accompaniments for breakfast or lunch .

2¹/₂ cups (625 ml) coconut milk
1 teaspoons salt
2 pandan leaves, tied into a knot, or 1 salam leaf
2 cups (400 g) long-grain rice, washed and
  drained

Crisp-fried Anchovies
¹/₃ cup (85 ml) vegetable oil
2 cups cleaned dried anchovies
¹/₂ cup (75 g) raw peanuts
6 shallots, processed until coarsely ground
2 teaspoons sugar
¹/₂–1 teaspoon chili powder
¹/₄ teaspoon turmeric powder
1–2 small round green limes, halved, or
  wedges of lime or lemon, optional

Additional Accompaniments
2 eggs, lightly beaten, cooked to make a thin
  omelette, shredded, or 4 fried eggs
¹/₂ small cucumber, skin raked with a fork, sliced
Malay Chili & Dried Shrimp Paste Dip
  (page 175)

Put the coconut milk, salt, and pandan or salam leaves in a saucepan with a heavy base. Bring to the boil over low-medium heat, stirring constantly. Pour in the rice, stir, then partially cover the pan. Cook over low heat until coconut milk is completely absorbed, about 5 minutes.

Cover the pan firmly and remove from heat. Stand 5 minutes. Wipe the inside of the lid with a towel and cover again. Put over the lowest possible heat and cook for 15 minutes. Remove from the heat, fluff up the rice with a fork, cover and let it stand until required, up to 20 minutes. Remove the pandan leaves before serving.

To prepare the Crisp-fried Anchovies, heat all but 2 tablespoons of the oil in a wok. Add the anchovies and stir-fry over moderate heat until crisp and golden brown. Remove from the wok and drain on paper towel. Discard the cooking oil and wipe the wok clean with paper towel. Reheat the wok, then add the peanuts, and stir-fry over low-medium heat until the peanuts are cooked, about 8 minutes. Remove from the wok.

Heat remaining 2 tablespoons of oil in the wok and add the shallots. Stir-fry over low heat for 2 minutes, then add sugar, chili powder, and turmeric and cook another minute or two, until fragrant. Return the anchovies and peanuts to the wok and stir for about 1 minute to mix thoroughly. Allow to cool before serving. Serve the rice as an accompaniment to other dishes, or if serving traditional accompaniments, put one-quarter of the rice on each of four plates. Add some of the omelette, peanuts, cucumber, and sambal to each portion and serve hot.

Serves: **4**   Preparation time: **20 min**   Cooking time: **40 min**

rice soup with minced pork or chicken *khao tom*

I really love this easy, home-style dish, which many housewives in Thailand (as well as neighboring countries) whip up for a quick breakfast using rice left over from the night before. Minced pork — or chicken if you prefer — is simmered in chicken stock, then cooked rice and fish sauce are added, plus an egg if you like. The garnishes and dip are an important part of the overall flavor.

5 cups (1.25 liters) chicken stock
7 oz (200 g) minced lean pork or chicken
3 cups (400 g) cooked rice
1 tablespoon fish sauce
4 teaspoons sugar
4 teaspoons rice vinegar or white vinegar
4 eggs, optional
2 tablespoons Crisp-fried Shallots or Garlic
  (page 17)
sprigs of coriander leaf
crushed dried chili flakes to taste
Simple Thai Fish Sauce & Chili Dip (page 175)

Put the chicken stock in a large saucepan and bring to the boil. Add the minced pork or chicken (broken up with a fork) and simmer uncovered for 3 minutes. Add the rice and simmer another 2 minutes, then add the fish sauce.

Put 1 teaspoon sugar and 1 teaspoon vinegar into each of four large bowls, stirring to dissolve the sugar. Break an egg into bowl, then ladle the piping hot soup over the top. Garnish with crisp-fried shallots and garlic and sprigs of coriander leaf. Let the soup stand for a minute or two so the egg starts to set, then stir before eating. Serve hot accompanied by crushed dried chili flakes and Thai Fish Sauce & Chili Dip for adding to taste.

Serves: **4**   Preparation time: **10 min**   Cooking time: **12 mins**

a flash in the pan

All too often, it's simply not possible to spend a lot of time preparing a meal. You've come home late, you're tired and hungry and you want something delicious in a hurry — but you're not interested in pulling out a packet of instant noodles or opening a can. With the recipes in this chapter, you don't have to. All of these seafood, poultry or meat dishes can be ready within 30 minutes, and this includes measuring, slicing, chopping, seasoning, and cooking. This is fast food, Southeast Asian style.

Several of the following recipes are for stir-fried combinations of meat, seafood or poultry with vegetables and seasonings; basically, a meal in a wok, to be served with rice. These include Chicken Stir-fried with Green Curry Paste, Stir-fried Beef with Lemon Grass & Capsicum, and Pork with Salad & Cambodian Dip. In fact, there are plenty of variations on this stir-fried theme, each of them tasting quite different. One of my favorites, however, just has to be the Vietnamese recipe for Stir-fried Chicken with Mango & Cashews — this is a real winner on any occasion.

There are also a few simple but wonderful seafood recipes. Try Fragrant Squid, an easy room-temperature dish, or Thai Fried Fish in Ginger Sauce and you'll see what I mean. Larb, a Thai, Cambodian, and Lao combination of minced beef or chicken with herbs, is a popular restaurant dish in the West, so two versions of this have been included.

There's a particularly elegant modern recipe for Roasted Duck and Vegetables on Crispy Noodles; even though it's quick and easy to prepare, it could star at any dinner party.

Eggs come quickly in the form of the simple but really good Pork Omelette and one of our family stand-bys, Vietnamese Scrambled Egg with Chinese Sausages. So put your rice on to cook, then get to work preparing one of these recipes and you'll be enjoying a marvellous meal within just 30 minutes. And don't forget, you'll find plenty of other quickly prepared dishes in the Salads, Rice, and Noodles chapter too.

stir-fried chicken with mango & cashews *ga xao hot dieu*

Chicken stir-fried with cashew nuts is a Chinese restaurant cliché in the West, but this Vietnamese combination has a more complex (and in my opinion, infinitely superior) flavor. The Vietnamese add juicy sweet mango, tomato, and snow peas, flavoring it all with a touch of fish sauce, lime juice, pepper, and sugar. Not only does this dish look beautiful, it has a perfect balance of salty, sweet, and sour flavors.

1 large ripe but firm mango (about 7 oz or 200 g flesh after slicing)
3 tablespoons fish sauce
1 teaspoon lime juice
1 teaspoon sugar
$1/2$ teaspoon salt
$1/4$ teaspoon freshly ground black pepper
1 cup (250 ml) vegetable oil
1 lb (500 g) boneless chicken breast, cut in $3/4$ in (2 cm) pieces, dried with paper towel
2 teaspoons very finely minced garlic
1 teaspoon very finely minced large red chili
7 oz (200 g) sugar snap or snow peas, tips, tails, and strings removed (halved diagonally if large)
1 medium ripe tomato, peeled and cut in $1/2$ in (1 cm) dice
$1/2$ cup (70 g) dry-roasted cashew nuts

Using a sharp-pointed knife, cut the mango lengthways, following the stone to remove the two "cheeks" of flesh. Cut diagonal slashes across each mango cheek, $1/2$ in (1 cm) apart, taking care not to cut right through the skin. Use a spoon to ease out the mango slices.

Combine the fish sauce, lime juice, sugar, salt, and pepper in a small bowl, stirring to dissolve sugar and salt.

Heat the oil in a wok until very hot, then add the chicken and deep-fry in two separate batches, stirring frequently, until just cooked, 2 minutes. Remove with slotted spatula and drain on paper towel.

Pour out all but 3 tablespoons of oil from the wok. Re-heat the oil and stir-fry the garlic and chili over medium heat for a few seconds. Increase the heat, add the snow peas, and stir-fry 1 minute. Add chicken and fish sauce mixture, stirring to mix well, then put in the reserved mango slices, tomato, and cashews. Stir for about 30 seconds until heated through, taking care not to smash the mango. Transfer to a dish and serve with steamed white rice.

Serves: **4**   Preparation time: **15 min**   Cooking time: **7 mins**

stir-fried chicken with lemon grass, chilies & tamarind *ga xao sa ot me*

To make this simple dish, chicken thighs are briefly marinated in a mixture of fish sauce, crushed chili, garlic, lemon grass, and sugar. The sugar helps give the chicken a rich brown color when it is stir-fried, but the sweetness is offset by the sour fruitiness of tamarind juice, another example of the clever balance of flavors typical of Vietnamese cuisine.

1 lb (500 g) chicken thigh fillets, cut in $1^3/_4$ in (4 cm) pieces
1 tablespoon fish sauce
$1^1/_2$ tablespoons sugar
1–3 large red chilies, ground to a paste
$^1/_4$ teaspoon freshly ground black pepper
1 stem lemon grass, tender inner part of bottom 3 in (8 cm) only, very thinly sliced
3 cloves garlic, very finely minced
1 tablespoon vegetable oil
$^1/_2$ cup (125 ml) chicken stock
1 heaped tablespoon tamarind pulp, soaked in $^1/_4$ cup warm water, squeezed and strained to obtain juice
salt to taste
sprigs of coriander leaf to garnish

Put the chicken in a bowl and add the fish sauce, sugar, chili, pepper, lemon grass, and half of the garlic, stirring to mix well. Cover and marinate 15 minutes.

Heat the oil in a wok 30 seconds, then add the remaining garlic and stir-fry 5 seconds. Add the marinated chicken and stir-fry over high heat until it has turned brown, about 2 minutes.

Reduce the heat and add the remaining sugar, chicken stock, and tamarind juice. Simmer until tender, stirring frequently, about 3 minutes. Taste, adding salt if desired. Transfer to a serving dish and garnish with fresh coriander.

Serves: **4** Preparation time: **20-25 min** Cooking time: **5 mins**

pork with salad & cambodian dip   *loc lac chrouk*

This uncomplicated recipe uses just a few basic ingredients, but it has a delightfully fresh flavor thanks to the unique Cambodian salt, black pepper, and lime dip. Serve this stir-fried pork and salad with rice as part of a main meal; you might like to add a soup (Creamy Pumpkin Soup, page 49, or Piquant Fish Soup with Pineapple & Bean Sprouts, page 57); if time is short, just toss together some Fresh Bean Sprout Pickle (page 179) before starting this recipe.

1–1¼ lb (500–600 g) pork fillet or loin, thinly
  sliced, shredded
1 tablespoon crushed and finely minced garlic
2 teaspoons fish sauce
1 teaspoon sugar
¼ teaspoon freshly ground black pepper
lettuce leaves, to line a serving plate
1 small red or brown onion, thinly sliced,
  rings separated
2 medium ripe tomatoes, each cut in
  8 wedges
2 tablespoons vegetable oil
Cambodian Salt, Black Pepper & Lime Dip
  (page 178)

Put the pork in a bowl and add the garlic, fish sauce, sugar, and pepper. Massage to mix well and set aside while preparing the salad. Line a serving plate with lettuce leaves. Scatter with onion rings and surround with tomato wedges. Set aside.

Heat oil in a wok, add pork and stir-fry over high heat until cooked, about 3 minutes. Arrange the cooked pork in the center of the lettuce and serve, accompanied by the dip and steamed white rice. Each person squeezes lime or lemon juice to taste into the dipping sauce. A little of the pork can be rolled up with a tomato wedge in a lettuce leaf and seasoned with the dip before eating.

Serves: **4**   Preparation time: **15 min**   Cooking time: **3 mins**

chicken stir-fried with chilies & basil *gai pad bai horapa*

The flavor of this dish is so good no one will believe how ridiculously quick and easy it is to make (once you've located the bird's-eye chilies and fragrant Asian basil). The bruised chilies add pungency and flavor to the chicken, but be sure to warn anyone who is not a chili addict to put them to one side rather than eating them whole, as the Thais do.

3 tablespoons vegetable oil
1¼ lb (600 g) boneless chicken thigh fillet or
  breast, cut in ½ in (1 cm) dice
1–2 tablespoons whole bird's-eye chilies,
  preferably green, lightly bruised
1 cup firmly packed Asian basil leaves,
  coarsely torn
2 tablespoons fish sauce

Heat the oil in a wok, then add the chicken, and stir-fry over high heat for 3 to 4 minutes. Add the chilies and ½ cup of the basil and stir-fry for another minute. Splash on the fish sauce, stirring to mix thoroughly. Transfer to a serving dish and scatter the rest of the basil on top.

Serve immediately with plain rice and a salad; a simple chicken stock with some diced bean curd would be good to help moisten the rice when eating, as this chicken dish is dry.

Serves: **4**   Preparation time: **7 min**   Cooking time: **7 mins**

chicken stir-fried with green curry paste *pad bai horapa keow wan gai*

If you've got some Thai Green Curry Paste ready (preferably home-made) this is one of the easiest chicken recipes around, and wonderfully fragrant too. All you need do is stir-fry the curry paste for a moment, add some chicken breast and flavor it with kaffir lime leaves, Asian basil, and a splash of fish sauce. Yes, that's really all there is to it.

3 tablespoon vegetable oil
3 tablespoons Thai Green Curry Paste
  (page 159)
1 lb (500 g) chicken breast fillet, cut in 1 1/2 in
  (3 cm) pieces
2 kaffir lime leaves, edges torn, optional
1/2 cup loosely packed Asian basil leaves
2 tablespoons fish sauce

Heat the oil in a wok 30 seconds, then add the curry paste and stir-fry over medium heat for 1 minute. Increase the heat and add the chicken, then stir-fry until it has changed color and is almost done, about 3 minutes. Add the kaffir lime leaves and half the basil and stir-fry over high heat for 1 minute. Sprinkle with fish sauce to taste and stir to mix well. Transfer to a serving dish and scatter with remaining basil leaves. Serve hot with white rice.

Serves: **4-6**   Preparation time: **7 min**   Cooking time: **7 mins**

spicy minced beef *larb neua*

The first time I tried this Lao dish (which is also popular in northeast Thailand), I was presented with raw minced buffalo, moistened with a liberal splash of fresh blood and mixed with herbs and lashings of chili. To my surprise, it actually tasted great, but I'm not advocating that you strive for total authenticity. Use good ground beef, stir-fry it briefly, and take a rain check on the blood. Add the seasonings, herbs, and crunchy rice powder and you'll love the result.

1 lb (500 g) lean rump or sirloin beef, finely ground
1 teaspoon vegetable oil
1 tablespoon Roasted Rice Powder (page 18)
3 stems lemon grass, tender inner part of bottom 3 in (8 cm) only, thinly sliced
4–6 shallots, thinly sliced
1 teaspoon crushed dried chili flakes, or more to taste
1 large red chili, thinly sliced
1/4 cup (60 ml) lime juice, or more to taste
2 tablespoons fish sauce
1/2 cup loosely packed mint leaves, coarsely chopped
cabbage or lettuce leaves, optional

Break up the beef with a fork. Heat the oil in a wok and when very hot, add the beef and stir-fry just until it starts to change color, about 1 minute. Transfer to a large bowl and leave to cool.

Add all other ingredients to the beef, tossing to mix well, and serve immediately. Traditionally, the larb is spooned into cabbage or lettuce leaves and eaten with steamed rice, although you could just serve it beside the rice and omit the leafy wrappers if you like.

Serves: **4**   Preparation time: **10 min**   Cooking time: **3 mins**

fragrant minced chicken with herbs *larb muan*

This mild yet fragrant Cambodian chicken dish is similar to the spicy beef popular in Laos and northeastern Thailand. Minced chicken is stir-fried with a fragrant spice paste, seasoned with fish sauce and accentuated with aromatic roasted rice powder and herbs. Plenty of black pepper (rather than the crushed dried chili flakes of Thailand) and lime juice give a very Cambodia accent. You can serve this either straight from the wok or at room temperature, together with rice and other dishes.

3 cloves garlic, minced
2 tablespoons finely minced galangal
2 large red chilies, minced
2 teaspoons dried shrimp paste
3 tablespoons vegetable oil
2 spring onions, thinly sliced
1 1/4 lb (600 g) minced chicken
3 tablespoons fish sauce
1/2 cup (125 ml) water
3 tablespoons Roasted Rice Powder (page 18)
3 tablespoons minced polygonum or mint
2 tablespoons minced Asian basil
3 tablespoons lime juice, or more to taste
salt to taste
1/2 teaspoon freshly ground black pepper

Process the garlic, galangal, chilies, and shrimp paste to a smooth paste in a spice grinder, adding a little of the oil if necessary to keep the blades turning.

Heat the oil in a wok, then add the processed mixture and stir-fry over low heat until fragrant, 2 to 3 minutes. Increase the heat and add the minced chicken and spring onions. Stir-fry until chicken has changed color all over, about 2 minutes, then splash with fish sauce and stir-fry for about 30 seconds. Add the water and cook, stirring occasionally, until the liquid has dried up and the chicken is done, 3 to 4 minutes.

Remove from the heat and stir in the toasted rice powder, polygonum, basil, and lime juice. Taste and add salt if you like, and more lime juice if you think it needs it. Sprinkle with black pepper and transfer to a serving bowl. Serve hot or at room temperature.

Serves: **4**   Preparation time: **15 min**   Cooking time: **10-12 mins**

opposite **spicy minced beef**

stir-fried beef with lemon grass & capsicum *sach ko cha kroeung*

In this Cambodian recipe, beef is mixed with a seasoning paste of fragrant lemon grass, kaffir lime leaves, fresh coriander, chilies, and garlic. There's no waiting around for it to marinate — just toss it in the wok with onion, capsicum, and spring onions, splash in some fish sauce, add a bit of sugar, salt, and crushed peanuts and there you have it: a really tasty meal to serve with rice.

1–1 $1/4$ lb (500–600 g) sirloin or fillet steak, thinly sliced
3 tablespoons vegetable oil
3 tablespoons fish sauce
1 tablespoon sugar
$1/2$ teaspoon salt
1 large red or brown onion, $1/2$ in (1 cm) cut off root end and discarded, cut in wedges
1 large red capsicum, julienned
$1/3$ cup (55 g) coarsely crushed dry-roasted peanuts
4 spring onions, white part halved length-ways, white and green parts cut in $1^3/4$ in (4 cm) lengths
sprigs of coriander leaf to garnish

Seasoning Paste
3 shallots, minced
4 cloves garlic, minced
2–3 dried chilies, cut in 1 in (2 cm) lengths, soaked in hot water to soften, or $1/2$–1 teaspoon chili powder
1 tablespoon finely minced fresh coriander stem and leaf
5 kaffir lime leaves, central ribs discarded, torn
2 stems lemon grass, inner tender part of bottom 3 in (8 cm) only, thinly sliced
1 tablespoon finely minced galangal
$1/2$ teaspoon turmeric powder
$1/2$ cup (125 ml) water

Make the Seasoning Paste by processing the shallots, garlic, chilies, coriander, lime leaves, lemon grass, and galangal in a spice grinder until smooth, adding a little water if needed to keep the mixture turning. Transfer to a bowl and stir in the remaining water. Add the beef, stirring to coat thoroughly.

Heat the oil in a wok. Add the beef, fish sauce, sugar, and salt and stir-fry over high heat for 2 minutes. Add the onion and stir-fry until it starts to soften, about 1 minute.

Add the capsicum and stir-fry over high heat, 1 minute. Reserve 1 tablespoon each of the peanuts and the spring onion. Add the remaining peanuts and spring onion to the wok, stir-fry 1 minute, then transfer to a serving dish.

Garnish with the remaining peanuts and spring onion, and the coriander sprigs, and serve hot with rice. You could also serve Fresh Bean Sprout Pickle (page 179) or Vinegared Cucumber Salad (page182), and perhaps a simple soup for an even more sumptuous meal which will, of course, take a little longer.

Serves: **4**   Preparation time: **20 min**   Cooking time: **5 min**

roasted duck & vegetables on crispy noodles

This is one of my favorite dinner party dishes, a modern Singapore recipe combining elements of both Chinese and Western cuisines. Chinese-style roasted duck (found in just about any Chinatown in the world) is tossed with shredded raw vegetables and a tangy dressing, then laid on a bed of crisp deep-fried rice vermicelli. Gravy is normally provided together with the roasted duck, so if you can lay your hands on some of this, be sure to include it in the sauce.

2 cups (500 ml) oil for deep frying
1³/₄ oz (50 g) rice vermicelli, broken into
  short lengths
¹/₂ small green capsicum, very finely julienned
2¹/₂ in (6 cm) carrot, very finely julienned
2¹/₂ in (6 cm) white daikon radish very
  finely julienned
1 cup (75 g) finely shredded red cabbage
¹/₂ roasted duck, preferably Chinese style,
  skin discarded, meat cut in ¹/₂ in (1 cm)
  slices

Sauce
¹/₂ teaspoon very finely minced garlic
¹/₄ teaspoon salt
¹/₂ teaspoon French Dijon mustard
liberal sprinkling white pepper
3 tablespoons rice or white vinegar
3 tablespoons peanut or other vegetable oil
¹/₂ teaspoon sesame oil
1 tablespoon roasted duck gravy (see Note)

Prepare the Sauce. Crush the garlic, salt, and mustard in a small bowl with the back of a spoon, then stir in pepper, vinegar, peanut, sesame oil, and gravy, mixing well. Set aside.

Heat oil in a wok 30 seconds. When smoking hot, add a small handful of noodles and deep-fry until puffed and crisp, about 3 to 4 seconds. Remove with a wire basket or slotted spatula and drain on paper towel. Repeat until all noodles are cooked. Arrange the fried noodles on a large serving plate.

Combine the capsicum, carrot, radish, cabbage, and duck in a bowl. Add the Sauce, tossing to mix well. Lay the salad over the center of the noodles and serve immediately.

This dish is best eaten as a separate course; you could begin the meal with a non-fried appetizer, follow it with a soup and then serve the duck.

Note: If you can't get the roasted duck gravy, use 1 tablespoon chicken stock mixed with 1 teaspoon oyster sauce and a large pinch of five-spice powder.

Serves: **4**   Preparation time: **15 min**   Cooking time: **3 min**

thai fried fish in ginger sauce *pla priu wan*

It always impressive when you serve a whole fish, and this Thai dish tastes even better than it looks. The fish is bathed with a piquant sweet and sour sauce, enhanced by plenty of fresh and pickled ginger, fish sauce, and fresh coriander leaf. Although it won't look as impressive, you could use fish fillets as a quicker alternative.

2–2¹/₂ lb (1–1.25 kg) whole fish or fresh
  white fish (snapper bream or sea bass), or
  1¹/₄ lb (600 g) fish fillets
2 tablespoons cornflour
oil for deep frying
1 heaped tablespoon very finely shredded
  pickled ginger
cucumber slices to garnish
sprigs of coriander leaf to garnish

Sauce
2 cloves garlic, finely minced
¹/₂ cup (125 ml) water
¹/₄ cup (60 g) brown sugar
¹/₄ cup (60 ml) rice vinegar
4 teaspoons fish sauce
2 teaspoons cornflour
3 tablespoons water
2¹/₂ in (6 cm) ginger, julienned
1 fresh red chili, seeded and very finely
  shredded
3 spring onions, cut in 1¹/₄ in (3 cm) lengths

Wash the whole fish, dry thoroughly, and cut two deep diagonal slashes on each side. Heat the oil in a wok and when smoking hot, sprinkle the cornflour on both sides of the fish, rubbing it in with your fingers. Shake the fish to the remove excess flour. If using fish fillets, coat them with cornflour in a similar way.

Lower the fish carefully into the oil and fry, turning once, until the fish is golden brown and cooked through, about 10 to 12 minutes, flicking the hot oil up over the surface of the fish during cooking. If you are using fish fillets, they will need around 4 minutes. Drain fish on paper towel and keep warm in a low oven.

To make the Sauce, pour out all but 1 tablespoon of oil from the wok. Re-heat the oil and fry the garlic until golden, then add the water, sugar, vinegar, and fish sauce. Bring to the boil. Mix the cornflour and water together and add to the wok, stirring over moderate heat until the Sauce thickens and clears, about 30 seconds. Add the fresh ginger, chili, and spring onions and simmer 1 minute.

Put the fish on a serving dish, pour over the hot sauce, and scatter with pickled ginger. Surround with cucumber slices and decorate with fresh coriander.

Serves: **4** Preparation time: **15 min** Cooking time: **15 min**

grilled fish with spicy filling *sambal ikan panggang*

It doesn't take long to make the fragrant spicy filling that lifts these Malay-style fish out of the ordinary. To be honest, Malays are more likely to fry fish now that the wood or coconut husk fire has virtually disappeared from modern kitchens, but I prefer to use a grill or broiler because it reduces the consumption of fat and the fish still tastes great. For best results, you need really fresh fish. Work quickly and you'll have the fish ready and waiting to be devoured in just 30 minutes.

4 small whole fish, about 1½–2 lb (750g–
  1 kg) preferably mackerel or herring,
  scaled and cleaned, heads left on
1 teaspoon salt
1 teaspoon turmeric
1–2 tablespoons vegetable oil

Spicy Filling
4 shallots, minced
1 clove garlic
2 teaspoons ground galangal
4 large red chilies, sliced, some seeds
  removed if preferred
4 candlenuts, minced
1 stem lemon grass, tender inner part of
  bottom 3 in (8 cm) only, thinly sliced
½ teaspoon dried shrimp paste
2 tablespoons vegetable oil
½ teaspoon sugar
½ teaspoon salt

Pat the fish dry inside and out with paper towel. Make slits right along both sides of the back bone of each fish to create a pocket. Sprinkle the fish on both sides with the salt and turmeric and leave to marinate while you prepare the filling.

To make the Spicy Filling, process the shallots, garlic, galangal, chilies, candlenuts, lemon grass, and shrimp paste in a spice grinder until smooth, adding a little of the oil if needed to keep the mixture turning.

Put your grill on to heat so that it will be hot immediately the fish are ready for cooking. To finish the stuffing, heat the oil in a small pan. Add the filling, sugar, and salt and stir-fry over low heat until it starts to smell fragrant, 3 to 4 minutes.

Use a teaspoon to push some of the stuffing into both pockets of each fish. Brush the fish on both sides with oil, then grill or broil until golden brown on both sides and cooked through, about 4 minutes for each side. Serve with rice and a cooked vegetable and salad, such as Cucumber and Pineapple Salad (page 182).

Serves: **4**   Preparation time: **15 min**   Cooking time: **12 mins**

fragrant squid *yam pla muk*

Fresh squid or calamari has a delicate flavor and texture, provided you start with really fresh squid and cook it just until it turns white — over-cooking makes the flesh tough. In this Thai recipe, the squid is mixed with a tangy dressing of chili, garlic, lime juice, and fish sauce. Add lemon grass, shallots, and mint and you have a superb salad to serve with rice. If you prefer, you could substitute some of the squid with prawns and fish for a mixed seafood salad.

2 lb (1 kg) whole squid (calamari), or 1³/₄ lb
  (800 g) squid hoods
2 cups (500 ml) water
2 large red chilies, finely minced
4 shallots, thinly sliced
1 stem lemon grass, inner part of bottom
  3 in (8 cm) only, very thinly sliced
2 teaspoons caster sugar
¹/₄ cup (60 ml) lemon juice
¹/₄ cup (60 ml) fish sauce
¹/₄ cup firmly packed mint leaves, torn

If you're using whole squid, pull out the heads, and cut the tentacles off just above the eyes. Squeeze to remove the hard portion in the center of the tentacles, then keep the tentacles aside. Pull off the flaps from the squid bodies and put with the tentacles. Remove the reddish-brown skin from the squid and clean out the central cavity. Cut the squid bodies (hoods) in half lengthways and pat dry on both sides with paper towel.

For a decorative "pine cone" look to the squid, score the soft inside of the squid pieces with diagonal lines using a very sharp knife, taking care not to cut right through the flesh. Turn the piece of squid and score diagonally across the lines already made, resulting in a fine criss-cross pattern. Cut each squid half into bite-sized pieces. If you don't have time to score the squid, just cut it into bite-sized pieces.

Bring the water to the boil in a saucepan, then add the squid, and cook uncovered just until squid turns white, about 1 minute. Tip into a colander, rinse under cold water, drain well, and cool to room temperature.

Put the squid in a serving bowl leave to cool. Add the chilies, shallots, lemon grass, sugar, fish sauce, and mint, tossing to mix well. Serve at room temperature.

Serves: **4**   Preparation time: **15 min**   Cooking time: **1 min**

pork omelette *gai tod gup moo*

I particularly enjoy this omelette with a salad for lunch, but you could just as well serve it as part of a main meal with rice (adding a soup and a salad or vegetable dish). Omelettes with a filling of ground seasoned pork are common in Thailand, but in this easy recipe, the meat is mixed with the egg before cooking. The omelettes are not chili-hot, so are good for those who prefer mild food. For the genuine Thai taste, however, spoon over liberal amounts of the chili-spiked Simple Thai Fish Sauce & Chili Dip when eating.

8 eggs
$1/2$ tablespoon fish sauce
$1/2$ lb (250 g) finely ground lean pork, separated
  with a fork
3–4 shallots, finely minced
2 cloves garlic, crushed and minced
3 tablespoons finely minced coriander leaf
1 tablespoon vegetable oil
$1/4$ teaspoon freshly ground black pepper
sprigs of coriander leaf to garnish, optional
Simple Thai Fish Sauce & Chili Dip (page 175)

Serves: **4**   Preparation time: **7 min**
Cooking time: **7 min**

Whisk the eggs with the fish sauce, then stir in the pork, eggs, shallots, garlic, and minced coriander, mixing well.

You can either cook 1 large omelette and cut it in quarters to serve (the quicker option), or use a small frying pan to make individual omelettes. Assuming you're taking the latter option, put about 12 teaspoons of oil in a small frying pan (about 6 in or 14 cm in diameter) and heat, swirling the pan to grease the sides as well as the bottom. When moderately hot, pour in $1/4$ of the egg mixture and cook until the edges are starting to set, about 1 minute. Lift the edges of the omelette with a spatula and let the liquid portion of egg run underneath. Cook until the bottom of the omelette is golden brown and the top almost set, 1 to 2 minutes. Slide the omelette out onto a plate, then flip it over into the pan and continue cooking until the other side is golden brown, about another 2 minutes.

Put the omelette on a plate and continue cooking, adding a little oil to grease the pan each time, to make four omelettes. Arrange the omelettes on a serving plate and garnish each with a sprig of coriander leaf if desired. Serve at room temperature accompanied by the Dip.

stir-fried squid with garlic & black pepper *pla mok phat*

A Thai dish without chilies might seem strange, but before chilies were introduced to Southeast Asia, black peppercorns were relied on for heat. This recipe is quickly prepared, although if you want to impress everyone by scoring the squid decoratively, it'll take a little longer. Despite the use of only a few seasonings, the flavor is excellent. Be sure to use fresh, not frozen, squid.

1 1/4 lb (600 g) small fresh squid or calamari
  with tentacles intact, or 1 lb (500 g) fresh
  squid hoods
2 teaspoons black peppercorns
6 cloves garlic, minced
1 teaspoon oyster sauce
1 teaspoon fish sauce
1 teaspoon light soy sauce
1/2 teaspoon sugar
1/4 cup (60 ml) vegetable oil
2 spring onions, cut in 1 3/4 in (4 cm) lengths

Serves: **4**   Preparation time: **10 min**
Cooking time: **4 min**

If you're dealing with whole squid, pull out the heads and cut the tentacles off just above the eyes. Squeeze to remove the hard portion in the center of the tentacles, then keep the tentacles aside. Remove the reddish-brown skin from the squid and clean out the central cavity. Cut the squid hoods in half lengthways and pat dry on both sides with paper towel. For a decorative "pine cone" look to the squid, score the soft inside of the squid pieces with diagonal lines using a very sharp knife, taking care not to cut right through the flesh. Turn the piece of squid and score diagonally across the lines already made, resulting in a criss-cross pattern. Cut each squid half into bite-sized pieces. If you don't have time to score the squid, just cut it in bite-sized pieces. Dry the squid pieces and tentacles on paper towel and set aside.

Process the peppercorns in a spice grinder until very coarsely ground. Add the garlic and process another few seconds to get a coarse paste; you do not want a fine paste for this dish. If you have a mortar and pestle, you can do the job quickly and easily. Put the oyster sauce, fish sauce, soy sauce, and sugar in a small bowl, stirring to dissolve the sugar. Set aside.

Heat oil in a wok until smoking hot, then add the squid pieces and stir-fry over maximum heat for 1 minute. Add the pepper-garlic mixture and stir-fry for 2 minutes, then pour in the prepared sauce, mixing well. Add the spring onions and stir-fry just until they are wilted, about 30 seconds. Serve hot with rice.

scrambled eggs with chinese sausages *trung ga xot xet*

This recipe (based on one by Vietnamese culinary authority, Nicole Routhier) is one of my stand-by dishes for days when I "haven't a thing in the fridge." I always keep dried Chinese sausages in my store cupboard (they seem to last forever), and these lift the usual scrambled eggs to the level of a gourmet treat. You can serve this dish with either rice or crusty French bread and a simple salad for a delicious light meal.

3 dried Chinese sausages, cut in $1/2$ in (1 cm) slices
8 large eggs
2–3 spring onions, thinly sliced
2 tablespoons fish sauce
1 tablespoon finely minced shallot or onion
3–4 cloves garlic, crushed and minced
3 small-medium tomatoes, diced
2 tablespoons coarsely chopped coriander leaf
freshly ground black pepper to taste

Put the sausages in a saucepan, preferably with a non-stick surface. Cook over moderate heat, stirring from time to time, until the sausages release their fat and just start to brown, about 2 to 3 minutes.

While the sausages are cooking, break the eggs into a bowl whisk lightly. Stir in the spring onions (use only two if they are large) and the fish sauce.

Add the shallot and garlic to the sausages and stir-fry for 30 seconds, then put in the tomatoes. Stir-fry until the tomatoes soften, about 2 to 3 minutes. Add the egg mixture to the pan and cook over low heat, stirring constantly with a wooden spoon, until the eggs are set but not too firm. Add the fresh coriander and stir to mix well. Transfer the cooked eggs to a serving dish and grind plenty of black pepper over the top. Serve hot.

Serves: **4** Preparation time: **10 min** Cooking time: **3 min**

time to impress

There's no denying that some Southeast Asian dishes take time, although the recipes for seafood, poultry and meat which appear in this section are not necessarily complex. Some are actually very easily and quickly prepared, but need time to cook slowly to perfection: Burmese Braised Pork with Green Mango, Thai Red Beef Curry with Bamboo Shoots, Spicy Balinese Pork, Laotian Beef & Vegetable Stew, and a Nonya favorite, Braised Pork in Black Sauce, all fall into this category.

Others recipes — such as Thai Barbecue Chicken and Honey-glazed Chicken — don't really require that much preparation time, but need to be left aside for the fragrant marinade to penetrate. There are even a couple of fish recipes, Grilled Fish with Your Choice of Sambal, and Pan-fried Fish with Tamarind Mint Sauce, that take only a little more than 30 minutes from start to finish.

But finally, it must be admitted, there are a number of recipes where you really do need to spend time peeling, chopping, squeezing, processing, or wrapping in banana leaf. These are the times when you might wish you were part of an extended Asian family, with plenty of willing hands to help, or that you were one of those cooks lucky enough to have household help. But when you try them, you're sure to agree that these more time-consuming recipes are well worth every moment.

Pick a day when you have plenty of time, or can persuade someone to join you in the kitchen to help peel the shallots and garlic, slice the lemon grass, process curry pastes or wilt squares of banana leaf so that you can enjoy such wonderful dishes as Thai Spicy Fish Mousse in Banana Leaf Cups; Thai, Indonesian, and Malay curries; Singapore's fantastic Chili Crab; and Thai Deep-fried Eggs with Pork & Prawn Filling.

balinese seafood satay on lemon grass   *sate lilit*

I've made these sublime satay so many times that friends joke this is my signature dish. (The recipe is based on one created by Lother Arsana and Heinz von Holzen, with whom I worked on *The Food of Bali*.) Spicy fish, prawn, and coconut paste are molded around lemon grass skewers, which give the most incredible fragrance to the satay, although you could use alternatives if fresh lemon grass is not available.

10 oz (300 g) boneless skinned white fish
  fillets (such as snapper, bream, or grouper),
  cubed
10 oz (300 g) raw prawns, peeled and
  deveined
2 cups (200 g) fresh or frozen grated
  coconut, or 1 1/2 cups (125 g) desiccated
  coconut, moistened with 3/4 cup
  (185 ml) milk
5 kaffir lime leaves, very finely shredded
1 teaspoon freshly ground black pepper
1 teaspoon salt
1 tablespoon finely minced palm sugar
2–3 fresh red or green bird's-eye chilies,
  minced, optional
20–24 stems fresh lemon grass, cut in 5–6 in
  (12–14 cm) lengths, or 16 trimmed pieces
  fresh or canned sugar cane, or bamboo
  skewers
1/4 cup (60 ml) vegetable oil

Seasoning Paste
4 large red chilies, seeded and minced
6 shallots, minced
3 cloves garlic, minced
2 tablespoons grated ginger
5 candlenuts, minced
1/2 teaspoon dried shrimp paste
60 ml (1/4 cup) vegetable oil
2 teaspoons freshly ground coriander powder
1/2 teaspoon turmeric powder
1 small-medium tomato (about 3 1/2 oz or
  100 g), peeled and minced
1 heaped tablespoon tamarind, soaked in
  1/4 cup water, squeezed and strained to
  obtain the juice
1 salam leaf, optional
1 stem fresh lemon grass, bottom 5 in
  (12 cm) bruised and cut in 3 pieces

Prepare the Seasoning Paste by processing the chilies, shallots, garlic, ginger, candlenuts, and shrimp paste to a smooth paste in a spice grinder; you may need to do this in two batches. Heat the oil in small pan, preferably non-stick. Add the ground ingredients and coriander and stir-fry over low-moderate heat, 3 minutes. Add the turmeric, tomato, tamarind juice, salam leaf, and lemon grass and cook, stirring frequently, until the liquid has dried up and the oil starts to come out, about 10 to 12 minutes. Transfer to a bowl to cool, then remove the salam leaf and lemon grass. (The paste can be refrigerated in a covered container for up to a day before using, or even deep-frozen.)

Pulse the fish and prawns in a food processor until they turn into a smooth paste. Put the coconut, Seasoning Paste, lime leaves, pepper, salt, sugar, and chilies in a bowl and mix to combine well, then add the processed mixture and mix thoroughly, using your hand to make sure everything is evenly distributed.

Spread 2 tablespoons of the oil on a large plate. Make a shallow slit about 2 in (5 cm) long in the thick end of each lemon grass stem and bruise the stem lightly with pestle or back of a cleaver to help release the fragrance. Oil your hands lightly, then mold 2 to 3 heaped tablespoons of the seafood mixture around the thick end of each lemon grass stem, pressing firmly with your hands to make a cylinder about 4 in (10 cm) in length. Put each satay on the oiled plate, turning to cover with a little oil.

Grease the grill of a barbecue or broiler with oil. Cook the seafood skewers over moderate heat until golden brown, about 4 to 5 minutes, turning frequently and taking care they don't burn. Serve hot as an appetizer or as part of a main meal, with rice and other dishes.

Serves: **6-8**   Makes: **about 20-24 sticks**   Preparation time: **1 hour**   Cooking time: **10 min**

fragrant diced fish in banana leaf packets   *pepes ikan*

My friend Rani, with whom I lived in Ubud while working on a book on Balinese cuisine, was always making little banana-leaf packets of chopped fish, poultry, meat, or even eels caught in a nearby paddy field. This is her version of diced fish fillets mixed with a chili-coconut sauce, scented with lemon basil and lime juice. These packets can be prepared in advance and steamed or (even better) cooked over a grill just before they're needed. If you can't obtain banana leaf (which does wonderful things to the texture and flavor) you could steam the mixture in four to six small heat-proof bowls.

1 1/4 lb (600 g) white fish fillets, skinned, boned, and cut in 1/2 in (1 cm) dice
3 tablespoons minced lemon basil leaves (see Note)
1 teaspoon lime or lemon juice
12 pieces of banana leaf, each about 8 in (20 cm) square, softened in boiling water or in a gas flame

Spice Paste
4 shallots, minced
2 cloves garlic, minced
1 tablespoon finely minced galangal
1 stem lemon grass, tender inner part of bottom 3 in (8 cm) only, thinly sliced
2 fresh red chilies, minced, seeded if desired
4–6 bird's eye chilies, minced
4 candlenuts, minced
1 teaspoon salt
1/2 teaspoon dried shrimp paste, toasted
2/3 cup (170 ml) thick coconut milk

Prepare the Spice Paste by processing all the ingredients except coconut milk in a spice grinder until very smooth, adding a little of the coconut milk if necessary to keep the mixture turning. Put the paste in a small saucepan and stir the coconut milk. Bring to the boil over medium heat, stirring. Lower the heat and simmer uncovered, stirring frequently, for 3 minutes.

Transfer the mixture to a bowl and add the fish, lemon basil leaves, and lime juice, stirring to mix well.

Place a piece of banana leaf on a bench. Put about 2 heaped tablespoons of the fish mixture in a rectangle across the center of the banana leaf. Fold over the end closest you to cover the fish, then tuck in both sides, turning the package over to make an envelope. Repeat until the fish is used up, stirring the mixture each time to distribute the coconut milk evenly.

Cook over moderately hot charcoal or under a broiler for about 5 minutes on each side. Alternatively, put the packets in a steamer and cook over a wok of rapidly boiling water for 15 minutes, adding more boiling water after 10 minutes and making sure the water does not touch the packets during the steaming. If using heat-proof bowls, steam for 20 to 25 minutes. Serve hot or at room temperature.

Note: If lemon basil leaves are not available, add two finely shredded kaffir lime leaves or 1 teaspoon grated kaffir lime or lemon rind.

Serves: **4-6**   Preparation time: **35 min**   Cooking time: **10-20 mins**

spicy fish mousse in banana leaf cups   *hor mok pla*

This Thai favorite is a recipe to prepare when you really want to impress. The decorative banana-leaf cups filled with fish mousse not only look exotic but smell divine. (You can, however, take the easier option and cook the fish in small ramekins or soufflé dishes). The fish is processed to a smooth paste and flavored with red curry paste, fish sauce, and fresh herbs, giving it an incredible flavor. You can enjoy this either hot or at room temperature.

16 pieces of fresh banana leaf, 5 in (12 cm)
  square, softened in a gas flame or boiling
  water
1 lb (500 g) firm boneless white fish fillets,
  skinned and cubed
2 cups (500 ml) thick coconut milk
1 egg
2 tablespoons Thai Red Curry Paste
  (page 164)
1 tablespoon fish sauce
$^1/_4$ teaspoon salt
1 spring onion, minced
1 cup loosely packed Asian basil leaves
1 large red chili, seeded and sliced
2 kaffir lime leaves, cut into hair-like shreds

Serves: **4**   Preparation time: **20-40 min**
Cooking time: **20 mins**

If you are using banana leaf, fold in the sides of each square by about 1 in (2.5 cm), pressing to make a line. Lift up the marked edges to make a square container with sides 1 in (2.5 cm) high, and fold over at each corner, stapling to hold the shape.

Put the fish in a food processor and process at high speed until it forms a coarse paste. Add the coconut cream, egg, curry paste, fish sauce, salt, and spring onion and process until smooth.

Put two basil leaves in the bottom of each banana leaf cup. Fill with the fish mixture, repeating until all the cups have been filled. Lay one basil leaf, a slice of chili, and a few shreds of kaffir lime leaf across the top of each cup. If you are using four to six small bowls instead of banana leaf cups, divide the basil, chili, and kaffir lime leaves between these.

Transfer the banana leaf cups or bowls to a steaming basket, or set on a perforated metal disc and place in a wok over boiling water. Steam over boiling water until the mousse is set, about 20 minutes (or up to 10 minutes longer if using bowls), adding more boiling water to the wok after 10 minutes to prevent it from drying out. Serve the fish cups either hot or at room temperature.

pork-stuffed prawns *kung tiparot*

You can find some amazing seafood at the coastal stalls in Thailand, but I was still surprised to find this sophisticated recipe in a simple shack on the beach near Songkla, on the southeast coast (perhaps the cook had learned it from someone in Bangkok). King prawns were filled with seasoned ground pork, dipped in a light batter, deep-fried until golden brown and served with sweet Thai chili sauce. I find that home-made Vietnamese Fish Sauce Dip, while not traditional, also works very well.

12 raw king prawns (about 5 in or 12 cm in length)
$1/4$ teaspoon black peppercorns
1 teaspoon finely ground coriander root
$2^1/2$ oz (75 g) lean ground pork
2 teaspoons fish sauce
$1/2$ teaspoon sugar
vegetable oil for deep-frying
3 tablespoons rice flour
2 tablespoons plain flour
$1/4$ teaspoon salt
2 eggs, lightly beaten
sweet Thai chili sauce or Vietnamese Fish Sauce Dip (page 175)

Serves: **4-6**   Preparation time: **30 min**
Cooking time: **15 mins**

Remove the heads and shells from the prawns, but leave on the final tail section. Cut down the back of each prawn with a sharp knife. Remove the black vein and use the palm of your hand to press gently on each prawn to open out the back, taking care not to squash it completely flat. Set aside.

Process the peppercorns to a powder in a spice grinder or mortar, then add the coriander root and process to a paste. Transfer to a bowl and stir in the pork, fish sauce, and sugar, mixing well with your hand.

Spread some of the pork filling down the back of each prawn, carefully pushing it in with your fingers and smoothing the top. When all the prawns have been filled, heat oil for deep-frying in a wok.

Combine both lots of flour and salt in a bowl, and have the beaten eggs in a separate bowl nearby. Hold a prawn by the tail over the flour mixture and spoon it over to coat the prawn. Shake the prawn gently to dislodge any excess flour, dip it in egg to coat all over, then lower it into the hot oil. Repeat with another three to four prawns, and deep-fry until they are golden brown and cooked, about 3 to 4 minutes. Drain on paper towel and keep warm while cooking the remaining prawns. Serve hot with a bottled sweet Thai chili sauce or Vietnamese Fish Sauce Dip.

singapore chili crab

Back in the late 1960s in Singapore, it was still possible to sit at a table with your feet in the sand, and to inspect the live crabs kept in huge baskets under the coconut trees before ordering the famous Palm Beach chili crab. Singapore has changed enormously since those days, but its chili crab is still one of the great seafood dishes of the world. This recipe takes time, but believe me, it's worth every moment. The crab is traditionally eaten with chunks of crusty bread to mop up the sauce.

3–4 lb (1.5–2 kg) live mud crabs
2 tablespoons vegetable oil
6 shallots, minced
6–8 large cloves garlic, crushed and minced
2–3 tablespoons minced ginger
3–4 red bird's-eye chilies, minced
3½ cups (875 ml) chicken stock
4 tablespoons hot bean paste, or 3 tablespoons salted soybean paste plus
  2 extra bird's-eye chilies
¼ cup (60 ml) bottled chili sauce
½ cup (125 ml) bottled tomato sauce
1 tablespoon sugar
2 tablespoons Chinese rice wine (preferably
  Shao Hsing)
2 teaspoons salt
1 teaspoon white pepper
2 eggs, lightly beaten
2 tablespoons cornflour, mixed with
  3 tablespoons water

Chili-Ginger Sauce
6 large red chilies, minced
5–6 cloves garlic, minced
2 tablespoons finely minced ginger
2 teaspoons sugar
½ teaspoon salt
1 teaspoon rice vinegar
1 tablespoon water

Put the crabs in the freezer for 15 to 20 minutes to immobilize them. Cut in half length-ways with a cleaver and remove the back and spongy grey matter. Remove the claws and crack in several places with a cleaver. Cut each body half into two to three pieces, leaving the legs attached.

Make Chili-Ginger Sauce by blending all ingredients in a spice grinder and set aside.

Heat the oil in a wok and add shallots, garlic, ginger, and bird's-eye chilies. Stir-fry over low-medium heat until fragrant, about 3 minutes, then add the Chili-Ginger Sauce, chicken stock, hot bean paste, chili sauce, tomato sauce, sugar, rice wine, salt, and pepper. Bring to the boil, then lower heat and simmer 2 minutes. Add the crab pieces and simmer uncovered, turning several times, until the shells are bright red and the crabs are cooked, about 10 minutes.

Add the cornflour mixture and stir until the sauce thickens and clears. Add the eggs and stir until set, then transfer the chili crab to a serving dish and serve with crusty French bread.

You could follow the crab with something simple, perhaps some steamed rice with stir-fried mixed vegetables and a soup.

Serves: **4-6**   Preparation time: **40 min**   Cooking time: **20 mins**

grilled fish with your choice of sambal

One of the easiest, healthiest, and most delicious ways of cooking fish is grill it over hot charcoal (or use a table-top griller or broiler). If green mangoes are available, try the grilled fish with piquant Thai Green Mango & Cashew Salad spooned over the top, or make the Indonesian dip of sweet soy sauce with lime or lemon juice, shallots, chili, and lemon-scented or Asian basil. Both options are really tasty — the choice is yours. (You could also grill one large fish rather than four small ones.)

4 small whole fish or 1 whole fresh fish, about 3 lb (1.5 kg) (such as snapper, bream, trevally, grouper, or barramundi), cleaned and scaled
1–2 teaspoons salt
2–3 tablespoons vegetable oil
half quantity of Green Mango & Cashew Salad (page 64)
1/2 cup (125 ml) sweet soy sauce
1/4 cup (60 ml) lime or lemon juice, or more to taste
2 shallots, thinly sliced
1 large fresh red chili, seeded if desired, thinly sliced
2 tablespoons coarsely chopped lemon basil or Asian basil

Wash the fish, drain well, then wipe inside and out with paper towel. Cut two deep diagonal slashes on each side of each fish and sprinkle both sides with salt.

Grease the grill of a barbecue, table-top grill or broiler liberally with oil. Brush both sides of the fish with oil and put it on the grill. Cook small fish for 3 to 5 minutes on each side, until golden brown and cooked through. A large fish will take 20 to 30 minutes to cook, depending on the thickness. Check to see if it is cooked through by inserting the tip of a knife to ensure that the flesh in the center is white. If not, put it back and cook a little longer.

While fish is cooking, make the Green Mango & Cashew Salad. To prepare the Spicy Soy Sauce Dip, combine soy sauce, lime or lemon juice, shallots, chili, and basil. Taste, adding more lime juice if desired, then divide between four small sauce bowls.

Transfer the cooked fish to a large platter. If using Green Mango Salad, spoon this over the top of the fish, or serve with the bowls of Spicy Soy Sauce Dip.

Serves: **4**   Preparation time: **15 min**   Cooking time: **30 mins**

pan-fried fish with tamarind mint sauce   *ca chien sot me chua*

I'm not usually a fan of fish fillets, preferring to buy whole fish (it's easier to check the freshness) and cook it whole so that I don't waste any of the flesh. However, when I can be sure of really fresh fillets (or if I have time to cut them off a whole fish), I love to prepare this Vietnamese recipe, a beautifully orchestrated blend of taste sensations — sweet, sour, salty, spicy, and aromatic with mint. Use a non-stick pan so that you can minimize the amount of oil needed for frying.

1$^1/_2$–2 heaped tablespoons tamarind pulp, soaked in $^3/_4$ cup warm water, squeezed and strained to obtain juice
4 tablespoons fish sauce
3 tablespoons sugar
1 teaspoon light soy sauce
1$^1/_4$–1$^1/_2$ (600–750 g) white fish fillets (snapper or bream), cut in 4 serving pieces, bones removed but skin left on
$^1/_2$ teaspoon freshly ground black pepper
$^1/_3$ cup (40 g) cornflour
3 tablespoons vegetable oil
1 tablespoon crushed and minced garlic
1 tablespoon finely minced ginger
1 large red chili, minced
2 tablespoons minced fresh mint
additional mint sprigs for garnish

Combine the tamarind juice, water, fish sauce, sugar, and soy sauce in a bowl, stirring to dissolve the sugar. Set aside. Dry the fish with paper towel, then sprinkle both sides with black pepper. Dip into cornflour to coat both sides, shaking to remove the excess.

Heat 2 tablespoons of the oil in a frying pan (preferably non-stick) until smoking hot. Add the fish pieces, skin side down. Reduce the heat to medium and cook until the skin is crisp and golden brown, about 4 to 5 minutes. Turn the fish and fry until cooked through, about another 2 minutes. Transfer to a serving plate and keep warm.

Heat the remaining tablespoon of oil in the frying pan and stir-fry garlic, ginger, and chili over medium heat for 30 seconds. Add the tamarind mixture and simmer 1 minute, stirring constantly. Stir in the mint leaves and immediately pour the sauce over the fish. Garnish with additional mint sprigs and serve.

Serves: **4-6**   Preparation time: **15 min**   Cooking time: **20 mins**

laotian chicken with onion & tomatoes *kai pad som mak kheua khua dong*

In this simple Laotian recipe, chicken pieces are seasoned with garlic, pepper, and salt before being gently braised with shallots, onion, and spring onions. This combination of types of onion ensures a really good flavor and fragrance, while the sliced tomatoes, chicken stock, and fish sauce cook down to make a delicious sauce.

2$^1/_4$–3 lb (1.25–1.5 kg) chicken, cut in serving pieces, or 2 lb (1 kg) chicken pieces
1 tablespoon crushed and minced garlic
$^1/_2$ teaspoon salt
$^1/_2$ teaspoon freshly ground black pepper
2 tablespoons oil
6 shallots, finely minced
2 tablespoons fish sauce
1 large red or brown onion, sliced lengthways
6 spring onions, white part finely minced, green part cut in 1$^1/_4$ in (3 cm) lengths to make $^1/_2$ cup (keep remainder for some other use)
3 medium ripe tomatoes (about 13 oz or 400 g), sliced
$^1/_2$ cup (125 ml) chicken stock, preferably home-made
salt to taste
1 heaped tablespoon minced coriander leaves

Put the chicken pieces in a bowl and rub in the garlic, salt, and pepper. Set aside for 10 minutes.

Heat the oil in a wok, then add the shallots and stir-fry over low-medium heat for 1 minute. Add the chicken pieces and cook gently, turning so that they change color all over. Sprinkle with fish sauce, then add the sliced onion and cook until the onion softens, 4 to 5 minutes.

Add the white part of the spring onions, the $^1/_4$ cup of spring onion greens and the tomatoes. Cook, stirring several times, until the tomatoes start to soften, 2 to 3 minutes. Add the chicken stock, bring to the boil, cover the wok and simmer, stirring from time to time, until the chicken is tender, 15 to 20 minutes. You may need to add a little more stock if the sauce threatens to dry out before the chicken is cooked. Taste and add a little salt if desired, then sprinkle with a few extra grindings of black pepper. Transfer to a serving dish and garnish with coriander.

Serves: **4**   Preparation time: **20 min**   Cooking time: **25 mins**

chicken in lightly spiced coconut milk   *opor ayam*

If you're not in the mood for chili-hot food, try this Indonesian chicken, fragrant with coriander, cumin, and fennel and simmered in coconut milk. There is plenty of sauce, which is aromatic with lemon grass, salam leaves, and kaffir lime leaves. Even if you are unable to obtain all of these herbs, you can be sure of a beautiful mild chicken curry.

3 cups (750 ml) coconut milk
1 stem lemon grass, bottom 4 in (10 cm),
 bruised
2 salam leaves, optional
2 kaffir lime leaves, torn
1 thin slice galangal, bruised
1 teaspoon finely minced palm sugar
$^3/_4$–1 teaspoon salt
1 fresh chicken, about 3 lb (1.5 kg),
 cut in 14 pieces
1–2 teaspoons lime or lemon juice
1 tablespoon crisp-fried shallots

Spice Paste
1 tablespoon coriander seeds
$^3/_4$ teaspoon cumin seeds
$^1/_4$ teaspoon fennel seeds
4 candlenuts, minced
6 shallots, minced
2 cloves garlic, minced
1 tablespoon minced ginger
$^1/_2$ teaspoon white pepper

Prepare the Spice Paste by toasting the coriander, cumin, and fennel seeds in a dry saucepan over low heat, shaking the pan frequently, until fragrant, 1 to 2 minutes. Process to a fine powder in a spice grinder, then transfer to a small bowl. Add the candlenuts, shallots, garlic, and ginger to the spice grinder. Process to a smooth paste, adding a little of the coconut milk if necessary to keep the blades turning. Put in with the ground spices, add the white pepper and stir.

Transfer the Spice Paste to a large saucepan. Place over low-medium heat and stir in the coconut milk, a little at a time. When well mixed, add the galangal, salam, and lime leaves, sugar, and salt. Bring to boil, stirring frequently, then simmer uncovered for 2 minutes. Add chicken pieces and cook uncovered, stirring from time to time, until chicken is tender, about 30 minutes. Just before serving, add lime or lemon juice to taste. Transfer to a serving dish and garnish with crisp-fried shallots.

Serves: **4**   Preparation time: **25 min**   Cooking time: **35 mins**

thai barbecued chicken *gai yang*

Years ago, my young son made it his mission to try barbecued chicken in as many places as possible every time we visited in Thailand. After a few years of research, he finally declared that the best version was the chicken served on the bridge linking Thailand with Burma at Mae Sai. I must confess that we never tired of eating this chicken, which is marinated in the Thai trinity of garlic, black pepper, and coriander root. Cook it over charcoal for that authentic Thai flavor, and serve it with sweet Thai chili sauce.

2¹/₂ lb (1.25 kg) fresh chicken pieces (thighs, drumsticks, and breast)
1 tablespoon black peppercorns
6 large cloves garlic, minced
1¹/₂ tablespoons coarsely minced coriander root
1¹/₂ tablespoons coarsely minced coriander stems and leaves
1¹/₂ teaspoons salt
1 tablespoon Thai Mekong whisky or Chinese rice wine (preferably Shao Hsing), optional
vegetable oil for brushing
sweet Thai chili sauce to serve

Remove any excess skin and fatty deposits from the chicken and prick the skin all over with a fork to allow the marinade to penetrate.

Pound or process the pepper to a coarse powder in a mortar or spice grinder, then add the garlic, coriander root, stems, leaves, and the salt. Process to a smooth paste, adding the whisky or rice wine a little at a time.

Rub the chicken pieces all over with the mixture, then leave to marinate at least 4 hours, or refrigerate in a covered container up to 24 hours if preferred. Brush liberally with the oil and cook over hot charcoal, turning several times, until golden brown and cooked through, about 15 minutes. Alternatively, grill or broil until cooked. Serve with sweet Thai chili sauce.

Serves: **4-6** Preparation time: **10 min + 4 hours marinating** Cooking time: **15-20 mins**

spicy indonesian barbecued chicken   *ayam panggang menado*

If you're concerned about your fat consumption, here's a chicken recipe from northern Sulawesi, Indonesia, that doesn't contain coconut milk. Chicken pieces are simmered in a tangy mixture of fresh seasonings and chili, together with herbs, sweet soy sauce, and tomatoes, then barbecued for even more succulence and flavor. This is great for entertaining or taking on a barbecue picnic as most of the work can be done in advance.

4 chicken quarters (leg or breast portions), about 2 lb (1 kg)
1 tablespoon lime or lemon juice
1 teaspoon salt
1/4 cup (60 ml) oil
1 stem lemon grass, bottom 5 in (12 cm) only, slit and bruised
1/2 cup loosely packed lemon basil or Asian basil sprigs
2 pandan leaves, raked with a fork and tied in a knot
3 tablespoons sweet soy sauce, or 3 tablespoons thick black soy sauce with 2 teaspoons soft brown sugar
4 medium-sized ripe tomatoes, minced
1 cup (250 ml) water

Seasoning Paste
6–8 large red chilies, sliced
10–12 shallots, minced
2 tablespoons minced ginger
2 cloves garlic, minced

Rub chicken pieces with lime juice and salt and set aside.

Prepare the Seasoning Paste by processing all the ingredients to a smooth paste in a spice grinder, adding a little of the oil if necessary to keep the mixture turning.

Heat 3 tablespoons of oil in a wok, then add the Paste and stir-fry until fragrant, about 4 minutes. Add the lemon grass, basil, pandan leaves, soy sauce, and tomatoes. Cook, stirring frequently, until the tomatoes have reduced to a pulp, about 5 minutes. Add the water and chicken, cover the wok and simmer, turning the chicken several times, until the sauce has dried up and the chicken is tender, about 25 minutes. Take care that the sauce does not burn, because of the sugar content of the sweet soy sauce; if it threatens to dry up before the chicken is cooked, add a little more water to the wok. When the chicken is tender, remove from wok, picking off any pieces of herb or tomato skin, and leave to cool.

Shortly before the chicken is required, brush each piece with remaining oil and cook over charcoal or under a hot grill until golden brown on both sides, taking care that it does not burn. Chop with a cleaver into smaller pieces before serving.

Serves: **4**   Preparation time: **25 min**   Cooking time: **35 mins**

honey-glazed chicken *ga quay mat on*

To make this sophisticated Vietnamese recipe, chicken — first marinated with black pepper, sugar, salt, and sesame oil — is brushed during cooking with a piquant glaze. This is a good recipe if you're entertaining, not just because it's sure to be enthusiastically received, but because the chicken can be marinated and the honey glaze prepared several hours in advance. Then all you need to do is start roasting the chicken about an hour before you want to eat.

1 whole fresh chicken (about 2½–3 lb or 1.25–1.5 kg)
2 teaspoons salt
2 teaspoons freshly ground black pepper
2 tablespoons sugar
2 teaspoon sesame oil
2 stalks lemon grass, bottom 5 in (12 cm) only, bruised and cut in 4 pieces

Honey Glaze
1 tablespoon vegetable oil
2 teaspoons annatto seeds or a little red food coloring, optional
¼ cup (60 ml) honey
2 tablespoons sweet soy sauce, or 2 tablespoons dark soy sauce mixed with 2 teaspoons soft brown sugar
4 teaspoons lime or lemon juice
1 teaspoon sesame oil

Remove any fatty deposits and excess skin from the chicken, then pat it dry with paper towel. Mix the salt, pepper, sugar, and sesame oil in a small bowl. Rub half the mixture inside the chicken, and the remainder over the outside. Leave chicken to marinate at room temperature for 1 hour, or cover and refrigerate for several hours if preferred.

Prepare the Honey Glaze by heating the oil in a small saucepan. Add annatto seeds and cook over moderate heat until the oil turns light orange, 2 to 3 minutes. Strain the oil into a large bowl, discarding seeds. Add honey, soy sauce, lime juice, and sesame oil, mixing well. If using red food coloring, just mix all the Honey Glaze ingredients together, including the vegetable oil. (The sauce can now be kept aside for several hours if you are preparing the recipe in advance.)

To finalize the dish, put the lemon grass inside the chicken and place it in a baking dish. Use a pastry brush to paint the Honey Glaze over the outside of the chicken, reserving the remaining glaze. Roast the chicken at 425°F (200°C), breast side up, for 15 minutes.

Stir the glaze thoroughly, baste the chicken again and return it to the oven. Reduce the heat to 350°F (180°C) and cook 15 minutes. Brush the chicken with the glaze and oil which has run into the baking dish, then with the reserved glaze. Turn the chicken breast side down, and cook another 15 minutes. Brush again and roast for a final 15 minutes. Cut the chicken with a cleaver into 14 to 16 serving pieces, put on a serving dish and serve hot with the glaze from the baking dish poured over.

Note: It is important to baste the chicken every 15 minutes so that the skin becomes crisp and turns a rich golden brown. Stir the marinade each time before basting to amalgamate the honey.

Serves: **4**   Preparation time: **20 min + 1 hour marinating**   Cooking time: **1 hour**

thai green chicken curry *gaeng kiew wan gai*

Intensely aromatic Thai green curry paste — which gets its color from green chilies and coriander— goes particularly well with chicken and duck, and is sometimes also cooked with beef. You can either add bamboo shoots or straw mushrooms to the pot — or both if you like. This recipe uses home-made curry paste, which has a really fresh taste; if you decide to use the commercial variety, you may need to adjust the amount as the intensity varies from brand to brand.

$1/2$ cup (125 ml) thick coconut milk
3–4 tablespoons Thai Green Curry Paste
  (see below)
1 fresh chicken (about $2^{1}/_{4}$ lb or 1.25 kg),
  cut in 12–14 pieces, or 1 small duck, cut
  in bite-sized pieces
3 cups (750 ml) thin coconut milk
4 kaffir lime leaves
2 tablespoons fish sauce
$3^{1}/_{2}$ oz (100 g) sliced bamboo shoots, optional
$3^{1}/_{2}$ oz (100 g) fresh or canned straw mushrooms, optional
4–6 green bird's-eye chilies, bruised
$1/2$ cup loosely packed Asian basil leaves

Thai Green Curry Paste
2 large green chilies, minced
8–12 bird's-eye chilies, green if possible,
  minced
3 shallots, minced
4 cloves garlic, minced
1 tablespoon minced galangal
2 teaspoons minced coriander root
2 teaspoons minced coriander stem
2 teaspoons dried shrimp paste
1 teaspoon freshly ground coriander
1 teaspoon salt
2 kaffir lime leaves, central rib discarded,
  minced
2 stems lemon grass, tender inner part of
  bottom 3 in (8 cm) only, thinly sliced
1 teaspoon grated kaffir lime rind or
  lemon rind
1 tablespoon vegetable oil

To make the Green Curry Paste, put all the ingredients except the oil in a spice grinder (you will probably need to do this in two batches) and process to a smooth paste, adding a little of the oil needed to keep the mixture turning. If using the paste for some other recipe, transfer to an airtight container and refrigerate for up to 1 week. Alternatively, store in small zip-lock bags in the freezer in two-tablespoon quantities for future use.

To prepare the chicken curry, put the thick coconut milk in a saucepan and stir in the Thai Green Curry Paste. Cook uncovered, stirring frequently, over low-medium heat until the oil comes out and the mixture starts to fry and smells fragrant, about 8 to 10 minutes.

Add the chicken pieces and stir-fry over medium heat for 10 minutes. Add the thin coconut milk, lime leaves, and fish sauce and bring to the boil, stirring constantly. Lower the heat and simmer very gently, uncovered, for 15 minutes. If you are using bamboo shoots and mushrooms, add these now and keep simmering until the chicken is tender. Stir in the chilies and basil just before serving.

Serves: **4-6**   Preparation time: **40 min**   Cooking time: **35 mins**

braised pork in black sauce   *tau yu bak*

The Nonyas of Malaysia and Singapore take a classic Chinese braised pork dish, add a cinnamon stick, substitute sweet little purple shallots for onions, and potatoes for bamboo shoots, then add a touch of sugar. You'll be surprised how these touches improve an already delicious dish, which embodies the best of home-style cooking — simple but oh, so good. A very close Chinese friend from Kuching, in Malaysian Borneo, paid me the ultimate compliment by saying this recipe is even better than the one prepared by his mother.

1 1/4 lb (600 g) belly or shoulder pork, skin left on
3 tablespoons dark soy sauce
3 tablespoons light soy sauce
2 teaspoons sugar
1/4 teaspoon white pepper
10 shallots, minced
4 cloves garlic, minced
2–3 tablespoons vegetable oil
2 in (5 cm) cinnamon
1 tablespoon salted soybeans
8 dried black Chinese mushrooms, soaked to soften, stems discarded, soaking water reserved
3–4 cups (750 ml–1 liter) water, (including water reserved from soaking mushrooms)
2–3 medium potatoes (about 10 oz or 300 g), peeled and quartered

Cut the pork in $^3/_4$ in (2 cm) thick slices, then cut into pieces about 1 1/4 x 2 1/2 in (3 x 6 cm). Sprinkle with both lots of soy sauce, sugar, and pepper. Mix well and leave to marinate for 30 minutes. Process the shallots and garlic in spice grinder until finely ground.

Heat the oil in a wok or large saucepan, then add the processed mixture and stir-fry over low-medium heat for 2 minutes. Add cinnamon and stir-fry for a few seconds, then add salted soybeans and stir-fry 30 seconds.

Put in the mushrooms and stir-fry 1 minute. Drain the meat in a sieve, saving the marinade. Increase the heat, add the meat, and stir-fry until it changes color, 3 to 4 minutes. Add enough water to just cover the meat and bring to the boil. Reduce heat, cover, and simmer until the meat is just tender, about 45 minutes.

Add the potatoes and a little more water if needed, cover, and simmer, stirring occasionally, until the potatoes are cooked and the meat is very soft, about 15 to 20 minutes. Serve hot with steamed white rice. You can make this well in advance and reheat it if you like, or even refrigerate it for 24 hours.

Serves: **4**   Preparation time: **20 min + 30 min marinating**   Cooking time: **1 hour 10 mins**

braised pork with green mango *wettha thayet thi chet*

It won't take you long to prepare this Burmese pork dish, which can be left to simmer gently for about an hour while you get on with other things. Although it has only a few seasonings — garlic, ginger, onion, chili, and turmeric, plus the ubiquitous dried shrimp paste and a touch of sesame oil —what lifts it out of the ordinary is sour green mango. If you can't find unripe mangoes, there are alternative suggestions for obtaining that irresistible sour tang.

1 large red or brown onion, minced
2–3 cloves garlic, minced
1 3/4 in (4 cm) ginger, minced
1 teaspoon dried shrimp paste
3 tablespoons vegetable oil
1 teaspoon sesame oil
2–3 teaspoons crushed dried chili flakes, or
  1 teaspoon chili powder
1/4 teaspoon turmeric powder
1 1/4 lb (600 g) boneless pork shoulder, cut in
  3/4 in (2 cm) slices, about 1 1/2 in (4 cm)
  square
1 1/2 tablespoons fish sauce
1–2 unripe green mangoes (about 1/2 lb
  or 250 g), peeled and coarsely grated
  (see Note)
1 1/2–2 cups (375–500 ml) water
sugar to taste
salt to taste

Process the onion, garlic, ginger, and shrimp paste to a smooth paste.

Heat both lots of oil in a saucepan and add the processed paste, chili, and turmeric. Stir-fry over low-medium heat until fragrant, about 4 to 5 minutes. Add the pork and stir-fry until it changes color and is well coated with the seasonings, about 5 minutes.

Splash in the fish sauce, stir for about 1 minute, then add the green mango and stir-fry for 5 minutes. Add just enough water to cover the pork and bring to the boil. Cover the pan, lower the heat, and simmer until the pork is tender and sauce has reduced, about 1 hour. (I sometimes add a couple of cubed potatoes towards the end of the cooking time.) Taste and add sugar and salt if needed to balance the flavors. Serve hot with steamed rice.

Note: If you can't find green mango, you could use 1 grated sour green apple to replace unripe green mango; add this with the pork for stir-frying, then add 1 tablespoon lime or lemon juice with the water after the pork has been stir-fried. Taste at the end of cooking and add more lime juice as needed for a sour tang.

Serves: **4**   Preparation time: **15 min**   Cooking time: **1 hour 10 mins**

spicy balinese pork   *babi masak kecap*

Like many Indonesian dishes, this excellent recipe doesn't contain any dried spices but what is does have is plenty of chilies, shallots, garlic, ginger, and dried shrimp paste, with sweet soy sauce offset by a touch of lime juice. This dish is one of my personal favorites, and makes me very glad that the Balinese are Hindu and therefore not forbidden to eat pork like Indonesia's Muslims.

4–6 large red chilies, sliced
8 shallots, minced
4 cloves garlic, minced
2 in (5 cm) ginger, minced
1 teaspoon dried shrimp paste, toasted
3 tablespoons oil
1$^1/_4$ lb (600 g) pork shoulder, in $^3/_4$ in (2 cm) slices, cut in 1$^1/_4$ in (3 cm) squares
3 tablespoons sweet soy sauce, or 3 tablespoons thick black soy sauce with 2 teaspoons soft brown sugar
1 tablespoon lime juice
1$^1/_2$ cups (375 ml) water
salt to taste

Process the chilies, shallots, garlic, ginger, and shrimp paste to a smooth paste in a spice grinder, adding a little of the oil if necessary to keep the blades turning.

Heat the oil in a wok or saucepan with a heavy base, then add the chili paste and stir-fry over low-medium heat, 4 minutes. Add the pork and stir-fry over medium heat until it has changed color, about 5 minutes.

Add the soy sauce, lime juice, and water. Bring to the boil, cover, and simmer over low heat, stirring occasionally, until the pork is tender and sauce has thickened, about 1 hour. Taste and add salt if desired. Transfer to a serving dish and serve hot with steamed white rice and vegetables.

Serves: **4**   Preparation time: **12 min**   Cooking time: **1 hour**

deep-fried eggs with pork & prawn filling *kai sawan*

These eggs looking pretty much like regular whole eggs, cooked in a light batter. When you cut into them, however, you realize that half the egg is actually a mixture of pork and prawns. These delicious Thai-style eggs can be served as part of a main meal with rice, or you could enjoy them as a snack or starter.

3 1/2 oz (100 g) minced lean pork
7 oz (200 g) raw prawns, peeled and
   deveined, or 4 oz (125 g) cooked crabmeat
4 large eggs, hard-boiled
1 tablespoon minced coriander leaves
2 tablespoons thick coconut milk
2 teaspoons fish sauce
1/2 teaspoon salt
freshly ground black pepper
vegetable oil for deep-frying

Batter
1/3 cup (40 g) plain flour
2 teaspoons vegetable oil
1/4 teaspoon salt
1/3 cup plus 1 tablespoon (100 ml) water

Process the pork, prawns, coriander leaves, coconut milk, fish sauce, salt, and pepper in a food processor.

Peel the eggs, halve lengthways, and remove the egg yolks. Add the yolks to the food processor and pulse the mixture several times until finely ground. Using wet hands, fill each half of egg white with one-eighth of the pork mixture, pushing it into the hollow left by the yolk and molding it with your hands to make the shape of a complete egg.

Prepare the Batter by putting the flour, oil, and salt in a small bowl, gradually stirring in the water to make a smooth thick batter.

Heat the oil in a wok until very hot, then dip the eggs into the Batter and put, filling side down, into the oil. Cook for 3 to 4 minutes, until golden brown underneath, then turn over and fry the other side for a couple of minutes. Remove from the wok, drain and serve hot.

Note: If you prefer to omit the crabmeat, increase the amount of prawns to 10 oz (300 g).

Serves: **8**   Makes: **16**   Preparation time: **20 min**   Cooking time: **10 mins**

thai red beef curry with bamboo shoots   *gaeng ped neua normai*

This Thai classic is a really gutsy dish, with the no-nonsense flavor of beef emphasized by the robust and fragrant Thai Red Curry Paste. You can make your own following the recipe below; if you use commercial curry paste, you may need to adjust the amount slightly as the intensity seems to vary from one brand to another. Coconut milk helps soften the bite of the chilies and the rather neutral flavor of bamboo shoots (or eggplant, if you prefer) acts as foil to the spicy sauce.

$^1/_2$ cup (125 ml) thick coconut milk
4 tablespoons Thai Red Curry Paste
  (see below)
3 cups (750 ml) thin coconut milk
1$^1/_4$ lb (600 g) topside beef, in $^3/_4$ in (2 cm)
  slices, cut in 1$^1/_4$ in (3 cm) squares
4 kaffir lime leaves, torn
$^1/_2$ lb (250 g) canned bamboo shoots, boiled
  in fresh water 10 minutes, drained and
  sliced, or 1–2 slender Asian eggplant, cut in
  1$^1/_4$ in (3 cm) slices
1–2 tablespoons fish sauce
salt to taste

Thai Red Curry Paste
2 teaspoons coriander seeds
1 teaspoon cumin seeds
1 teaspoon black peppercorns
10–12 dried red chilies, cut in $^3/_4$ in (2 cm)
  lengths, soaked in hot water to soften
$^1/_3$ cup minced shallots
$^1/_4$ cup minced garlic
2 tablespoons finely minced galangal
2 tablespoons thinly sliced lemon grass
1 tablespoon ground coriander root
1 teaspoon dried shrimp paste, toasted
$^1/_2$ teaspoon grated kaffir lime rind, or
  1–2 kaffir lime leaves, minced

Prepare the Thai Red Curry Paste if you are not using the commercial variety. Put the coriander, cumin, and pepper in a small dry pan and cook, shaking the pan, until fragrant, 1 to 2 minutes. Transfer to a spice grinder and grind to a fine powder, then keep aside in a small bowl.

Process all the other curry paste ingredients to a smooth paste in a spice grinder; you will probably need to do this in several small batches. You may need to add a teaspoon or two of water to keep the mixture turning during processing; the resulting paste must be absolutely smooth. Combine this paste with the ground spices, stirring to mix well. Refrigerate in an airtight jar for about three weeks, or deep-freeze in small portions if not using for this curry.

To make the beef curry, put the thick coconut milk into a saucepan and stir in the red curry paste. Cook uncovered, stirring frequently, over low-medium heat until the oil comes out and the mixture starts to fry and smells fragrant, about 8 to 10 minutes. Add the thin coconut milk and bring to the boil, stirring constantly. Put in the beef and lime leaves and simmer uncovered until beef is tender, 1 to 1$^1/_4$ hours.

Add the bamboo shoots or eggplant and continue cooking until the vegetables are done and the meat is very tender; if the sauce seems to be drying out before the cooking is done, add a little water. Just before serving, add fish sauce to taste, and a little salt if you desire. Transfer to a serving dish and serve with rice.

Serves: **4**   Preparation time: **20 min**   Cooking time: **1 hour 30 mins**

laotian beef & vegetable stew   *or lam*

When I asked the women vegetable sellers at a street market in Luang Prabang what went into the popular local beef stew, I was shown bundles of woody sticks. I was skeptical when they insisted that these were cooked together with the meat, vegetables, and herbs, but I later found out that this vine is related to the pepper family and gives a faintly bitter flavor. Even without this esoteric ingredient and using the easily available vegetables and herbs suggested here, you'll find this is still a very tasty dish.

2 tablespoons preserved fish, or 3 table-spoons chopped canned anchovies
1¼ lb (600 g) topside or chuck steak, cut in ¾ in (2 cm) slices, about 1¼ in (3 cm) square
1 stem lemon grass, tender inner part of bottom 3 in (8 cm) only, thinly sliced
6 shallots, thinly sliced
4–6 slender Asian eggplants (about 1½ lb or 750 g), left whole
4 large red chilies, left whole
3–4 cups (750 ml–1 liter) water
6 spring onions
13 oz–1 lb (400–500 g) leafy greens (water-cress, water spinach, English spinach, ama-ranth, silver beet, etc), coarsely chopped
½ teaspoon freshly ground black pepper
salt to taste
½ cup loosely packed Asian basil leaves, minced
small bunch of dill or mint, minced

If using preserved fish, put it in a small bowl and add enough warm water to cover. Stir, then leave to soak for a few minutes before pouring the contents into a sieve. Press down on the solids to extract the salty liquid.

Put the meat in a wide saucepan and add the preserved fish liquid (or chopped anchovies), lemon grass, shallots, chilies, eggplants, and enough water to cover. Bring to the boil, then reduce the heat, cover and leave to simmer until the eggplants and chilies are very soft, 15 to 20 minutes. Lift out the eggplants and chilies and remove the stem end of each. Slice the eggplants in half and scoop out the flesh. Chop the chilies, then process the eggplants and chilies to a paste; alternatively, you can mash them finely with a fork. Return to the pan.

Cut the spring onions in 1¾ in (4 cm) lengths, then mince enough of the green portion to make 2 tablespoons. Set aside the finely minced spring onions and add the rest to the pan, together with the leafy greens. Bring to the boil, cover, and continue cooking until the meat is very tender, about 1¼ hours. If there is still a lot of liquid in the pan, uncover and cook over moderately high heat to reduce it slightly.

Add black pepper and salt to taste, then stir in the basil and the dill or mint. Transfer to a serving bowl and scatter with the reserved spring onion greens.

Note: You can use just one type of leafy green vegetable, or a combination of several.

Serves: **4**   Preparation time: **30 min**   Cooking time: **1 hour 30 mins**

malay lamb curry

A genuine Malay curry that uses commercial curry powder? Yes, local cooks do sometimes use blended spice mixtures (see Curry Powder, page 214), but also add whole spices, fresh seasonings, and lemon grass for a more complex blending of flavors. The seasoning is softened with a little coconut milk and given a touch of sourness with tamarind juice. Add a few potato cubes and you have a fragrant, mouth-watering dish. You can make this curry a day before you intend to serve it, as the flavors actually improve with keeping.

3 tablespoons curry powder for meat
$1/2$ teaspoon fennel powder
3 tablespoons water
3 tablespoons oil
$1^1/_4$ lb (600 g) lean lamb leg, in $1/_2$ in (1 cm) thick slices, cut in $1^3/_4$ in (4 cm) squares
2 cups (500 ml) water
1 stem lemon grass, bottom 6 in (14 cm) only, slit and bruised
1 teaspoon salt, or more to taste
2 potatoes, peeled and cubed
$1/_2$ cup (125 ml) coconut milk
1 heaped tablespoon tamarind pulp, soaked in $1/_4$ cup (60 ml) warm water, squeezed and strained to obtain juice
1 teaspoon sugar

Seasoning Paste
6 shallots, minced
3 cloves garlic, minced
$1^1/_2$ tablespoons minced ginger
4 dried chilies, cut in $3/_4$ in (2 cm) lengths, soaked in hot water to soften, seeds discarded

Whole Spices
$1^1/_2$ in (4 cm) cinnamon
2 petals of star anise
2 cardamom pods, slit and bruised
2 cloves

Prepare the Seasoning Paste by processing the shallots, garlic, ginger, and chilies in spice grinder to make a smooth paste, adding a little of the oil if necessary to keep the mixture turning. (You may need to process the shallots first to reduce them and make enough space in your grinder jar before adding the remaining ingredients.)

Combine the curry powder, fennel, and water in a small bowl, stirring to make a smooth paste. Set aside.

Heat the oil in a wok, then add the whole spices and stir-fry over low-medium heat until fragrant, about 1 minute. Add the Seasoning Paste and stir-fry for 2 minutes, then add the curry powder paste and stir-fry for another 2 minutes. Add the lamb and stir-fry until it changes color and is covered with spices, 3 to 4 minutes.

Add the water, lemon grass, and salt and bring to the boil, stirring to remove any spice paste stuck to the bottom of the wok. Cover and simmer until meat is just tender. Add the potato cubes and a little more water if needed, and simmer until both the potatoes and meat are tender. Add the coconut milk, tamarind juice, and sugar and simmer gently, uncovered, until the sauce has thickened, about 5 minutes. Serve hot with white rice or Lacy Malay Pancakes (page 32).

Serves: **4**   Preparation time: **30 min**   Cooking time: **1 hour**

a little something on the side

Whether you call them dips, sauces, sambals, or salsas, tangy accompaniments are an integral part of Southeast Asian food. No matter how simple the meal, there'll always be a little something on the side for extra flavor. Serve a bowl of noodle soup or some grilled chicken and you'll probably want to add Simple Thai Fish Sauce & Chili Dip, or Vietnamese Fish Sauce Dip. Malaysian and Singaporean noodle dishes just wouldn't be the same without the emphatic Sambal Belacan (Malay Chili & Shrimp Paste Dip). Many Cambodian dishes respond instantly to Cambodian Salt, Black Pepper & Lime Dip, and it's impossible to imagine a plate of deep-fried spring rolls without the famous Vietnamese Fish Sauce Dip.

Although you can enjoy most of these dips as a condiment, you can also scoop many of them up with an array of ingredients called "dippers." Dips together with the dipper of your choice (such as pungent Thai Shrimp Paste Dip with Crispy Rice Cakes, or the Burmese Tangy Tomato Dip with deep-fried bean curd skin or pork cracklings, for example) are often served as a between-meal snack, but they could just as well be enjoyed as the prelude to a main meal or put on the table together with the rice and other dishes.

It's not just dips and sambals that add extra zing to a meal; there are various relishes, freshly-made pickles and side-salads too. The ubiqituous Vietnamese Long White Radish & Carrot Relish, excellent Cambodian Red Capsicum Relish, and Malay Cucumber and Pineapple Salad are just some of the side-dishes that add a refreshing note to meals based on rice.

Cooked vegetable dishes are never dull. For example, this chapter includes Cabbage Simmered in Coconut Milk, Stir-fried Pumpkin & Sugar Snap Peas, a classic recipe for Stir-fried Green Vegetables with Oyster Sauce, some interesting bean curd dishes and even a recipe for Sour Spicy Pineapple Curry.

tangy tomato dip   *khayan chin thi pantwe pyaw*

This roasted tomato dip is a specialty of the Shan tribe of Burma, who usually add their distinctive dried fermented soybean wafers for extra flavor; however, easily available salted soybean paste makes an adequate substitute. Roasting the tomatoes, chilies, shallots, and garlic over charcoal gives this dip a wonderful flavor, but even if you have to use a grill, broiler, or a dry wok, you'll still be delighted with the result.

8 shallots, unpeeled
8 cloves garlic, unpeeled
4 large chilies, green if possible
4–6 small tomatoes (about 10 oz or 300 g)
1 tablespoon salted soybean paste
$^1/_2$–$^3/_4$ teaspoon chili powder
salt to taste
1 heaped tablespoon finely minced fresh
   coriander leaf

Put the shallots, garlic, and chilies on a fine mesh grill over a barbecue or under a hot grill; alternatively, put them in a dry wok. Cook over medium heat, turning several times. Remove the chilies as soon as they soften, taking care the skin does not blacken, but keep cooking the shallots and garlic until they the skins start to blacken and the inside is soft.

Slice off the stem end of the chilies. Cut each chili lengthways and discard the seeds. Slice the chilies put in a mortar or spice grinder. Remove the blackened skins from the shallots and add to the chilies. Cut the rounded end off each garlic clove, grab the skin of the other end, and squeeze out the garlic, adding it to the chilies and shallots.

Cook the tomatoes in the same way as the other ingredients, turning until they start to soften. Transfer to a plate, peel, then chop coarsely.

Pound or process the shallots, garlic, chilies, soybean paste, and chili to make a coarse paste. Add the tomatoes and pound or process briefly, just enough to mix them well with the other ingredients but not to make a smooth paste. Add salt to taste, then stir in the coriander leaf. Serve at room temperature with dippers or as a condiment with rice. (Any left-over can be refrigerated in a covered container for up to a week.)

Serves: **4-6**   Preparation time: **15 min**   Cooking time: **10 min**

all-purpose dippers

The most interesting (and often inadvertently amusing) Burmese cookbook I've come across is Mi Mi Khiang's *Cook and Entertain the Burmese Way*. When suggesting food to enjoy with dips, she lists what she calls "dippers," and it's hard to come up with a better name for the food that you use to help scoop up a dip. Mi Mi Khiang includes in this category such exotic items as the young leaves of the acacia thorn, young mango leaves, fish bladder chips, buffalo-hide chips, and dried milk sheets. You'll be happy to know you can also used somewhat more accessible ingredients such as those suggested below.

Something crunchy
deep-fried prawn or fish crackers (*krupuk*)
Crispy Rice Cakes (page 30)
deep-fried pork skin/pork cracklings (sometimes sold as *chicharon*)
deep-fried dried bean curd skin (use dried bean curd skin sold in thick, crinkled strips about 1 $^1/_4$ in or 3 cm wide)

Raw vegetables
cucumber
long white radish
carrot
yam bean (*jicama*)
celery
broccoli
cauliflower
young winged beans
baby corn
button or oyster mushrooms
capsicum
young long beans

Leafy greens
young passionfruit leaves
cabbage leaves
sprigs of water spinach

Fruit
segments of pomelo
sticks of unripe green mango, pineapple, or half-ripe papaya
apple guava
rose apple, wood apple, or cashew apple
slices of star fruit

simple thai fish sauce & chili dip *nam pla prik ki noo*

An indispensable accompaniment to Thai food, and served just as salt would be served with Western food, this dip is simplicity itself. If you can't be sure of a constant supply of bird's-eye chilies, keep some in the freezer so you're always equipped to make this dip for serving with just about anything Thai.

1/2 cup (125 ml) fish sauce
1 teaspoon lime juice
8–10 fresh red or green bird's eye chilies, coarsely chopped

Combine all ingredients in a bowl and transfer to small sauce bowls when serving. Any left-over dip can be kept in a covered container in the fridge. You can keep adding fish sauce and a squeeze of lime juice to the left-over chilies, which will keep their bite for quite some time.

Serves: **4**   Preparation time: **2 min**

vietnamese fish sauce dip *nuoc mam*

This is the "serve with everything" Vietnamese dip, a clever blending of flavors, sour yet with a touch of sweetness, salty with fish sauce, fragrant with lime juice, and with a judicious touch of garlic and chili. The proportions vary from one cook to the next; this recipe happens to be my favorite. Some cooks add a tablespoon or two of finely grated carrot to the sauce before serving.

1 clove garlic, minced
1 large red chili, minced
2 tablespoons caster sugar
2 tablespoons lime juice
1/4 cup (60 ml) rice vinegar
1/4 cup (60 ml) fish sauce
1/4 cup (60 ml) water

If you have a mortar and pestle, pound the garlic and chili together with a little of the sugar until coarsely ground. Stir in the rest of the sugar and remaining ingredients, mixing until the sugar dissolves. If you prefer to use a blender, process all ingredients until the chili is fairly fine. Pour into a bowl and allow the pink froth to disappear before serving. This makes about 3/4 cup of dip; double the amounts if you like and refrigerate any left-over in a covered container for up a week.

Serves: **4-6**   Preparation time: **5 min**

malay chili & dried shrimp paste dip *sambal belacan*

The most popular accompaniment in Malaysia and Singapore, this is a pungent mixture of fresh red chili and toasted dried shrimp paste. It is always served with a small round green lime, its fragrant juice mixed into the sambal just before eating. Perfectionists claim that the ingredients should be pounded in a mortar, and that the toasted dried shrimp paste should still be warm for maximum flavor. I find the sambal is perfectly acceptable if processed in a spice grinder, but agree that the shrimp paste should be freshly toasted. The sambal keeps refrigerated in a covered jar for about two weeks, but is best freshly made.

5–6 large red chilies, sliced
1 1/2 teaspoons dried shrimp paste, freshly toasted (page 18)
1/4 teaspoon salt, or more to taste
4 small round green limes (*limau kesturi, kalamansi* or calamondin), top sliced off, or 1 lime or lemon, quartered

Process or pound the chilies, shrimp paste, and salt until the chilies are finely ground, but not turned into a smooth paste. Transfer to four small sauce dishes and put a lime on each. Each person squeezes in lime juice to taste, stirring it before using the dip as a condiment with rice. Any unused sambal can be refrigerated for several days in a covered container.

Serves: **4**   Preparation time: **8 min**

opposite, top left (foreground) **simple thai fish sauce & chili dip**   (background) **vietnamese fish sauce dip**   top right **malay chili & dried shrimp paste dip**
below **thai shrimp paste dip** (recipe on page 176)

thai shrimp paste dip *nam prik kapi*

To make this popular Thai dip, cooks start with freshly toasted dried shrimp paste, then set off on a culinary journey adding lashings of garlic, as many hot chilies as they can tolerate, a pinch of salt and fish sauce for saltiness, a squeeze of lime juice balanced with a little palm sugar. Tiny pea-sized eggplants are often lightly pounded and added, and some cooks also throw in a few pounded dried prawns. This recipe is a starting point, which you can adjust to taste. Scoop up with any of the dippers (page 172), or put a big dollop next to your rice.

1 tablespoons dried shrimp paste, freshly
 toasted (page 18)
4 cloves garlic
1 tablespoon ground palm sugar
$1/4$ teaspoon salt
4–8 red or green bird's-eye chilies
3–4 pea-sized eggplants, optional
1 tablespoon lime juice
2 teaspoons fish sauce

Put the warm shrimp paste in a mortar or spice grinder and add the garlic, palm sugar, and salt. Pound or process until smooth. Add the chilies (and pea-sized eggplants, if you are using these) and pound just a few times until they are just broken up; a coarse texture is characteristic of this dip. If you are using a spice grinder, process a couple of times for a second or two. Transfer to a bowl and stir in the lime juice and fish sauce. This dip can be refrigerated in a covered container in the refrigerator for about one week, but is best enjoyed freshly made.

Serves: **4**   Preparation time: **5 min**

burmese crispy dried prawn sprinkle *sambal balachaung*

Although this condiment is not well known outside Burma, it certainly deserves to be. It's crunchy, salty, full of dried prawns, shallots, and garlic, as hot as you like, and normally served an accompaniment to rice-based meals. This recipe is based on one from Charmaine Solomon's classic *Complete Asian Cookbook*. Charmaine, whose grandmother lived in Burma, suggests that Balachaung addicts like myself can try it as a sandwich relish; I also sprinkle it over vegetables, salads, and some soups.

$1/2$ cup (125 ml) vegetable oil
3 tablespoon sesame oil
10 shallots, sliced
10 cloves garlic, thinly sliced
$1/4$ cup (125 g) dried prawns
$1/4$ cup (60 ml) rice or white vinegar
1–3 teaspoons crushed dried chili flakes
1 teaspoon salt
$1/2$ teaspoon toasted dried shrimp paste
 (page 18)

Heat both lots of oil in a wok. Add the sliced shallots and cook over low heat, stirring frequently, until they are golden brown and crisp. Lift out with a slotted spoon and drain on paper towel, leaving the oil in the wok. Add the sliced garlic and cook as for the shallots, making sure it does not turn dark brown. Drain and set aside.

Do not soak the prawns but put them into a food processor and process to a powder. Reheat the oil left in the wok and add the prawn powder. Stir-fry over low heat for 5 minutes, then add the vinegar, chili flakes, salt, and shrimp paste. Cook, stirring frequently, for 5 minutes. Remove from the wok and spread on a couple of layers of paper towel to absorb the oil. When completely cold, put the prawn mixture in a bowl and toss with the fried shallots and garlic. Transfer to a tightly sealed jar.

Note: It is important that the shallots and garlic are sliced evenly, so that the slices will all be cooked at the same time. Ensure the temperature is kept low throughout the cooking.

Makes: **about 2 cups**   Preparation time: **15 min**   Cooking time: **25 min**

opposite, top **burmese crispy dried prawn sprinkle**   bottom left **salted soybean, pork & peanut sauce**   bottom right **long white radish & carrot relish (recipes on page 178)**

salted soybean, pork & peanut sauce   *nuoc leo*

Traditionally served with Barbecued Pork Balls and Happy Pancakes, this sauce normally contains a tiny amount of minced pork and pork liver, although I prefer to use the more readily available chicken liver. If you like, you could omit the liver altogether and increase the amount of pork to three tablespoons. It might seem like a nuisance to have to buy a tiny amount of pork for the sauce, but remember, you're going to be using pork in the accompanying dish. You could also serve this sauce as a dip.

I tablespoon vegetable oil
2 cloves garlic, crushed and minced
I chicken liver, minced
I tablespoon finely minced lean pork
3 tablespoons salted soybean paste, mashed
2 teaspoons sugar
I tablespoon chunky peanut butter
3/4 cup (185 ml) water
2 tablespoons coarsely crushed dry-roasted
  peanuts
1/2–I teaspoon lime juice

Heat the oil in a small saucepan and add the garlic. Stir-fry for a few seconds until it starts to smell fragrant, then add the chicken liver and pork. Stir-fry for 1 minute, then add the soybean paste and sugar and stir-fry over medium heat for another minute. Add the peanut butter, stirring until it dissolves, then add the water, bring to the boil and simmer for 3 minutes. Transfer to a bowl and stir in the peanuts. Add lime juice to taste and leave to cool before serving.

Serves: **4**   Preparation time: **8 min**   Cooking time: **2 min**

long white radish & carrot relish   *cu cai ca-rot chua*

This relish seems to be everywhere in Vietnam, as well as in Laos and Cambodia. Try to use an Asian vegetable shredder, which produces match-stick shreds, rather than a normal grater.

I cup (100 g) finely shredded long white
  radish (daikon)
I cup (100 g) finely shredded carrot
I tablespoon salt
I tablespoon sugar
1/4 cup (60 ml) rice vinegar
1/4 cup (60 ml) water

Put the radish and carrot in a bowl and sprinkle with the salt. Rub with your hands and set aside for 10 minutes. Squeeze to remove as much moisture as possible, and pour it out of the bowl. Fill the bowl with cold water, rinse, squeeze again and drain well. Put into a bowl and sprinkle with sugar, then add vinegar and water, stirring to mix well. Refrigerate for around 30 minutes before serving. Drain off the liquid before serving with noodle dishes, barbecued meats and also as an accompaniment to rice.

Serves: **4**   Preparation time: **8 min**

cambodian salt, black pepper & lime dip   *tik marij*

The first time I first saw this dip was in the packed lunches of workers taking a break in the shade of the stunning temples of Angkor in Cambodia. This mixture of salt and black pepper, with lime wedges for adding juice to taste, is such a universal favorite that I'm sure if I'd examined more closely the cooking and eating scenes carved into the wall of the 12th-century Bayon temple, I'd have seen it there too. It does wonders with plain rice, and to just about anything you fancy to dip in it.

I tablespoon freshly ground black pepper
2 teaspoons salt
I lime or lemon, quartered

Combine the pepper and salt in a small bowl. Transfer to four tiny sauce bowls and put a lime or lemon piece on each bowl for squeezing in according to taste. Give the dip a stir with a spoon before using.

Serves: **4**   Preparation time: **2 min**

fresh bean sprout pickle   *dua gia*

This lovely fresh Vietnamese pickle or relish is quickly made and goes well with just about everything. Start it before you put your rice on to cook; it takes just a couple of minutes to measure the ingredients and add the bean sprouts, then leave it all to marinate for half an hour while preparing the rest of the meal.

$^3/_4$ cup (185 g) caster sugar
I teaspoon salt
I cup (250 ml) rice vinegar
$2^1/_2$ cups (200 g) bean sprouts, straggly tails
  removed

Serves: **4**   Preparation time: **10 min**

Put the sugar, salt, and rice vinegar in a bowl, stirring to dissolve the sugar. Add the bean sprouts and toss gently. Leave to marinate 30 minutes, tossing once or twice during this time. Drain before serving with just about any fish, meat, or poultry dish and rice. Any left-over pickle can be refrigerated in a covered container for up to 24 hours; make sure it is well drained before storing.

roasted thai chili paste   *nam prik pao*

Ready-made versions of this are widely available in jars outside Thailand, but you might like to try making it at home. To get the real Thai flavor, the ingredients should be roasted over hot coals, but you can get a reasonable approximation by dry-roasting the basics in a wok or under a hot grill or broiler. This paste is added to a number of dishes, including hot sour soups, and can also be served as a condiment with rice.

6–8 large dried chilies, left whole, rinsed,
  and dried
5 shallots, unpeeled
4–5 cloves garlic, unpeeled
I tablespoon dried shrimp paste
I heaped tablespoon tamarind pulp, soaked
  in $^1/_4$ cup (60 ml) warm water, squeezed,
  and strained to obtain juice
I tablespoon ground palm sugar
$^1/_2$ teaspoon salt
2 tablespoons vegetable oil

If it's convenient to use a barbecue, put the chilies, shallots, and garlic on a fine mesh grill and cook over a moderately hot fire or gas flame, or cook under a hot grill or broiler. Turn the chilies just until they are crisp but not blackened, taking great care as they burn very quickly. Remove the chilies and continue cooking the shallots and garlic, turning until they are soft and the skin has started to blacken. Remove from the grill and leave aside until cool enough to handle. (Alternatively, you could cook the chilies, shallots, garlic, and shrimp paste in a dry wok.)

Spread the shrimp paste into a thin layer on aluminum foil, enclose, then grill on both sides until fragrant.

Break the stem end off each chili, break the chilies into small pieces, then transfer to a spice grinder and grind coarsely. Remove the skins from the shallots, then cut the rounded end off each garlic clove. Grab the skin of the other end and squeeze out the garlic. Add the shallots, garlic, and shrimp paste to the spice grinder and process until finely ground.

Heat the oil in a small pan and add the paste. Cook over low-medium heat, stirring frequently, until fragrant and cooked, about 4 to 5 minutes. Cool, then refrigerate in a covered jar.

Makes: **about I cup**   Preparation time: **10 min**   Cooking time: **30 min**

red capsicum relish *chrourk m'teh*

This is one of the most delicious relishes you'll find in anywhere, and goes well with almost any food, Southeast Asian or Western. Capsicums are grilled until the skin blackens, giving them a marvelous smoky flavor, then mixed with garlic, fish sauce, and vinegar, balanced by a little sugar. This recipe is based on one from Longtein de Monteiro's *The Elephant Walk Cookbook*.

2 large red capsicums (about $^1/_2$ lb or
  250 g each)
$^1/_4$ cup (60 ml) rice vinegar
$^1/_4$ cup (60 ml) fish sauce
2 tablespoons sugar
1 teaspoon salt
4 large cloves garlic, thinly sliced
a few sprigs of Asian basil, optional

Cook the capsicums, either over charcoal, under a very hot grill, or on a rack directly over a gas flame, turning until the skin had blackened all over and the flesh is slightly softened, about 10 minutes. (You want fierce heat so that the skin will be blackened before the capsicums become over-cooked.) Put the capsicums in a plastic bag, close, and set aside for 15 minutes to loosen the skins. Hold the capsicums under running water and rub to remove the skin. Discard the seeds and membranes and chop the flesh into pieces roughly $^3/_4$ in (2 cm) square.

Combine the vinegar, fish sauce, sugar, and salt in a bowl, stirring to dissolve sugar. Add garlic, capsicum, and Asian basil (if using), stirring to mix well. Marinate for at least 30 minutes. Serve with rice and other dishes; it is particularly good with any fried food, and also with Steamed Pork Sausage (page 29). Any left-over portion can be refrigerated for about 1 week.

Serves: **6**   Preparation time: **10 min**   Cooking time: **10 mins**

vinegared cucumber salad   *yam tan gwa*

Variations of this easy salad — my standby for when I don't have a variety of vegetables on hand — are found through-out the region, partnering the cool crunchiness of cucumber with sweet, sour, salty, and sometimes hot flavors. This Thai version add peanuts for extra crunch, though you could omit these if you prefer. This palate-cleansing salad is good at just about any meal, especially when fried food is served.

4 tablespoons rice vinegar
3 tablespoons water
3 tablespoons caster sugar
1 teaspoon salt
1 cucumber (about 1 lb or 500 g), peeled
1 large red chili, seeded if desired, thinly sliced
2 shallots, thinly sliced
2 tablespoons coarsely crushed dry-roasted
   peanuts, optional

Put the vinegar, water, sugar, and salt in a bowl and stir until dissolved. Cut the cucumber in half lengthways and scrape out the pulpy portion only if the seeds are well formed. Cut across in $^1/_2$ in (1 cm) slices and toss with the vinegar mixture. Add chili and shallots, mix, then cover and refrigerate at least 30 minutes. Transfer to a serving bowl and scatter the top with the peanuts.

Serves: **4**   Preparation time: **15 min**

cucumber & pineapple salad   *kerabu timun & nenas*

I'll admit that if you're not fortunate enough to live in Southeast Asia, it's pretty hard to find the intensely fragrant wild pink ginger bud (usually called torch ginger, although botanists are still arguing whether it's *Nicolaia* sp or *Phaemeria* sp). Even without such an exotic ingredient, you can still make this refreshing salad. Its crunchy texture and sweet-sour tang make it particularly good with braised or fried food, or curries.

1 cucumber (about 1 lb or 500 g)
1 teaspoon salt
2 thin slices fresh pineapple (about 10 oz
   or 300 g), peeled, cored, and diced
2 tablespoons thinly sliced ginger bud
   (see Note)

Dressing
4 tablespoons dried prawns, toasted in a
   dry wok, 4–5 minutes
1–2 large red chilies, sliced
1 teaspoon dried shrimp paste, toasted
1–2 tablespoons lime juice, depending
   on sweetness of pineapple
2 tablespoons water
1 tablespoon sugar
1 teaspoon salt

Rake the skin of the cucumber with a fork and then rub all over with the salt. Rinse under running water, squeeze the cucumber, then cut in four lengthways. Cut across into $^1/_2$ in (1 cm) dice and put in a bowl with the pineapple and ginger bud (if using).

   To make the Dressing, put all the ingredients in a spice grinder or blender and process until finely ground. Add to the cucumber and pineapple, toss and serve immediately.

Note: If you can't get ginger bud, cook $^1/_2$ cup freshly grated or desiccated coconut in a dry wok over very low heat, stirring until it turns rich brown, taking care it does not burn. While the coconut is still hot, process or pound it to an oily paste. Cool, then add to the cucumber and pineapple together with the dressing.

Serves: **4-6**   Preparation time: **20 min**

sour spicy pineapple curry   *pacheri nanas*

Pineapples are often used as a vegetable when they're still a little under-ripe, as in this Malay/Indonesian recipe, which you'll often find at weddings. This is partly because of pineapple's bright yellow color — yellow is the color of royalty, and a bride and groom are regarded as "king and queen" on their marriage day — and also because this hot, sour, fragrantly spiced dish is irresistible. Be sure not to use ripe pineapple for the best result.

1 medium under-ripe fresh pineapple (about 3 lb or 1.5 kg), peeled, quartered lengthways, core discarded, each quarter halved across
3–4 cups (750 ml – 1 liter) water
1 1/2 teaspoons turmeric powder
3 tablespoons vegetable oil
1 large red or brown onion, thinly sliced
1 whole star anise
6 cardamom pods, slit and bruised or 1/4 teaspoon cardamom seeds or ground cardamom
2 in (5 cm) cinnamon
8 cloves
4 cloves garlic, minced
2 in (5 cm) ginger, minced
1 teaspoon salt
1 tablespoon sugar, or more to taste
2–3 large red chilies, halved lengthways, leaving stem attached

Put the pineapple in a medium saucepan and add just enough water to cover. Add the turmeric, stir, then bring to the boil. Lower the heat and simmer uncovered for 10 minutes, then drain, discarding the liquid. Cut the pineapple into bite-sized pieces.

Wash and dry saucepan and return to heat with the oil. When moderately hot, add the onion, star anise, cardamom, cinnamon, and cloves and stir-fry over medium heat for 2 minutes. Add the garlic and ginger and stir-fry over low-medium heat, 2 minutes. Add 1 cup (250 ml) water, salt, and sugar. Bring to the boil and simmer uncovered, 2 minutes.

Put in the pineapple and chili and simmer 2 minutes. Taste and add more sugar if desired. Serve hot with rice and other dishes.

Serves: **4-6**   Preparation time: **15 min**   Cooking time: **15 mins**

laotian grilled eggplant *yam makheua*

Eggplant, a rather neutral vegetable, is never dull in Southeast Asia. You can find variations of grilled eggplant salad in Cambodia and Thailand, but what gives this Laotian version its distinctive flavor is the roasted shallots, garlic, and chilies. Combine these with the smoky flavor of the roasted eggplant and you get a really flavorful salad. It is easy for Lao cooks to grill the ingredients over hot coals, but you'll still get a good result using a gas or electric grill or dry-roasting in a wok.

2–3 (about 13 oz or 400 g) slender
  Asian eggplants
3 shallots, unpeeled
3–4 cloves garlic, unpeeled
2–3 large chilies, preferably green
$1/4$ cup coarsely chopped coriander leaf or dill
$1/4$ cup coarsely chopped mint
1 spring onion, thinly sliced
2–3 tablespoons fish sauce
3 tablespoons lime juice
2 teaspoons sugar
salt to taste

Prick the eggplants in a several places with a fork, then cook over hot charcoal or under a very hot grill, turning until the skin has started to blacken and the eggplants are soft. Alternatively, you could set the eggplants on a rack directly over a gas flame or under a broiler and cook until done. Leave until cool enough to handle, then half lengthways and scrape out the flesh with a spoon. Chop coarsely and put in a bowl.

Put the shallots, garlic, and chilies on a fine mesh grill and cook over charcoal, a gas flame or under a broiler, turning until slightly blackened and soft; you could cook these at the same time as the eggplants. Alternatively, put them all in a heavy dry wok and cook, turning several times, until they darken and become soft; the chilies and garlic will be ready before the shallots. When cool enough to handle, cut off the stem end off the chilies and slice. Peel the shallots. Cut the rounded end off each garlic clove, then grab the skin of the pointed end and squeeze out the garlic. Pound or process the shallots, garlic, and chilies in a spice grinder just until they turn into a coarse paste.

Put the eggplants in a bowl and stir in the shallot paste, herbs, fish sauce, lime juice, and sugar. Taste and add a little salt if desired. Serve with rice and other dishes.

Serves: **4**   Preparation time: **10 min**   Cooking time: **10-15 min**

stir-fried bean curd, bean sprouts & chinese chives

Isn't it nice when really healthy vegetable dishes also taste great? This recipe gives you the protein and phytoestrogens of bean curd, together with the rich beta-carotene, iron, and vitamin C content of the garlic chives. The garlic chives also add an earthy flavor, but if you can't find these, spring onions work well. Fish sauce, sugar, and black pepper give a Cambodian accent to this easy and deliciously healthy vegetable dish.

3 tablespoons vegetable oil
2 cloves garlic, finely julienned
13 oz (400 g) hard bean curd, dried, cut in
  $^1/_2$ in (1 cm) dice
bunch of Chinese chives, or 6 spring onions,
  cut in 1 $^1/_2$ in (4 cm) lengths
7 oz (200 g) bean sprouts, scraggly tail ends
  removed, washed, and well-drained
3 tablespoons fish sauce
1 tablespoon sugar
$^1/_4$ teaspoon freshly ground black pepper

Heat oil in a wok 30 seconds, then add garlic and stir-fry for 5 seconds. Add the bean curd and stir-fry over medium-high heat until crisp and golden all over, about 3 minutes. Add the garlic chives or spring onions and stir-fry 30 seconds, then add the bean sprouts and stir-fry for another 30 seconds.

Sprinkle over the fish sauce, sugar, and pepper and stir-fry for 30 seconds. Transfer to a serving dish and serve hot with rice.

Serves: **4**   Preparation time: **20 min**   Cooking time: **4 mins**

long beans & bean curd with red curry paste   *tua fak yow tau hu*

It's amazing what a difference a little Thai red curry paste and Asian basil makes to this simple combination of bean curd and long beans. You can use either home-made or bought curry paste (page 214) for this tasty vegetable dish, which is ready in moments.

$1/4$ cup (60 ml) chicken stock or water
1 tablespoon fish sauce
1 teaspoon sugar
$1/2$ cup (125 ml) oil
7 oz (200 g) hard bean curd, patted dry with paper towel
2 teaspoons minced garlic
2–3 teaspoons Thai Red Curry Paste (page 164)
13 oz (400 g) long beans, cut in $1 1/4$ in (3 cm) lengths
$1/4$ cup firmly packed sprigs of Asian basil

Combine stock or water, fish sauce, and sugar in a small bowl, stirring to dissolve the sugar. Set aside.

Heat the oil in a wok, add the bean curd, and fry until golden brown and crisp on both sides. Drain well on paper towel, then cut in $1/2$ in (1 cm) dice.

Discard all but 2 teaspoons of the oil. Re-heat the oil, add the garlic, and stir-fry over medium heat for a few seconds, then add the curry paste and stir for just 15 seconds. Add the long beans and stir-fry for 2 minutes. Add the stock mixture, stir to mix well, then add the diced bean curd. Stir-fry over medium heat until the beans are cooked, about 2 to 3 minutes. Add the basil, stir, and then transfer to a serving dish. Serve hot with rice and other dishes.

Serves: **4**   Preparation time: **10 min**   Cooking time: **10 mins**

cabbage simmered in coconut milk   *kobis masak lemak*

It makes sense in areas where ripe coconuts literally drop from the trees (if not plucked with the help of a trained monkey) to use coconut milk in cooking, its creamy sweetness transforming everything from meat to poultry, seafood, and vegetables. This Malay recipe for cabbage simmered in lightly seasoned coconut milk can be adapted to many other vegetables, and makes a perfect accompaniment to rice and other dishes, particularly fried or grilled food that is dry.

1 tablespoon oil
4 shallots, finely sliced
1 clove garlic, minced
1 large fresh red or green chili, sliced
3 cups (750 ml) coconut milk
$^1/_2$ small round cabbage (1 lb or 500 g),
   halved lengthways, cored, and coarsely
   sliced across
2 tablespoons dried prawns, soaked in warm
   water to soften
$^1/_2$ teaspoon salt, or more to taste

Heat the oil in a saucepan, then add the shallots, garlic, and chili and stir-fry over low-medium heat until soft, 3 minutes. Add the coconut milk, increase the heat slightly and bring almost to the boil, stirring constantly.

Put in the cabbage, dried prawns, and salt, stirring to mix well. Bring almost to the boil, then lower the heat. Simmer gently with the pan uncovered until the cabbage is soft, about 15 minutes, stirring occasionally. Taste and add more salt if desired. Transfer to a serving bowl and serve hot or warm with plain white rice.

Note: Try using two small sweet potatoes, cut in chunks, with a bunch of English spinach or amaranth instead of the cabbage; pumpkin and long beans are also very good cooked in this way.

Serves: **4-6**   Preparation time: **10 min**   Cooking time: **20 mins**

fried bean curd in tomato sauce   *tua hu sot cha*

This easy recipe consists of firm bean curd, pan-fried until crisp and golden outside, served with a tomato sauce. Sounds simple — and it is — but the flavor is even better than you might expect. The fresh tomato sauce is accented with a perfect balance of fish sauce, soy sauce, garlic, sugar, and salt, another example of the delicacy and sophistication of the Vietnamese palate.

3 tablespoons vegetable oil
4 squares firm bean curd (about 13 oz
  or 400 g), dried with paper towel
sprigs of fresh coriander, to garnish

Sauce
1 teaspoon vegetable oil
1 teaspoon finely minced garlic
2 medium ripe tomatoes, skinned and diced
  (about 7 oz or 200 g)
$1/4$ cup (60 ml) water
4 teaspoons fish sauce
2 teaspoons light soy sauce
2 teaspoons sugar
2 teaspoons tomato paste
$1/4$ teaspoon freshly ground black pepper

Prepare the Sauce first by heating the oil in a medium saucepan. Add the garlic and stir-fry over medium heat until golden. Add the tomatoes and stir-fry until slightly softened, about 2 minutes. Add water, fish sauce, soy sauce, sugar, tomato paste, and pepper. Bring to the boil, lower heat, cover and simmer for 3 minutes. Remove from the heat but keep warm.

Heat the oil in a frying pan until very hot. Add the bean curd and fry until golden brown underneath, about 3 minutes. Turn and fry the other side, about 3 minutes. Drain on paper towel and transfer to a serving dish. Pour over the tomato sauce, garnish with coriander sprigs, and serve with steamed rice and other dishes.

Serves: **4**   Preparation time: **10 min**   Cooking time: **10 mins**

stir-fried pumpkin & sugar snap peas   *cha bonle*

This Cambodian recipe is the essence of simplicity: pumpkin stir-fried with sugar snap or snow peas and spring onion, flavored with garlic, fish sauce, a touch of sugar, and black pepper. Apart from looking beautiful —the golden orange pumpkin contrasting with bright green peas — this versatile recipe can be served as part of any Southeast Asian meal.

3 tablespoons vegetable oil
2–3 cloves garlic, very finely minced
1¹/₂–2 tablespoons fish sauce
1 teaspoon sugar
1 lb (500 g) butternut or other bright yellow pumpkin, peeled, seeds and fibers discarded, flesh julienned
7 oz (200 g) sugar snap or snow peas, tips and strings removed (if using large snow peas, cut in half diagonally)
2 spring onions, cut in 2 in (4 cm) lengths
¹/₂ teaspoon freshly ground black pepper

Heat the oil in a wok, then add the garlic and stir-fry for a few seconds. Add the fish sauce and sugar, stirring, then put in the pumpkin and stir-fry over medium-high heat, 2 minutes. Add the peas and stir-fry 2 minutes. Add the spring onions, stir-fry 30 seconds, then sprinkle with black pepper and transfer to a serving dish.

Note: In Cambodia, pork is often added to this dish; you could add 7 oz (200 g) shredded pork fillet after putting in the fish sauce and sugar, and stir-fry 1 minute before adding the pumpkin and snow peas.

Serves: **4-6**   Preparation time: **15 min**   Cooking time: **5 mins**

eggplant with dried prawn sambal   *sambal terong hay bee*

If you think eggplant is rather dull, this flavorful Nonya recipe is sure to change your mind. Most Nonya cooks deep-fry the eggplants first, but I prefer to keep the fat content low by cooking them whole in a tiny bit of oil in a covered pan. For maximum flavor, halve the eggplants before spreading them with sambal topping; this may be a bit tricky if using miniature eggplants, so try to find the regular slender variety.

4 tablespoons vegetable oil
1 lb (500 g) slender Asian eggplants, skin left on, stems trimmed
1 medium red or brown onion, halved lengthways, thinly sliced across
1 teaspoon sugar
$^1/_2$ teaspoon salt
juice of 1 small round green lime (*limau kesturi*), or lime juice to taste

Seasoning Paste
$^1/_3$ cup (35 g) dried prawns, dry roasted for 3–4 minutes
2 large red chilies, sliced
6 shallots, minced
1 large clove garlic, minced
1 teaspoon dried shrimp paste, toasted

Serves: **4-6**   Preparation time: **15 min**
Cooking time: **15 mins**

Heat 1 tablespoon of the oil in a wide saucepan or covered frying pan. Put in the whole eggplants. Cover the pan and cook the eggplants over low heat, turning until they are until cooked through. Remove the eggplants, cut in half lengthways, then cut across in two or three pieces, depending on their size. Keep warm.

While the eggplants are cooking, prepare the Seasoning Paste. Process the dried prawns to a powder in a spice grinder. Remove the prawn powder and add the remaining ingredients. Process to a smooth paste, adding a little of the oil if needed to keep the mixture turning.

Heat the remaining 3 tablespoons of oil in a wok then add the onion and stir-fry over low-medium heat until softened, about 2 to 3 minutes. Add the Seasoning Paste and dried prawns and stir-fry over low heat, until cooked and fragrant, about 4 minutes. If the mixture starts to stick, add a little more oil or about a tablespoon of water. When the mixture is cooked, stir the sugar and salt, stirring until dissolved.

Spread the cooked mixture over the top of each piece of eggplant. Squeeze over lime juice to taste and serve hot or at room temperature with rice and other dishes.

Note: If slender Asian eggplants are not available, miniature eggplants could be used.

silken bean curd steamed with vegetables *tau hu sawam*

The name of this elegant, Chinese-inspired Thai recipe translates as "heavenly bean curd" and that's a pretty good description of its appearance and flavor. The feather-light texture and relatively neutral flavor of silken bean curd is enhanced by a sauce, and is a perfect foil for decorative pieces of carrot and mushroom, surrounded by bok choy cabbage. It's great for serving at a special dinner, and tastes every bit as good as it looks.

2 rolls (250 g each) silken bean curd, cut in
  1 in (2.5 cm) slices
$^1/_2$ small carrot, very thinly sliced, blanched in
  boiling water 3 minutes
6–8 fresh or canned straw mushrooms,
  rinsed and drained, halved lengthways
2 teaspoons cornflour
$^1/_2$ cup (125 ml) chicken stock
2 teaspoons oyster sauce
1 teaspoon fish sauce
$^1/_2$ teaspoon sugar
$^1/_4$ teaspoon white pepper
2 teaspoons oil
1 teaspoon very finely minced garlic
4 baby bok choy cabbage, halved lengthways,
  blanched in boiling water 2 minutes,
  drained, or $^1/_2$ lb (250 g) broccoli florets,
  blanched until just cooked

Put the bean curd slices in a single layer in a shallow heat-proof bowl. Place 1 slice of carrot half on top of each piece of bean curd, then arrange 1 mushroom half on top of the carrot.

Combine the cornflour, stock, oyster sauce, fish sauce sugar, and pepper in a small bowl, stirring to dissolve sugar. Set aside.

Heat the oil in a small saucepan and stir-fry the garlic over low heat until golden. Add stock mixture, bring to the boil and stir until it thickens and clears, about 1 minute. Spoon over each piece of bean curd.

Put the dish of bean curd in a bamboo steamer or on a perforated rack set in wok of rapidly boiling water. Cover and steam 5 minutes. Remove the dish from the steamer. Dip the bok choy in boiling water to reheat, drain well, and place around the bean curd before serving.

Serves: **4**   Preparation time: **15 min**   Cooking time: **12 mins**

stir-fried green vegetables with oyster sauce *kanaa namman hoi*

Many Thai cooks prepare leafy green vegetables and *gai larn*, a type of *kale* sometimes known Chinese broccoli, using this basic method. It is very similar to the Chinese way of stir-frying vegetables, yet the use of fish sauce as well as oyster and soy sauce adds a definite Thai touch. You can use *gai larn*, regular broccoli, or any dark leafy Asian greens.

1 $^1/_4$ lb (600 g) *gai larn*, or 13 oz (400 g) broccoli, broken into florets, or a bunch of leafy Asian greens (Chinese flowering cabbage, Chinese white cabbage or bok choy)
1 tablespoon vegetable oil
2 cloves garlic, crushed and minced
1 teaspoon oyster sauce
1 teaspoon fish sauce
1 teaspoon light soy sauce
$^1/_2$ teaspoon sugar
water or chicken stock, if needed

Serves: **4**   Preparation time: **5 min**
Cooking time: **5 mins**

If using *gai larn*, cut the leaves away from the stems and discard (these are too tough to eat). Peel the stems if the skin seems thick, then cut the stems lengthways in $^1/_4$ in (0.5 cm) strips. Cut strips across into 2 in (5 cm) lengths. Bring a large saucepan of water to the boil and blanch the *gai larn* or broccoli for 1 minute. Transfer to a sieve, drain, then cool in a bowl of cold water.

If using Chinese greens, cut across in 2 in (5 cm) lengths, discarding the hard bottom part of the stems if using Chinese flowering cabbage. Do not blanch, but set aside.

Heat the oil in a wok for 30 seconds, then add the garlic and stir-fry for a few seconds until it starts to smell fragrant. Add the blanched *gai larn* or broccoli, or the raw leafy greens to the wok and stir-fry until they are just cooked, adding a tablespoon or two or water or chicken stock from time to time if the vegetables start to stick. Usually, the moisture from washing the vegetables (especially if you're using leafy greens) is enough to prevent this happening.

Add the oyster sauce, fish sauce, soy sauce, and sugar and stir-fry for a few seconds. Transfer to a serving dish and serve immediately.

sweet endings

Even though meals in Southeast Asia are likely to end with fresh fruit, this doesn't mean that you can't find all kinds of irresistible cakes and sweet concoctions — it's just that they're more likely to be eaten as a between-meal snack. A common (and welcome) sight on the streets of Thailand in particular is a mobile vendor of sweetmeats. Dozens of intricate and often beautifully colored or decorated cakes, some of them nestling in tiny cups of banana leaf, prepared by specialist cooks allow everyone to indulge in their passion for something sweet without having to spend time cooking.

Bananas are probably the most widely grown fruit in Southeast Asia, so it's not surprising to find them appearing in many cakes or desserts. Bananas are often partnered with coconut milk, such as in the Vietnamese recipe for Banana & Sago in Coconut Milk. Malay and Indonesian cooks often add other ingredients to this combination, including pieces of ripe jackfruit, young coconut, or diced sweet potato and yam.

Glutinous or sticky rice is readily available in most of Southeast Asia, inexpensive and with a delicious flavor and texture. It's almost always transformed into desserts, and you're sure to share the passion for this once you've tried Black Rice Pudding, the inimitable partnering of Thai Mango with Glutinous Rice, or Cambodia's banana-leaf packets of Glutinous Rice and Banana.

There are cooling, syrupy desserts too, such as Singapore's White Fungus & Lotus Seeds, and Red Rubies from Thailand. And did you know you can find pancakes and crêpes in Southeast Asia? Try Burma's Crisp Rice-Flour Crêpes with Cinnamon-flavored Peanut Filling and Indonesia's quaintly named "bachelor in a blanket" (Pancakes with Coconut Milk & Palm Sugar Filling).

banana & sago in coconut milk *che chuoi*

Variations on this banana and coconut milk theme are found throughout Southeast Asia. Nonya cooks in Malaysia may add diced sweet potato or yam to the basic mix, creating the delightfully named Bubor Cha Cha (which sounds to me like a South American dance), while other cooks add ripe jackfruit or pieces of jelly-like young coconut meat. This Vietnamese version is very simple: bananas, sago, and coconut milk, sweetened with palm sugar and sprinkled with sesame seeds.

3 tablespoons pearl sago, soaked in cold
  water 10 minutes, drained
4 cups (1 liter) coconut milk
4 tablespoons finely minced palm sugar,
  or more to taste
pinch of salt
8 very small finger bananas, or 4 ripe but firm
  medium bananas, cut diagonally in 3/4 in
  (2 cm) slices
2 tablespoons sesame seeds, toasted until
  golden brown

Put the sago in a sieve and shake over the sink to dislodge any loose starch. Put in a saucepan and add the coconut milk, sugar, and salt. Bring slowly to the boil, stirring occasionally, then lower the heat, and simmer uncovered until the sago balls are starting to turn transparent, about 10 minutes.

Add the banana slices and simmer for 5 minutes. Transfer to four to six serving bowls and serve warm or at room temperature, sprinkling with sesame seeds just before serving.

Serves: **4-6**   Preparation time: **25 min**   Cooking time: **10 mins**

sago with palm sugar & coconut cream *gula melaka*

An American friend, faced with this dessert for the first time, remarked unkindly that the sago looked like frog spawn. When I finally persuaded her to taste this soothing mixture of jelly-like sago, creamy coconut milk, and sweet palm sugar syrup, she was ecstatic. This Malaysian dish used to be a great hit with the colonial British, and was an essential item after a big curry tiffin. This is not difficult to make, and can be prepared well in advance.

1 cup (180 g) pearl sago
8 cups (2 liters) water
1 tablespoon milk
1 cup (250 ml) thick coconut milk
pinch of salt

Palm Sugar Syrup
4 oz (125 g) palm sugar, minced
3/4 cup (185 ml) water
1 pandan leaf, raked with a fork and tied in
  a knot, optional

Put the sago in a sieve and shake over the sink to dislodge any loose starch. Bring the water to the boil in a large saucepan. Slowly pour in sago, stirring constantly with a wooden spoon. Boil uncovered, stirring occasionally, until sago balls turn transparent, about 15 minutes.

Tip the sago into a large wire mesh sieve and hold under cold running water to wash away the starch, about 45 seconds. Shake the sieve until the liquid has gone, then stir in the milk, which will change the dull grey color of the cooked sago to a more appealing white. Transfer the sago to four glass serving dishes, and when cool, refrigerate.

Make the palm sugar syrup by combining sugar, water, and pandan leaf in a small saucepan. Bring to the boil, stirring until sugar has dissolved. Simmer until syrup has reduced to 1/2 cup. Remove the pandan leaf and leave to cool.

Transfer the palm sugar syrup and coconut milk to separate small jugs, adding salt to the coconut milk. Serve with chilled sago, each person adding syrup and coconut cream to taste.

Serves: **4**   Preparation time: **10 min**   Cooking time: **15 mins**

rice-flour crêpes with cinnamon-flavored peanut filling *ye mon*

Looking for an inexpensive and easily made dessert? Try this simple Burmese recipe, light and crispy rice-flour crêpes filled with crunchy peanuts and sweetened with cinnamon sugar. Even if you haven't a thing in the house (naturally, I'm assuming everyone has rice flour and peanuts), you can make this delightful dessert or mid-afternoon snack in minutes.

2 cups (320 g) rice flour
$^1/_4$ teaspoon bicarbonate of soda
   (baking soda)
pinch of salt
2$^1/_2$ cups (625 ml) cold water
$^1/_2$ cup (125 g) caster sugar, or slightly less
   if preferred
1 teaspoon cinnamon powder
1$^1/_4$ cups (190 g) dry-roasted peanuts,
   coarsely ground
2–3 tablespoons butter
2 tablespoons vegetable oil

Serves: **4-6**   Preparation time: **10 min**
Cooking time: **20 mins**

Put the rice flour, baking soda, and salt in a bowl and stir in the water to make a very thin batter. Combine the sugar and cinnamon in a small bowl, and set near the stove with the peanuts and butter.

Heat 2 teaspoons of oil in a 8 in (20 cm) frying pan, preferably non-stick, swirling it to coat the sides and base. When hot, pour in $^1/_3$ cup of batter, swirling the frying pan so that the batter spreads evenly. Cook over medium-high heat until the top of the batter is set and the bottom turns golden brown, about 2 minutes.

Take about $^1/_2$ to 1 teaspoon butter on the point of a knife and spread it over the top of the pancake so that it melts in. Sprinkle over 2 tablespoons peanuts and about 1 tablespoon of cinnamon sugar and cook for about 15 seconds. Carefully fold the pancake in two, cook a few seconds longer, then transfer to a serving dish. Repeat until the batter is used up, adding 1 teaspoon of oil to the pan each time, to make eight pancakes. Serve hot.

mangoes with glutinous rice *mamuang khao niaw*

This partnership of sweet ripe mangoes with glutinous white rice bathed in creamy coconut milk is deservedly a Thai classic, and is the only exception to my conviction that serving ripe mangoes any way but plain and simple is gilding the lily. When mangoes are in season, buy a couple, follow this recipe and paradise will be yours.

1 cup (200 g) glutinous (sticky) white rice
²/₃ cup (170 ml) thick coconut milk
¹/₄ cup (60 g) caster sugar, or more to taste
¹/₄ teaspoon salt
2 large ripe sweet mangoes
4 tablespoons coconut cream
2 teaspoons sesame seeds for garnish, optional

Serves: **4**   Preparation time: **7 min**
Cooking time: **20-40 mins**

Put the rice in a bowl and pour over boiling water to cover. Stand for 15 minutes, then drain. Spread a large clean piece of cheesecloth or tea towel inside a steamer, or over a perforated metal disk that fits in your wok. Spread the rice evenly over the cloth, cover the steamer with a lid and set in a wok over boiling water. Cook until the rice is tender, about 40 minutes, topping up the water in the steamer with additional boiling water every 10 minutes or so to ensure plenty of steam. When the rice is cooked, remove the steamer from wok and leave the rice to cool slightly.

Combine the coconut milk, sugar, and salt in a bowl, stirring to dissolve the sugar. Add the warm rice, mix well and leave the rice for 30 minutes to absorb coconut milk. Divide the rice between four serving plates.

Cut each mango in half lengthways, as close to the stone as possible. Cut each half into four lengthways slices and scoop out the flesh from the skin with a spoon. Put four slices on each plate next to the mango and serve, spooning coconut cream over the top of each portion of rice.

Note: Although mango is the best, you could try other fruit such as ripe papaya (pawpaw), canned or fresh jackfruit or even ripe bananas with the sticky rice. The Thais often add a sprinkle of lightly toasted sesame seeds or crushed dry-roasted peanuts to the top of the rice when serving.

new year glutinous rice & banana packets *nom n'sahm chaek*

It's always exciting to buy banana-leaf wrapped packages in those parts of Southeast Asia where you don't speak enough of the local language to be certain what's inside. This Cambodian concoction was one of my more successful stabs in the dark, banana leaf filled with glutinous rice, coconut milk, banana, and grated coconut. You can either steam or grill the cakes, which are always served during the Chaul Chham or Cambodian New Year. Aluminum foil could be used to replace banana leaf, although the flavor and texture won't be the same.

1 cup (250 ml) coconut milk

$^1/_4$ teaspoon salt

1$^1/_4$ cups (250 g) glutinous rice, soaked 3–4 hours, drained

$^1/_2$ cup (50 g) freshly grated coconut, or $^1/_2$ cup (40 g) desiccated coconut moistened in 4 tablespoons milk

8 pieces of banana leaf, each about 9 in (22 cm) square, softened in a gas flame or hot water

8 tiny ladies' finger bananas (about 3$^1/_2$ in or 9 cm long), or 2 large bananas, halved lengthways, cut across in 3$^1/_2$ in (9 cm) lengths

Bring the coconut milk and salt slowly to the boil in a saucepan, stirring all the time. Add the drained rice, lower the heat, and cook over low heat, stirring constantly, until all the coconut milk has been absorbed and the rice has started to form a dry sticky mass, 4 to 5 minutes. Transfer to a bowl, stir in the grated coconut and leave until cool enough to handle. (Check the sweetness of the bananas; if not using the really sweet ladies' fingers, you may want to add about 1 tablespoon of caster sugar to the rice mixture.)

Put the banana leaf pieces, darker side down, on a bench or table top. Add one-eighth of the rice to each, spreading it to make a thin rectangle a little wider than the banana. Put a whole banana or a banana quarter down the center of the rice. Moisten your hands with water, lift the sides and ends of the banana leaf up and use to help to push the rice over the top of the banana, molding the rice so that it completely encloses the banana. Use your hands if necessary.

Fold over the end of the banana leaf closest to you, tuck in the sides, and roll up as firmly as possible so that the rice remains clinging around the banana; give the completed roll a gentle squeeze to make sure the rice is compressed. Put the packets in a steaming basket or on a perforated rack set well above the water level in a wok, and steam over rapidly boiling water for 25 minutes. Leave to cool slightly while still wrapped in the banana leaf.

If you prefer to grill the packets over charcoal, put over a moderate (not hot) fire, turning the packets a couple of times until the leaf starts to char slightly and the rice is cooked, 15 to 20 minutes. Check a roll to make sure the rice is translucent, which means it is cooked.

Serve the packets either warm or at room temperature. They are normally eaten while holding onto the banana leaf wrapping (which keeps your fingers from getting sticky). If you want to be a little more elegant, you could put a roll in a bowl and drizzle the top of each with coconut cream, or sprinkle with some lightly toasted sesame seeds.

Serves: **4-8**   Preparation time: **about 1 hour + 3-4 hours soaking**   Cooking time: **35 mins**

black rice pudding with coconut milk *bubor pulot hitam*

Just about everyone who tries this delicious nutty-tasting dish while travelling in Indonesia or Malaysia falls in love with it. Some cooks combine white and black glutinous rice, while Nonya cooks often add dried longans for a smoky flavor, but the basics of brownish-black glutinous rice (which turns a deep purple brown when cooked), palm sugar, and coconut milk remain constant. This can be enjoyed any time, for breakfast, as a between-meal snack or as a dessert.

1 cup (200 g) glutinous black rice, washed in several changes of water, drained
6 cups (1.5 liters) water
2 pandan leaves, raked with a fork, tied into a knot
2 tablespoons minced palm sugar
1 cup (250 ml) coconut milk
1–2 tablespoons sugar, or more to taste
1 cup (250 ml) coconut cream
pinch of salt

Put the rice in a large saucepan and add water. Bring to the boil, stirring occasionally. Cover, lower heat and simmer 30 minutes. Add the pandan leaves, palm sugar, and coconut milk.

Bring to the boil, stirring to dissolve the sugar, then lower the heat and simmer uncovered, stirring from time to time, until rice is soft and swollen, 20 to 25 minutes. Remove the pandan leaves.

Taste and add white sugar if desired. Divide between four bowls. Combine coconut cream and salt, then pour 2 tablespoons into the center of each serving. Put the remaining coconut cream in a jug for adding to taste. Serve warm or at room temperature.

Serves: **4**   Preparation time: **10 min**   Cooking time: **1 hour**

red rubies *tub tim krob*

Which would you prefer: a bowl of rubies or of sapphires for dessert? You can use either fresh or canned water chestnuts for this attractive Thai recipe, where a little red food coloring transforms them into rubies, or blue coloring produces sapphires, which are served floating in chilled sweetened coconut milk.

1 cup (250 ml) water
1 cup (250 g) sugar
few drops of red or blue food coloring
$^1/_4$ cup (40 g) tapioca flour
30 water chestnuts, peeled and finely diced
$2^1/_2$ cups (625 ml) coconut milk
rose or jasmine essence to taste

Bring the water and sugar to the boil, stirring to dissolve the sugar. Boil uncovered for 1 minute, then cool and refrigerate.

Bring a large saucepan of water to the boil and add enough food coloring to color the water. Put the tapioca flour in a plastic bag and add the water chestnuts. Hold the top of the bag closed and shake to coat the water chestnuts. Transfer the water chestnuts to a sieve or colander and shake to dislodge the excess flour.

Put the floured water chestnuts in the saucepan of boiling water and simmer uncovered for 2 minutes. Tip them into a colander and drain, then transfer to a bowl of iced water to cool. (The water chestnut pieces will be covered with a pale red or blue jelly-like coating.)

Just before serving, combine the chilled sugar syrup, coconut milk, and flavoring essence. Divide the rubies (or sapphires) between four to six bowls and add the coconut milk to each. Add an ice-cube or two to each serving if desired and serve immediately.

Serves: **4-6** Preparation time: **35 min** Cooking time: **8 min**

white fungus & lotus seeds in iced syrup   *ch'ng t'ng*

I include this Singapore favorite because it is so pleasantly light and makes a refreshing ending to just about any meal. White fungus might not sound particularly appealing, but although it is virtually tasteless, it absorbs other flavors and has a delightful, slightly chewy texture. The Chinese believe this soupy dessert is very cooling to the body, and sometimes add canned longans or other dried fruits to the basic recipe.

$2/3$ oz (20 g) dried white fungus
4 cups (1 liter) water
$2^1/_2$ oz (75 g) dried lotus seeds
4 oz (125 g) rock sugar, or $^1/_2$ cup (125 g) white sugar
2 tablespoons white sugar, or more to taste (only if using rock sugar)
crushed ice or 8–12 ice cubes
longans or lychee fruit, optional

Put the fungus in a large bowl and add hot water to cover it by about 3 in (8 cm). Leave to soften for 15 minutes, then cut away any hard portions. Cut the fungus into bite-sized pieces and put with the water in a saucepan.

Check the lotus seeds to make sure the bitter central core or endosperm has been removed (if so, the seeds will have a narrow slit on both sides). Sometimes, there are a few seeds with the core still intact; if you see a dark greenish center at the top of the seed, split the seed open and flick out the core.

Add the lotus seeds, rock sugar, and white sugar to the pan and bring to the boil, stirring to dissolve the sugar. Cover and simmer gently until the lotus seeds and fungus are soft, about 1 hour. Taste and add extra sugar to sweeten if desired, bearing in mind the syrup will be diluted with ice. Transfer to a bowl and when cool, refrigerate until required.

To serve, divide the syrup, fungus, and lotus seeds between four soup bowls. Add a generous portion of shaved ice and serve (with Chinese porcelain soup spoons if you happen to have these).

Note: If you like, add 1 cup of drained canned longans or lychees just before serving.

Serves: **4-6**   Preparation time: **10 min**   Cooking time: **1 hour including soaking time**

pancakes with coconut & palm sugar filling *bujang dalam selimut*

I love the Indonesian name for these pancakes, which translates as "bachelor in a blanket." Known as *kuih dadar* in Malaysia, the pancakes are filled with freshly grated coconut and palm sugar, although if you have to use desiccated coconut, this also works well. These pancakes (one of my daughters' favorites when she was young) are usually a great hit with children. For a more sophisticated version, try the sauce as described in the Note.

1 cup (125 g) plain flour
pinch of salt
1 egg, lightly beaten
1–1 1/4 cups (250–310 ml) milk
1–2 few drops green food coloring, optional
1–3 few drops pandan essence, optional
3 tablespoons vegetable oil

Filling
1/2 cup (90 g) ground palm sugar
1/3 cup (85 ml) cup water
1 1/2 cups (150 g) freshly grated coconut,
  or 1 1/4 cups (80 g) desiccated coconut
  moistened with 1 cup (250 ml) milk

Sift the flour and salt into a medium bowl. Make a well in the center and add egg and 1 cup milk. Mix to make a smooth thin batter, adding more milk if necessary. Add food coloring and pandan essence if using.

Prepare the Filling by putting palm sugar and water in a small saucepan. Heat gently, stirring until dissolved, then add the coconut. Stir over low heat for 1 minute. Spread out a plate to cool.

Heat a small non-stick diameter frying pan (about 6 in or 15 cm in diameter) with about 1/2 teaspoon of the oil, swirling to cover the bottom of the pan. Pour out any excess oil. Heat until moderately hot. Add almost 1/4 cup pancake batter, swirling to spread over the bottom of the pan. Cook until set underneath, about 45 seconds, then turn and cook another 30 to 45 seconds. Stack on plate and continue until the batter is used up.

When pancakes are cool, put 3 tablespoons of filling in the center of each pancake. Roll up the end closest to you, tuck in the sides, then roll up to enclose filling firmly. Serve at room temperature.

Note: If fresh pandan leaves are available, use these instead of green food coloring and pandan essence; blend 4 pandan leaves, chopped, with 1/2 cup of the milk, then press through a sieve. Add the pandan-flavored milk to the batter along with the rest of the milk. You could also make a coconut sauce to pour over the pancakes. Combine 1/2 cup (125 ml) coconut cream, 1/2 cup (125 ml) water, 1 teaspoon sugar, 1 teaspoon cornflour and, if desired, a few drops of pandan essence. Cook over low heat, stirring constantly, until the sauce thickens and clears, 2 to 3 minutes. Serve at room temperature.

Serves: **4-6**   Makes: **about 12 pancakes**   Preparation time: **20 min**   Cooking time: **30 mins**

water chestnut or sweet corn creams   *tar kor haed*

You can use either fresh or canned water chestnuts, or sweet corn kernels, to give texture and flavor to these lovely creamy sweetmeats, which are particularly good after a meal of spicy food. Although normally served in tiny banana leaf cups, these are time consuming to make and since the cakes are not steamed (when the moisture of the banana leaves would be an important factor), it's more practical to use small bowls.

5 pandan leaves (about 12 in or 30 cm in length), cut in 2 in (5 cm) lengths, or a few drops each of pandan essence and green food coloring (only if using water chestnuts)
$1^{3}/_{4}$ cups (435 ml) water
few drops jasmine or vanilla essence (only if using sweet corn)
$^{1}/_{2}$ cup (60 g) tapioca flour
$^{1}/_{3}$ cup (85 g) caster sugar
$^{1}/_{2}$ cup (about 100 g) finely diced fresh or canned water chestnuts, or $^{1}/_{2}$ cup drained canned sweet corn kernels
3 tablespoons rice flour
$1^{1}/_{2}$ cups (375 ml) thick coconut milk
large pinch of salt

If you are using water chestnuts, put the pandan leaves and $^{3}/_{4}$ cup of the water into a blender and process until the leaves are finely pulverized and the water has turned bright green. Strain through a fine sieve, pressing down to obtain as much juice as possible. Put the juice or a few drops of pandan essence with remaining water, tapioca flour, and sugar in a medium saucepan. If using sweet corn, combine $1^{3}/_{4}$ cups water and jasmine or vanilla essence with the tapioca flour and sugar.

Cook over low heat, stirring constantly with a wooden spoon, until the mixture becomes very thick and clear, leaving the side of the pan. If using fresh water chestnuts, blanch in boiling water for 1 minute. Drain and add the blanched or canned water chestnuts (or the sweet corn kernels if using) to the cooked mixture, reserving about 2 tablespoons for decoration. Transfer the mixture to six or eight small glass dessert bowls, about $^{1}/_{2}$ cup in capacity.

Combine the rice flour, coconut milk, coconut cream, and salt in a small pan. Cook over low heat, stirring constantly, until the mixture has become very thick. Spoon the rice-flour mixture over the top of each tapioca cream, spreading evenly. If using sweet corn, decorate the top of each portion with a few of the reserved kernels. Cool, then refrigerate until required.

Serves: **4-6**   Preparation time: **10 min**   Cooking time: **8 min**

southeast asian ingredients

Amaranth (Chinese spinach) is a leafy green vegetable that tastes fairly similar to true or "English" spinach. It is widely available in Southeast Asia, as well as in many Asian stores in the West. The color of the leaf varies from pale to dark green; some varieties are streaked with purple-red, while others with completely red leaves are often called red amaranth. The leaves may be rounded or narrow and pointed, but all types of amaranth have the same pleasant taste.

Anchovies are available dried, either whole or cleaned, and range in size from about ¹/₄ in to 2¹/₂ in (1.5 cm to 6 cm). They are salted and sun-dried to make a seasoning and snack item. They are particularly popular in Malaysia and Indonesia (where they're known as *ikan bilis* and *ikan teri* respectively). Dried anchovies are often cooked in a little oil to flavor vegetable dishes and soups; instant stock powder made from dried anchovies is now available. If possible, buy cleaned anchovies which have had the head and dark intestinal tract removed; otherwise, you'll need to snap off the heads and flick out the intestinal tract of each tiny fish with the point of a sharp knife. Check that packets of dried anchovies do not look powdery or stale before buying. Store in a tightly closed container on the shelf.

Bamboo shoots of several types of bamboo are inexpensive and readily available in most of Southeast Asia,

very often gathered wild by villagers. Although deep-frozen and dried bamboo shoots are usually available elsewhere, I recommend using canned bamboo shoots if fresh ones are not available. Provided canned shoots are briefly boiled in fresh water before being added to recipes, they have an acceptable flavor and texture.

Banana leaf is indispensable as a food wrapper, used to wrap food for steaming or grilling, to provide little trays to hold food for steaming, and used as a kind of cookie cup for sweetmeats. The moisture within the banana leaf makes a difference to the texture and flavor of the food, but if you can't find fresh or frozen banana leaf, use aluminum foil. For how to prepare banana leaf, see page 17.

Basil, Asian (*bai horapa* in Thai, *rau que* in Vietnamese) is the most common type of basil used in Southeast Asia, generally known outside the region as Asian or Thai basil. It has a wonderful aniseed aroma, making it quite different to the common Mediterranean or sweet basil, and has medium to dark green leaves with a purple tinge to the upper stems and purplish flower heads. Use regular sweet basil as a substitute if unavailable.

Basil, lemon (known in Thai as *bai manglak*) has smaller, soft pale green

leaves and is usually cooked (when the flavor intensifies) rather than eaten raw; unfortunately it is not widely found outside the region. Nor is holy basil (*kaprow*), which is used in only a few dishes.

It is not difficult to strike Asian or lemon basil for growing at home; put a few stems in ¹/₂ in (1 cm) of water in a glass and keep in a sunny spot until rootlets appear from the bottom of the stem. Transfer to a pot of well-dug soil or plant in the garden in a sunny place. You could also plant Asian basil seeds, which are sometimes available in Asian food shops or nurseries.

Bean curd (tofu) was introduced by the Chinese, and has become part of the local diet in much of Southeast Asia. The two most commonly used forms are regular or soft bean curd, which is reasonably soft and sold in blocks, and hard bean curd, which has been compressed to expel most of the moisture and form a solid cake. Soft bean curd is generally used in soups and braised dishes, while hard bean curd is normally deep-fried. Silken bean curd (Japanese in origin) is very soft; it is found in some cities in the region, and either steamed or added to soups, particularly by cooks of Chinese origin. Fresh bean curd should be covered with water and refrigerated; it can be kept for several days. Pasteurized bean curd is sold in vacuum packs or plastic tubs outside Southeast Asia; refrigerate until the expiry date.

Another type of bean curd sometimes added to braised dishes or soups is dried deep-fried bean curd, which is generally sold in small rectangles. These are often sold on strings in Asia, but are elsewhere usually packed in plastic. They are light and spongy in

texture, and need to be dipped briefly in boiling water to remove the oil before being used. Dried deep-fried bean curd has an almost nutty flavor and is particularly appreciated for the way it soaks up the liquid to which it is added. It can be kept refrigerated for at least two weeks.

Tiny squares of salty fermented bean curd, often reddish brown on the outside, are sold in jars and used exclusively as a seasoning (especially with pork), and as a condiment which is often served with rice porridge.

Bean sprouts are made by soaking small, round, green mung beans, then keeping them moist in a warm place until the crisp white shoots emerge 3 to 4 days later. One of the most important vegetables in the region, they are eaten raw, briefly blanched, stir-fried, or made into a pickle.

Buy crisp shoots with no sign of green leaves appearing at the seed end. Refrigerate covered in water for up to one week, changing the water each day. Pinch off the straggly tails before using the sprouts and discard any loose black skins, but do not remove the seed heads.

Black mushrooms (often known by their Japanese name, *shiitake*) are cultivated in most of Southeast Asia and enjoyed for their firm texture and meaty flavor when fresh. The **dried mushroom**, often imported from China, is even more widely used, and is often preferred for its more intense flavor and keeping ability. Buy dried black mushrooms that do not show any signs of powder under their gills, which would indicate they are deteriorating. Store in a dry place in a closed container. Before using, soak in hot water until they soften; this will range from about 15 minutes to 1 hour, depending on the thickness of the cap; "flower mushrooms," which have creamy white streaks making them look a bit like a chrysanthemum, are particularly tough and need a full hour to soften. Discard the stem before using the cap.

Cabbage is found in several varieties in Southeast Asia. The round white cabbage common in temperate climates is grown in cooler areas around the region, and eaten both raw and cooked. More frequently found in local markets is Chinese celery cabbage or Napa cabbage, with very long, pale green to almost white overlapping leaves, used both raw and cooked. Another type popular for stir-frying is Chinese white cabbage. This name is somewhat misleading because although the stems are usually bright white, the leaves are either pale or mid-green. This delicately flavored cabbage is widely known abroad as *bok choy*. Another variety of this cabbage, with green instead of white stems, is often called Shanghai *bok choy*.

Chinese flowering cabbage (*choy sam* or *cai sin*) is one of the most delicious members of the cabbage family, with soft mid-green leaves and stems, sometimes sold with delicate yellow flowers visible.

Chinese mustard cabbage or mustard greens comes in two basic varieties: one is occasionally stir-fried or braised, while the other is so bitter that it is most often salted and sold as a moist pickle known as Chinese salted cabbage. Usually available in vacuum packs, this pickle is used sparingly in soups and some braised or stir-fried dishes, mainly as a seasoning.

Chinese pickled cabbage (*tang cai*) is a beige-brown mass of salted and seasoned finely chopped leaves sold in plastic or cellophane packs. It is used as a flavoring, mainly for rice porridge and some noodle dishes.

Candlenuts are waxy, cream-colored nuts related to the macadamia. Sold raw, they must be cooked (generally crushed and fried in seasoning pastes) before being eaten. They add texture and a faint flavor to food. Choose candlenuts that are light cream in color, not golden brown, as the latter may be rancid. Candlenuts have a high oil content, so are best refrigerated. Substitute one unsalted macadamia or two cashews for each candlenut.

Cardamom is a Southwest Indian native used to flavor some curries and sweet dishes. Whole cardamom pods have a fibrous straw-colored bark that encloses about 12 to 16 intensely fragrant black seeds. Generally, whole pods — slit with a knife and bruised to help release their fragrance — are used. You could substitute a pinch of cardamom seeds for one whole cardamom; ready-ground cardamom is not recommended as it loses its fragrance very quickly.

Chayote originated in Central America is also known as choko, christophene, custard marrow, and vegetable pear. The last name describes its size and shape perfectly. Chayote has a delicate flavor and, when young and raw, a pleasant crisp texture. In most of Southeast Asia, however, the vegetable is cooked. Be sure to peel off the wrinkled, somewhat prickly skin; the central seed is edible.

Celery, Chinese is a small pungent plant, with leaves resembling large, dark green coriander leaves. It is used as a flavoring herb and not as a vegetable, particularly in Malaysia and Indonesia. The leaves are often used as a garnish for soups (in fact, the Malay name for this translates as "soup leaf") and for noodles. Chinese celery plants can be refrigerated for up to one week with the roots in a jar containing a little water; cover the plant and jar with a large plastic bag.

Chick pea flour is known as *besan* in India, where it is widely used as a thickener and to flavor to savories and other dishes. It is also used in Burmese cuisine. It is often available in health food shops as well as stores specializing in Indian ingredients.

Chili is a Central American native, and available in Southeast Asia in many different varieties of varying heat and flavor. The heat comes from an enzyme known as capsaicin, which is present in the seeds and membranes. Take care to wash your hands carefully after dealing with chilies, as the juice will sting — don't ever rub your eyes or nose when working with chilies.

Fresh chilies are used either green (unripe) or more commonly when they are ripe and bright red. The most common type (referred to in these recipes as "large chilies") are about finger length, and of moderate intensity. Large chilies are often crushed to use as a seasoning; one large chili is roughly equal to one teaspoon of crushed chili. It is possible to buy jars of crushed chili (generally mixed with a little salt), which can be kept refrigerated, and these are an acceptable substitute for large fresh chilies. Crushed chili is sometimes sold under the Dutch-Indonesian name, *sambal oelek* or *ulek*.

Generally speaking, the smaller and thinner the chili, the greater the heat. Small bird's-eye chilies are much hotter and also have a different flavor and aroma to large chilies. Bird's-eye chilies can range in size from the aptly (if indelicately) named "rat's dropping chili" which can be as tiny as $^1/_2$ in (1 cm), up to chilies $1^1/_4$ to $1^3/_4$ in (3–4 cm) in length. Green, orange (half-ripe), and red bird's-eye chilies are all used, generally in spicy dips and relishes. Fresh chilies can be stored whole in a plastic bag in the freezer; remove them and slice or chop while they are still frozen. If you want the full flavor of chilies, but less heat, discard some of the seeds before using.

Dried chilies give a much deeper red color to food and lack the smell of fresh chilies. They are usually cut in short lengths and soaked in hot water until they soften, 10 to 15 minutes depending on the thickness of the chili. Dried chilies vary in intensity; the hottest I have tasted come, surprisingly, from China; Thai dried chilies are hot but not unbearably so, while some Indian varieties are actually quite mild. When buying dried chilies, make sure they still have a good deep color; any which are fading in color or breaking up will be passing their use-by date pretty soon. Dried chilies should keep a few months on the shelf, or almost indefinitely refrigerated.

Toasted or dry-roasted dried chilies are coarsely crushed to make crushed dried chili flakes, sometimes sold as "chili flakes." These are always served on the table in Thailand as a condiment. You can easily make your own (see page 17).

Dried red chilies ground to a very fine powder are sold as chili powder; do not confuse this with American chili powder which contains black pepper and oregano, and is used in Mexican dishes. Chili powder is sometimes added during cooking to provide heat when other types of chili are not used.

A final tip for when someone has eaten a fiery chili and is suffering: don't drink water, eat a spoonful of sugar instead. This is remarkably effective.

Chili sauce is widely used in Southeast Asia as a condiment. Many manufactured chili sauces have added garlic or ginger; some are sweet, others quite acidic, and the chili content (read heat factor) differs considerably. One of the most widely exported chili sauces is a Thai blend of chili, garlic, and vinegar sold as Sriracha chili sauce. Perhaps the most versatile dipping sauce is the mild combination of chilies, ginger, and sugar often labeled "sweet Thai chili sauce;" this is particularly good with grilled chicken and fish. Most brands of chili sauce can be kept on the shelf, although you might like to refrigerate it if you want to store it for many months.

Chinese sausage (*lap cheong*) is particularly popular as a seasoning among the Vietnamese. Perfumed with rose-flavored wine, they are never eaten alone, but cooked with rice or other food. They keep well in a dry place, although if you live in a humid climate, you may prefer to refrigerate them.

Chinese chives (or garlic chives) resemble coarse flat blades of dark green grass. When raw, they have a strong flavor, which becomes more delicate after brief cooking. Sometimes, the flowering heads of this are sold as a vegetable, and are considered a delicacy by the Chinese. They are also very decorative; a spray or two transforms any dish. Spring onions are the best substitute.

Cinnamon may have been specified in these recipes, but the flavoring bark used in Southeast Asia is in fact from the cassia tree, a related species with a thicker, darker, and more pungently flavored bark than true Ceylon cinnamon. Since cassia is generally labeled "cinnamon" when sold, I've used this name throughout the recipes, but cassia is what you should be using.

Coconut is one of the most useful plants in the region, although not found everywhere in Southeast Asia. In areas where it is abundant, the flesh of the mature coconut is grated and squeezed to make coconut milk, used in almost all types of food, from soups through to cakes (see page 17). The water from inside young coconuts (often sold abroad in cans as "coconut juice") is sometimes used to simmer meat (it has a tenderizing effect), and also enjoyed as a cooling drink.

Although nothing matches fresh coconut milk for use in cakes and desserts, adequate substitutes are available. If I can't get fresh coconut milk, I prefer to use small packets of concentrated coconut cream (the one I use is reduced from two whole coconuts to make 200 ml of liquid). This can be used straight from the packet as coconut cream; diluted with two parts of water, it makes thick

coconut milk, and diluted with three parts of water it becomes equivalent to regular coconut milk. Some brands of concentrated canned coconut milk are also quite good, although I've come across some very mediocre products that I've had to throw away. I suggest you experiment with what you can find locally, buying products labeled "coconut cream" or those which are clearly concentrated to give you the flexibility to create the type of coconut milk you require.

Packets of powdered coconut milk are a useful standby for when you need just a few spoons of coconut milk, but I do not recommend this product for general use. Once you've opened a packet, store it in the refrigerator.

Coriander (leaves, seeds & roots) is the world's most widely used herb and perhaps even more popular in Southeast Asia than in Central and South America and the Middle East. Coriander leaves have a distinctive smell and attractive appearance, and are the most important flavoring herb and garnish throughout the region. Coriander seeds are the most popular spice; for maximum freshness, local cooks prefer to use whole coriander seeds, heating them slightly to help release their volatile oils and make them easier to pound or grind whenever required.

Each time you have finished using the leaves of whole fresh coriander plants, cut off the roots, wash well, dry and slice very thinly. Store in a small airtight container in the freezer; do this each time you use coriander, and you will soon have a stock of coriander roots for use in Thai recipes. If you do not have enough roots when these are required in a recipe, you could use finely chopped coriander stem to make up the amount.

Fresh coriander plants can be stored for about one week by putting them in a jar with the stems ends standing in about $1/2$ in (1 cm) of water. Enclose the coriander and the jar with a large clear plastic bag and stand in the refrigerator.

Coriander, saw tooth, a long pungent blade with saw-tooth edges, tastes like a cross between coriander, mint, and basil. It is known in Cambodia *chi bonla* or *chi barang*, *prik chee farang* in Thailand and *ngo gai* in Vietnam (elsewhere, it is sometimes referred to by its botanical name, *eryngo*). Saw tooth coriander is generally added to soups and served as part of a platter of fresh herbs with Vietnamese food. Fresh coriander leaf is the best substitute.

Curry powder is a mixture of ready ground spices, used particularly in Malaysia and Singapore. Different mixtures are available, prepared from a range of spices depending on the type of dish which is required, and are generally labeled accordingly. Curry powders labeled "for fish" or "for meat and poultry" are best bought in small quantities, and stored in an airtight container in the refrigerator for maximum flavor.

Curry leaves are used mainly in Burma and Malaysia (and particularly popular among cooks of southern Indian origin). These grow on trees and are generally sold in sprigs consisting of 12 to 16 small, slightly pointed dull green leaves. They release their distinctive flavor only when cooked. There is no substitute for curry leaves, although they are sometimes sold deep-frozen or found dried in Asian stores, especially those specializing in Indian ingredients.

Dill is a herb often associated with Scandinavian food, but found in some parts of Southeast Asia, including Laos, Cambodia, and Sumatra. It is used as a flavoring herb, or served as part of a herb platter.

Eggplant (also known as aubergine) comes in many different shapes, sizes, and colors, ranging from tiny pea-sized eggplants (generally lightly pounded and added raw to dips), to egg-shaped vegetables, and short or long slender eggplants. The color ranges from white through bright orange to pale green, pale purple, and deep purple, and there are even streaked green and purple varieties. Apart from the bitter pea-sized eggplant and a round, tough-skinned orange variety which is very sour, most Asian eggplants have the same mild flavor, which lends itself well to all types of seasoning.

Try to use slender Asian eggplants, which are less bitter than their Western counterparts and do not need pre-salting; they also have tender, edible skins. Some eggplants, especially Japanese varieties, are very short, about 5 to 6 in (12–14 cm) in length, while others can be up to 10 in (25 cm). The length is not important, so long as you can obtain slender Asian varieties, you'll find them much more palatable than the Western type.

English spinach is generally grown in highland areas of Southeast Asia, and is undoubtedly the finest of all leafy green vegetables, with a delicate flavor and melting texture. It is very fragile and the leaves bruise easily; refrigerate wrapped in kitchen paper for a day, or two at most.

Fish, salted is a standby in many Southeast Asian homes. The type used in recipes in this book is thick fillets of salted fish, often sold as Mergui fish (named after the region in southern

Burma reputed to produce some of the finest salted fish). Salted fish is not normally soaked before use; when thinly sliced and fried to a crisp, it makes a wonderful garnish (and, incidentally, a good substitute for crumbled bacon in Western salads).

Fish sauce is to most of Southeast Asia what soy sauce is to the Chinese and Japanese, the most widely used salty seasoning. Fish sauce has a unique fragrance which gives so much of the regional food its characteristic flavor and aroma. Made from the liquid poured off salted and fermented fish, fish sauce is a clear golden brown color. Thai and Vietnamese brands are usually readily available abroad; in general, Vietnamese fish sauce is slightly stronger in flavor than Thai brands. Keep fish sauce in the cupboard; it lasts almost indefinitely.

Fish, preserved is preferred to dried shrimp paste in Cambodia and Laos, where it is known as *prahok* and *padek* respectively. The Vietnamese call it *mam ca sac* and use both this and fermented anchovy sauce (*mam nem*) as a flavoring. Chunks of fresh fish are salted and packed in barrels with a little cooked rice to aid the fermentation.

Preserved fish is available in glass jars, often exported from Thailand. The English names vary, from Pure Pickled Gouramy Fish, to Pickled Grey Featherback Fish, to Preserved Mudfish, or something similar; the brand I am currently using also bears the French name *poisson en saumure*. You can recognize it by the pale beige or grey color of the thick paste, which has a few chunks of fish visible. This should be used sparingly. A jar will keep in the cupboard for at least a couple of years. Anchovy sauce or even fish sauce can be used a substitute.

Five-spice powder is a Chinese seasoning sometimes used in Thai and Vietnamese cooking. This finely ground mixture of cassia, cloves, fennel, Sichuan pepper, and star anise has a warm fragrance and flavor and is commonly used in braised dishes, or a pinch added to pork sausages or paté. To keep its freshness as long as possible, store in the refrigerator.

Flour is most commonly made from wheat, plain rice, glutinous rice, corn, and tapioca (cassava). Plain rice flour and glutinous rice flour

(sometimes labeled "sweet" or "sticky" rice flour, made from white glutinous rice) are both used in cakes and savories; they are not interchangeable. Cornflour or cornstarch is a fine white powder often used as a thickening agent. Tapioca flour is most commonly used in desserts (and is, incidentally, used like talcum powder against prickly heat), while plain wheat flour, made from imported wheat, is also used in some recipes. Mung pea flour made from the small green mung bean is a very refined starch used in some Indonesian cakes; it is often sold as *tepong hoen kwe*.

Fungus, wood ear is used for its slightly chewy texture and dark color. Wood or cloud ear fungus literally grows on trees and has virtually no flavor but is added to soups, salads, and vegetable dishes. Two varieties of dried wood ear fungus are available: one is small, thin, crinkly, and uniformly black, while the other is larger and thicker with a pale grey or beige underside. There is no difference in flavor, but the smaller version is less chewy and reconstitutes more quickly. It keeps almost indefinitely in a covered container on the shelf.

Before using, soak wood ear fungus in warm water until it softens and swells to about five times its dried size. Small thin fungus pieces will take 5 minutes, while thicker pieces need longer. Drain and cut out any hard central portion, then slice or chop according to the recipe.

Dried white fungus, sometimes called silver fungus, is generally a pale ivory

color, and very crinkly in appearance, almost like a dried chrysanthemum. It is used mostly in soupy desserts, where it is enjoyed for its slightly chewy texture and translucent appearance. It should be soaked in warm water to reconstitute.

Galangal is preferred to common ginger in much of Southeast Asia. It is pale cream with delicate pink tips while still young, and becomes quite tough and fibrous as it ages. The fragrance of this rhizome seems to embody the smell of the tropics: warm, exciting, and faintly spicy with a hint of camphor. Just the aroma alone is enough to get the taste buds going. If you can obtain fresh galangal, scrub it well, peel off any thick papery skin (but don't worry about the tender skin, which can be left on). Cut the galangal in thin slices and store in a sealed bag in the freezer; use the slices as required while still frozen.

Dried galangal slices are sometimes available, and can be soaked in hot water for about 30 minutes to reconstitute, but a better alternative to the fresh product is galangal packed in brine, usually sold in jars. This may be labeled with the Thai name, *kha*, or simply referred to as "rhizome." (Do not confuse it with Chinese keys or *krachai*). Avoid powdered galangal, which does not have anywhere near the same flavor as other substitutes.

Garam masala is a popular mild and fragrant Indian blend of several powdered spices.

Garlic is used liberally throughout the region. Choose whole garlic heads still with their outer covering for greater freshness and store in a cool, dry place. To peel garlic easily, lay a clove flat on a board and cut off the hard flat end. Hit the clove with your palm on the flat of a knife, then hold the skin at the pointed end while flicking the garlic clove out with the point of a knife.

Ginger is the best known member of a botanical family which has over 200 species in Southeast Asia. If possible, buy young ginger, which has a milder flavor and is juicier than mature ginger. The former is recognized by its paler color, often with faint pink tips if very young, and its very thin pale skin; the mature rhizome has brown wrinkly skin which needs to be scraped off before use. If you are not sure of a ready supply of fresh ginger, which can be stored for a month or so in a cool, dark place with plenty of circulation, slice fresh ginger and store it in the freezer. Use straight from the freezer.

Ginger bud is the unopened flower of pink torch ginger, known as *bunga kantan* or *bunga siantan* in Malaysia, and *kaalaa* in Thailand. It is eaten raw with a dip, added to salads or cooked in soups and curries. When cooked with fish, it has a flavor and fragrance somewhat reminiscent of polygonum. There is no substitute; if you are able to obtain the fresh buds, freeze whole for future use.

Ginger, pickled comprises slices of ginger pickled with salt and vinegar, either prepared at home, or bought in small amounts scooped out of big jars in local markets. Chinese and Japanese brands are usually readily available in Asian stores abroad. Pickled ginger is often shredded and added to sauces or salads.

Kaffir lime has an unattractive knobbly skin, which earns it the unappealing alternative name of leprous lime. It has very little juice but the fragrance of the grated rind or zest is incomparable. If you can ever lay your hands on fresh kaffir limes, put them whole in your freezer and pull them out to grate (while still frozen) whenever kaffir lime rind is needed.

Kaffir lime leaf is one of the region's most popular herbs, recognized by its double leaf that looks like a figure eight. The intense and inimitable fragrance of the kaffir lime leaf is essential in many Southeast Asian dishes. If you can buy the fresh leaves, store them in a bag in the freezer. The dried leaves are a poor substitute, but you can sometimes find frozen leaves in Asian stores. In most recipes, you could substitute $1/4$ teaspoon grated lime or lemon rind for 1 kaffir lime leaf.

Fresh kaffir lime leaves are often finely shredded for adding to salads and other dishes. Fold the leaf in half and cut out the tough central rib. Roll up the leaves from the tip to stem, like a cigar, then lay on a board and use a sharp knife to cut into hair-like shreds.

Lemon grass is one of the most important herbs in Southeast Asia, a type of grass that grows up to 32 in (80 cm) in height. The bottom portion (about 8 in or 20 cm) is a tightly packed bulb, a little like a miniature leek, while the top part of the lemon grass has coarse, broad leaves which are not used in cooking. The flavor and fragrance are concentrated in the bulb, which is either bruised and added whole (or cut in manageable lengths), or thinly sliced and often pounded or processed. Usually only the tender inner part of the bottom 3 in (8 cm) is used for slicing and pounding; peel off two or three of the tough outer leaves to get to the inner portion. As even the inner stem is fibrous, it must be sliced as finely as possible, or else processed, before being used.

Lemon grass is added raw to salads, and also cooked. If you can buy fresh lemon grass, trim off the leaves and keep about 5 to 6 in (12–14 cm) of the stem. Stand with the ends in about $1/2$ in (1 cm) of water in a glass and

keep in a warm place (a bench or window sill) for up to about 2 weeks for use when required. Alternatively, trim the lemon grass and store in the fridge for 2 to 3 weeks, or for several months in the freezer; slice while still frozen.

Small packets of thinly sliced, deep-frozen lemon grass are often available in Asian stores abroad; 2 tablespoons of sliced lemon grass are roughly equivalent to the inner part of the bottom 3 in (8 cm) of a stem of fresh lemon grass.

If you live in a moderately warm climate and would like to grow lemon grass, leave the cut stems of fresh lemon grass in water until they start to send out roots. Transfer to a large pot or a sunny spot in the garden and keep well watered. They should multiply during the summer.

Lime is medium-sized and round, with a thin green skin that ripens to a pale yellow color. These are commonly used to provide lime juice for countless sauces and other dishes in Southeast Asia. Tahitian or other varieties of lime, or even lemon, can be used as a substitute, although the flavor and fragrance are not identical. Small round green limes (as pictured), are 1 to $1^1/_2$ in (2.5–3 cm) in diameter and called *limau kesturi* in Malaysia and *lemo* in Bali, and have a mild and very fragrant juice. They are often sold as calamondin outside Asia, or may be known by their Filipino name, *kalamansi*. Substitute with regular lime juice, adding, if you like, a few drops of orange juice.

Long beans, also known as snake beans or yard-long beans, are the

most common type of green bean found in Asia. There are several different varieties; the thinner, dark green type (which sometimes has a purple tinge that disappears after cooking) tends to be firmer, and have a slightly more emphatic flavor. It also takes longer to cook than the fatter, pale green variety, which has a touch of sweetness. Young long beans are often eaten raw as part of a salad platter, as well as chopped and added to dishes such as green papaya salad and deep-fried fish cakes. They are also stir-fried and sometimes simmered in coconut milk. Regular green or French beans can be used as a substitute.

Long white radish is often known in the West by its Japanese name, *daikon*, although it's not just used in Japan but found throughout Asia. Use the smaller radishes around 6 to 7 in (16–18 cm) if possible, as these will generally have a milder flavor and finer texture than the larger ones. Long white radish has a very thin skin, which can be scraped off with a knife. It is normally eaten raw in Southeast Asia, generally after salting to remove some of the bitterness, and is frequently partnered with carrot.

Lotus seeds, dried have a pleasant flavor and texture, and are used in some soups, rice dishes, and desserts, particularly in Vietnam. Most lotus seeds have had the bitter central core or endosperm already removed (if so, the seeds will have a narrow slit on both sides). Sometimes, there are a few rogues with the core still intact, so check and if you see a dark greenish center at the top of the seed, split it open and flick out the core. Lotus seeds should be stored in an airtight container in the cupboard; they keep for many months.

Mango, green is universally loved throughout the region for its sour tang.

It is eaten with dips, made into salads and pickles, or stir-fried with other ingredients. The mango should be peeled with a vegetable peeler and the flesh cut away from the central oval stone. Green mangoes should be stored in the fridge and peeled only just before they are needed.

Ripe mangoes are generally eaten as they come from the tree, without any attempts to improve them. One exception is the favorite Thai dessert, where slices of ripe mango are partnered with glutinous rice drenched in coconut milk.

Mint grown in Southeast Asia has a very intense flavor, the closest equivalent elsewhere being spearmint. It is one of the most common herbs and an indispensable part of the Vietnamese and Thai salad platter. Refrigerate mint in a covered container lined with paper towel for about four days, if you don't have a ready supply in your own garden.

Noodles were introduced by the Chinese and have, over the centuries, become a firmly entrenched part of Southeast Asian cuisine, although they have never replaced rice as the staple food. Noodles made from rice flour predominate, although wheat flour noodles are also eaten, especially in the towns and cities where Southeast Asians of Chinese ethnic origin tend to congregate. Both fresh and dried noodles are used. Fresh noodles should be refrigerated until used; dried noodles will keep almost indefinitely in a cupboard.

Rice flour noodles, fresh are generally cut into flat strands about $1/2$ in (1 cm) in width, and are usually thin and light in texture. These are known as *sen men* in Thailand and *bahn pho* in Vietnam. Fresh rice noodles tend to be thicker and heavier in Singapore and Malaysia, where they are known as *kway teow* or *sa hor fun*. Spaghetti-like round fresh rice noodles are also found, and generally used in noodle soups. It is also possible to buy flat sheets of rice flour dough, which can be cut to the desired size. Very thin fresh rice vermicelli is also available in the region, but seldom seen abroad. All fresh rice noodles have been steamed before being sold; before using, they should be blanched in hot water for about 1 minute to remove any oil which has been used to stop them sticking together, then drained and used as directed in recipes.

Dried rice flour noodles come in

several forms. Rice vermicelli is very fine threads of rice noodle, rather like angel hair pasta. Rice-stick noodles (or rice-ribbon noodles) are flat and vary in width from about $1/8$ to $1/2$ in (3 mm–1 cm). (Some brands of rice vermicelli are confusingly labeled rice-stick noodles.) Dried rice flour noodles should be soaked in hot water for about 10 minutes to soften. They are then generally boiled until cooked, which will take 30 to 60 seconds for rice vermicelli, and about 3 to 5 minutes for rice stick noodles, depending on their thickness.

Transparent noodles, made from green mung bean starch, are also known as jelly noodles, glass noodles, cellophane noodles, and green bean threads. The dried noodles are very fine and white and difficult to cut before soaking, even using kitchen scissors. For this reason, try to choose very small packets so that you will not have to fight to separate as little as 1 oz (30 g), which a number of recipes require. Before using the noodles, put the required amount in a bowl and add warm water to cover. They should be soft after 10 minutes, when they can be drained and cut to size. Packets keep almost indefinitely on the shelf.

Wheat noodles in their fresh form are sold in flat ribbons of varying widths, or are round and vary in size from very thin noodles to fat, heavy yellow noodles looking like spaghetti. Wheat noodles are often called "egg noodles," even though most do not actually contain eggs and get their yellow color from food dye. Fresh wheat noodles can be kept refrigerated for 2 to 3 days. Wheat and egg noodles are also available dried, although the thickest variety is sometimes difficult to find.

Before using fine or medium fresh wheat or "egg" noodles, shake them to dislodge any starch (used to stop them sticking together) and blanch in boiling water for up to 1 minute to cook. Rinse under cold water (this is important) and drain.

Thick fresh wheat noodles (often known as Hokkien noodles) should be put into a bowl and blanched in boiling water for about 1 minute, to remove any oil or impurities. Drain and use as directed in the recipe.

Dried wheat noodles are normally added to boiling water to cook, without any pre-soaking; the cooking time will depend upon the thickness, but is usually around 3 minutes (check the time stated on the package). The

noodles should be separated with a long fork or chopsticks during cooking, and once cooked, rinsed in cold water, and drained. If this last step is omitted, the noodles may become gluey.

Onions are used although shallots and spring onions are usually preferred. These are either the mild, fragrant, pale purple-tinged onion with purplish-brown skin (often known as the Bombay or Spanish onion), or brown-skinned onions with creamy flesh and a mild flavor.

Oyster sauce is a Chinese seasoning sauce that does not actually taste of oysters (and often doesn't even contain them; check the label to see if you're buying real oyster sauce and not "oyster-flavored" sauce), and has the ability to intensify the flavor of food. It is often splashed on to cooked vegetables, or added to marinades; it is more popular in areas with a large Chinese community.

Pandan leaf is a long wide blade; it is a member of the pandanus family, and also called fragrant screwpine. The leaves grow up to about 20 in (50 cm) in length, but are often sold trimmed. Cooks throughout the region often rake a pandan leaf with a fork, then tie it into a knot and add it to the pot when cooking rice; it adds a subtle fragrance that makes the rice taste like prized newly-harvested rice. Pandan leaves are also used in some curries, but mainly in cakes and desserts. They can be deep-frozen. Pandan essence is the best substitute.

Papaya, also known as paw paw, is a Mexican native widely grown in Southeast Asia and found in almost every garden. Although they lack the high vitamin C content of the ripe fruit, young green papayas are used as a vegetable, either raw, steamed, or simmered.

Prawn crisps are dried wafers made from prawns and starch (generally tapioca flour) and are very popular as a garnish or snack, especially in Indonesia, where they are known as *krupuk*. Similar wafers are made with fish, vegetables, or the *melinjo* nut. All wafers should be stored in an airtight container and must be thoroughly dry before being dropped in very hot oil for a few seconds, until they puff up. (Some local cooks sun-dry them before frying, but you can also use a very low oven.)

Peanuts are grown in most countries in the region, and are an important food item, used as a garnish, ground for sauces, and eaten as a snack. Raw peanuts, still with their brown skin intact, are generally preferred, although skinned raw (white) peanuts, which are more expensive and considered to have slightly less flavor, are also used. Peanuts are usually dry-roasted just before use (see page 18) for maximum flavor, although if you like, you could keep some coarsely crushed dry-roasted peanuts in an airtight container in the refrigerator, ready for scattering on salads, noodles etc.

Polygonum is a pungent herb with dark, narrow green leaves known by a number of names in the West: polygonum (the botanical name), Vietnamese mint, hot mint, long-stemmed mint, and laksa leaf. To help

avoid any confusion, here are the major local names: Vietnam, *rau ram*; Thailand, *phak phai*; Laos, *phak pheo*; Malaysia *daun kesom*; Singapore, *daun laksa*. This distinctively flavored herb is frequently part of a platter of fresh herbs served with noodle soups in Laos, Cambodia, and Vietnam, and is added to laksa noodle soup in Singapore and some parts of Malaysia.

You can strike polygonum from plants bought in an Asian store if you live in either a hot or temperate climate. Stand a few stems in water in a glass set in a sunny spot (the window sill, perhaps); as soon as you see white roots appearing, plant it in the soil in a sunny position and water frequently.

Prawns, dried are used in countless ways throughout the region. Sometimes called dried shrimps, they are an important flavoring in their own right and not used as a replacement for fresh prawns. Although various sizes are available, the most common are around $3/4$ in (2 cm) long. They should look orangey-pink and plump; avoid any with a greyish appearance or with an unpleasant ammonia smell. It is possible to buy packets of powdered dried prawns (generally labeled "floss" or "powder"), but it is better to buy the whole prawns so you can check the quality. Dried prawns will keep for several months if refrigerated. Before use, dried prawns are usually soaked to soften slightly; 5 minutes in warm water should be sufficient. If prawn powder is to be used as a garnish or flavoring, the dried prawns have a better flavor if dry-roasted in a wok or saucepan for about 4 to 5 minutes (rather than being soaked) before being processed to a fine powder or floss.

Rice is a staple in the region and some of the finest rice in the world is grown in Thailand, which exports its fragrant long-grain white rice (often sold as jasmine rice) around the world. Unless otherwise specified, recipes in this book are made using Thai fragrant rice, generally the preferred rice throughout Southeast Asia. (Many hundreds of varieties of rice are found in the region, with hill rice, grown at higher altitudes and relying on monsoon rainfall rather than irrigated fields, being some of the tastiest. Unfortunately, these fine hill rice varieties are rarely exported.)

Glutinous white rice (also known as sticky or sweet rice) is the preferred staple in parts of Laos and northeastern Thailand. Elsewhere, it is used mainly for cakes and desserts. Black glutinous rice, which has long brownish-black grains, turns a lovely deep purple-brown when cooked; its nutty flavor makes it a favorite for desserts and cakes.

Rice paddy herb, known as *ngo om* in Vietnam and *ma om* in Cambodia, is a distinctive herb with a fleshy pale stem with narrow light green leaves. It tastes a bit like very strong fresh coriander leaf, which can be used as a substitute. Rice paddy herb is sometimes added to soups, served as part of a herb platter and also eaten with dips.

Rice paper is a wafer-thin disc made from a rice and water dough spread on woven bamboo trays to sun-dry (the disc retains the distinctive pattern of the tray when dried). Known in Vietnam as *bahn trang*, these discs are very brittle and need to be moistened in water to soften slightly before being used to roll up just about anything and everything Vietnamese. They are also filled and deep-fried to make the famous Vietnamese spring rolls.

Packets of rice papers (often made in Thailand) are available in three forms: large discs about 8 in (20 cm) in diameter; smaller discs 5 to 6 in (14 to 16 cm) in diameter, and wedges which have been cut from a large round rice paper. The last are preferable for making tiny deep-fried spring rolls. Advice on handling rice papers is given in recipes where these are required. They can be stored in a covered container in the cupboard for several months.

Rice vinegar is mild and faintly fragrant, and is the preferred vinegar throughout Southeast Asia. Inexpensive brands from China are usually readily available in the West (as well as in Southeast Asia). If buying a Japanese rice vinegar, make sure you do not buy what is labeled "sushi vinegar" as this has sweet rice wine, sugar, and salt added. If you cannot obtain rice vinegar, use distilled white vinegar.

Rice wine is used in Chinese-inspired recipes and sometimes added to marinades in other local dishes. The best rice wine is from Shao Hsing in China; use dry sherry as a substitute.

Sago, a starch extracted from the trunk of the sago palm, is sometimes eaten as a gluey staple in a few remote parts of Southeast Asia. However, it is more commonly dried to make tiny white balls, not much bigger than a pin head, used mainly in desserts and in a few soups. The balls soften and turn transparent when cooked, and help thicken coconut milk or water with their gluey texture. Tapioca balls, made from the starch of the cassava root, are virtually indistinguishable in taste (there isn't any!) and can be substituted for pearl sago. Some tapioca is the same size as pearl sago, although it is usually found in larger balls about the size of a tear drop.

Salam leaf is popular in Indonesian cooking. It is quite different to the Western bay leaf (or laurel), which is often incorrectly suggested as a substitute. Salam leaf grows on a large tree that is a member of the cassia family; it adds a distinctive aroma to food, even when used dried. If you can obtain

fresh salam leaves, keep them in a bag in the freezer; otherwise, store dried leaves in an airtight container in the fridge for long keeping. There is no substitute for salam leaves.

Salted soybean paste is richly flavored fermented soybean, known in Thailand by its Chinese name, *dau jiao*, and in Vietnam as *tuong cu da* or *tuong bac*. The beans are fermented in thick liquid and sold in jars; they vary from dark brown to light golden in color, and are sometimes labeled "yellow bean sauce." The basic salted soybean paste contains only soybeans, water, and salt. It is possible also to buy slightly sweetened versions, or those with added chili. The beans are usually mashed with the back of a spoon before being used.

Sesame oil is made by extracting the oil from toasted sesame seeds, giving it a rich flavor and aroma that is lacking in Middle Eastern sesame oils, extracted from raw seeds. Sesame oil is used sparingly as a seasoning, not as a cooking medium. Look for a Chinese brand if possible.

Sesame seeds are tiny tear-drop shaped seeds, creamy white in color, and rich in oil. In Southeast Asia (particularly Vietnam), they are generally toasted and used as a sprinkle on food, including desserts.

Shallots are small and purplish, each weighing about $^1/_3$ oz (10 g), and often preferred to larger onions for their sweetness and texture. If these are not available, the brown-skinned or "French" shallot (eschalot) can be substituted, taking into account any significant difference in size when measuring the quantity required for a recipe. Alternatively, use a red or brown skinned onion; a 3 to $3^1/_2$ oz (80–100 g) onion is roughly equivalent to eight shallots. In Vietnamese recipes, it's fine to use the white portion of spring onions if shallots are not available.

Shallots are frequently pounded and used to flavor and thicken sauces and curries, added raw to many salads, and also deep-fried until crisp as a popular garnish. Packets of crisp-fried shallots are normally available in Asian stores, but it is easy to make your own (see page 17).

Shrimp paste, dried is common everywhere from Burma (where it's called *nagpi*) through to Bali (where the local name is *terasi*), and some form of dried shrimp paste is an important part of Southeast Asian cuisine. Made from fermented salted shrimps pressed into a paste (which can range in texture from moist to firm and dry), dried shrimp paste varies in color from very dark brown through to a purplish pink. This paste is very strong smelling when raw, and must be cooked before being eaten (see page 18). It can be stored almost indefinitely in a firmly covered container in a store cupboard.

Shrimp paste, thick black should not be confused with dried shrimp paste, as it has a different flavor and texture (although it still declares its origin in terms of smell). This black, treacle-like paste is sold in jars, sometimes labeled "black prawn paste" or "*petis*." It is used in Malaysia and Singapore, particularly by Nonya cooks, and also in Indonesia, usually in sauces. The Chinese name is *hay koh*.

Soy sauce, introduced by the Chinese, is made from salted and fermented soy beans. Widely used in Southeast Asia, the most common type is light soy sauce, which is a clear medium brown liquid with a salty taste. Dark soy sauce (Chinese brands are often labeled "Superior Soy Sauce") is dense black and thicker, somewhat less salty and with a malty tang. In Indonesia, sweet soy sauce (*kicup manis*) is the most widely used variety. If you can't obtain this, add 1 teaspoon soft brown sugar to 1 tablespoon of dark soy sauce. If using light soy sauce which is naturally fermented (check the label, the best Japanese brands are made in this way), it is best refrigerated after opening. Other types of soy sauce can be kept in a cupboard for many months.

Spring onion is known by many other names (bunching onions, scallions, green onions, Welsh onions, and even shallots) around the world. These are slender stems with a white base and flat green leaves. Their delicate flavor makes them widely popular as a flavoring and a vegetable. Spring onions can be stored for up to one week by putting them in a jar with the stems ends standing in about $1/2$ in (1 cm) of water. Enclose the spring onions and the jar with a large clear plastic bag and refrigerate.

Star anise is native to Southern China, and looks like a small dried brown flower with shiny brown seeds within each of its eight petals. Sometimes some of the "petals" of this aniseed-flavored spice get broken; if a whole star anise is required, add more petals to make up the required number. Star anise is particularly popular with braised pork dishes and is essential in Vietnamese beef stock.

Sugar exists in different varieties in Southeast Asian kitchens, and regular white granulated sugar made from the sugar cane is just one of them. Refined cane sugar or caster sugar is sometimes preferred for its ability to dissolve quickly when stirred into sauces and dips.

Palm sugar is made from the boiled sap of several different types of palm,

including the coconut and palmyra. The flavor can be like a mild butterscotch, similar to maple syrup, or quite strong, while the texture varies from soft palm sugar sold in jars and spooned out, to hard round cylinders and wide oval cakes. (The oval shape comes from the coconut shell into which the sugar syrup is poured to set.) Palm sugar is not as sweet as regular cane sugar, and has a very pleasant aroma. Use soft brown sugar as a substitute, or if making palm sugar syrup, add a little maple syrup to the brown sugar syrup.

Rock sugar, made from combining refined and unrefined cane sugar with honey, is preferred for drinks and some desserts, and also added to braised dishes and Vietnamese paté; it has a slightly different flavor from granulated sugar, but this can be used as a substitute. Rock sugar is sold in pale, honey-colored chunks which can be broken up using a mortar and pestle.

Tamarind pods are from the huge and decorative tamarind tree. They contain flesh-covered seeds which are used either when young and green or, more commonly, picked when mature and used as a pulp.

Tamarind juice, which adds a fruity sourness to countless dishes throughout the region, is made from tamarind pulp, soaked in a little water, then squeezed and strained to provide the juice.

Tamarind pulp is usually sold as a dark brownish mass, pulp, seeds, fibers, and all. Some brands of tamarind pulp are compressed into a very hard brick and are best avoided, as is concentrated tamarind paste sold in jars. Try to find Thai brands of tamarind pulp, which are usually moist and of good quality. Stored in a jar or firmly covered container on the shelf, tamarind pulp keeps almost indefinitely.

Tapioca is also known as cassava. The tubers of this plant and even the

young leaves are sometimes eaten as a vegetable. The starch extracted from the tubers is sometimes dried and made into small balls (see Sago).

Turmeric belongs to the prolific ginger family. The plant has large soft leaves and is predominantly used for its intensely yellow rhizome. Fresh or frozen turmeric rhizome is sometimes available outside Asia; turmeric powder can be used as a substitute, but although it gives plenty of color, the flavor of turmeric powder is somewhat acrid compared to the fresh rhizome. Turmeric leaf is used as a herb in some Indonesian and Malaysian dishes; there is no substitute.

Water spinach is a popular and highly nutritious leafy green vegetable that grows in damp areas. It goes by a variety of names, including morning glory, water convolvulus, and swamp cabbage. It has hollow stems with pointed, mid-green leaves, which have a soft texture and appealing mild flavor when cooked. Young shoots are frequently eaten raw as part of a salad platter or with a dip, while the leaves and tender stems are usually braised. It does not keep well; wrap in damp newspaper or a cloth and refrigerate for one to two days.

Wild pepper leaves are sometimes incorrectly called betel leaves in English (*cha plu* in Thai, *bo la lot* in Vietnamese, *pak i leut* in Lao, and *daun kadok* in Malay). They have a pleasant, faintly peppery flavor and are used as a salad herb or, particularly in Thailand and Vietnam, as a food wrapper. These can sometimes be found in Vietnamese food shops and can be kept refrigerated in a cloth for a day or two.

Yam bean is neither a bean nor a yam, and is sometimes confusingly

called a turnip in Malaysia and Singapore. It is better known in some Western countries by its Mexican name, *jicama*. It is a roughly globe-shaped tuber, tapering slightly like a top, with papery beige skin covering crisp white flesh. Slightly sweet and juicy when small and young, yam beans tend to become fibrous with age. They are eaten raw (usually with a dip) when young, or cooked when mature.

Water chestnut is a Chinese vegetable grown in muddy waters. It has an almost milky sweetness and crisp white flesh that retains its delightful texture even after cooking. Rinse well to remove any dirt before peeling, then put into cold water immediately to avoid discoloring. Water chestnuts can be eaten raw or stir-fried. They are minced to add texture and flavor to fillings. They are also added to desserts and sweetmeats, particularly in Thailand.

Winged bean is also known as angled or Goa bean. It has a slight touch of bitterness and a pleasant crisp texture. Look for small young beans which snap rather than bend. Before cooking, pinch the tip and pull down any strings. Winged beans are either eaten raw, usually with a dip, or blanched briefly in boiling water, then sliced to make salads. They can also be stir-fried, but do not over-cook or they will lose their crisp texture.

index

Special thanks to the following for the loan
of their beautiful props:

Cecilia Choo
page: **31** embroidered placement

Galerie Cho Lon Pte Ltd
pages: **50** platters; **90** sauce cups and
  plate; **109** scroll table; **118** platter;
  148 metal tray and napkin; **166** placemat;
  202 platters; **205** tea set; **207** bowl

Published by Periplus Editions, with editorial offices
at 130 Joo Seng Road #06-01, Singapore 368357

ISBN-10: 0-7946-0230-4
ISBN-13: 978-0-7946-0230-7
Printed in Singapore

Book design by the Periplus Design Team

Distributors
North America, Latin America, and Europe
Tuttle Publishing, 364 Innovation Drive,
North Clarendon, VT 05759-9436, USA
Tel: 1 (802) 773-8930; Fax: 1 (802) 773-6993
info@tuttlepublishing.com
www.tuttlepublishing.com

Japan
Tuttle Publishing
Yaekari Building, 3F, 5-4-12 Osaki,
Shinagawa-ku, Tokyo 141 0032, Japan
Tel: (81) 03 5437-0171; Fax: (81) 03 5437-0755
tuttle-sales@gol.com

Asia Pacific
Berkeley Books Pte Ltd
130 Joo Seng Road #06-01, Singapore 368357
Tel: (65) 6280 1330; Fax: (65) 6280 6290
inquiries@periplus.com.sg
www.periplus.com

10 09 08 07   6 5 4 3